Easy Weekend Getaways from

Seattle

EASY WEEKEND GETAWAYS FROM

Seattle

Short Breaks in the Pacific Northwest

Anna Katz

The Countryman Press
A division of W. W. Norton & Company
Independent Publishers Since 1923

We would appreciate any comments or corrections. Please write to:
Countryman Weekenders Editor
The Countryman Press
A division of W. W. Norton & Company
500 Fifth Avenue
New York, NY 10110

For information about permission to reproduce selections from this book, write to
Permissions, The Countryman Press, 500 Fifth Avenue, New York, NY 10110

For information about special discounts for bulk purchases, please contact
W. W. Norton Special Sales at specialsales@wwnorton.com or 800-233-4830

Manufacturing by Versa Press
Series book design by Faceout Studio, Amanda Kreutzer
Production manager: Devon Zahn

The Countryman Press
www.countrymanpress.com

A division of W. W. Norton & Company, Inc.
500 Fifth Avenue, New York, NY 10110
www.wwnorton.com

Library of Congress Cataloging-in-Publication Data

Names: Katz, Anna, 1984- author. | W.W. Norton & Company.
Title: Easy weekend getaways from Seattle : short breaks in the Pacific Northwest / Anna Katz.
Description: First Edition. | New York : The Countryman Press, a division of W. W. Norton & Company, [2019] |
Series: Weekend getaways
Identifiers: LCCN 2019015375 | ISBN 9781682683903 (Paperback)
Subjects: LCSH: Northwest, Pacific—Guidebooks. | Seattle Region (Wash.)—Guidebooks.
Classification: LCC F852.3 .K38 2019 | DDC 917.950443—dc23 LC record available at
https://lccn.loc.gov/2019015375

10 9 8 7 6 5 4 3 2

For Troy

Contents

PART ONE | FOODIE GETAWAYS

PART TWO | ROMANTIC MINI-BREAKS

PART THREE | THE GREAT OUTDOORS

PART FOUR | QUIET TIME

PART FIVE | ITINERARIES

Welcome

It's impossible to account for just how many beautiful landscapes and seascapes there are to explore, how many innovative culinary creations there are to be consumed, how many charming scenes there are to inspire romance, how many pockets of quiet there are to inhabit within driving, biking, or busing distance of Seattle. This book is an effort in sorting the sheer awesomeness of the Pacific Northwest, to provide newcomers and the born-and-raised a guide for the region organized by type of activity rather than geography.

// TreeHouse Point, Issaquah

Foodie Getaways

Washington has an abundance of farmers
and foodies determined to grow and use
fresh, locally sourced, organic crops
for everything from huckleberry pie to
blueberry moonshine.

Romantic Mini-Breaks

Experience a spectrum of mushy feelings.
Long walks on the beach hand in hand,
leisurely afternoons getting high on a
bus, sunset sails, hotel fantasy packages,
candlelit dinners, couples massages—you
name it.

The Great Outdoors

There are a million ways to escape the
concrete jungle to hike lush halls of
moss, kayak open seas, ski down snowy
mountains, bike scenic back roads, or
camp under a thousand twinkling stars.

Quiet Time

For every looming deadline or jammed-
up inbox, there is an opportunity for
retreat, whether guided within a particular
modality, self-directed artistic seclusion, or
a simple solitary moment above the
tree line.

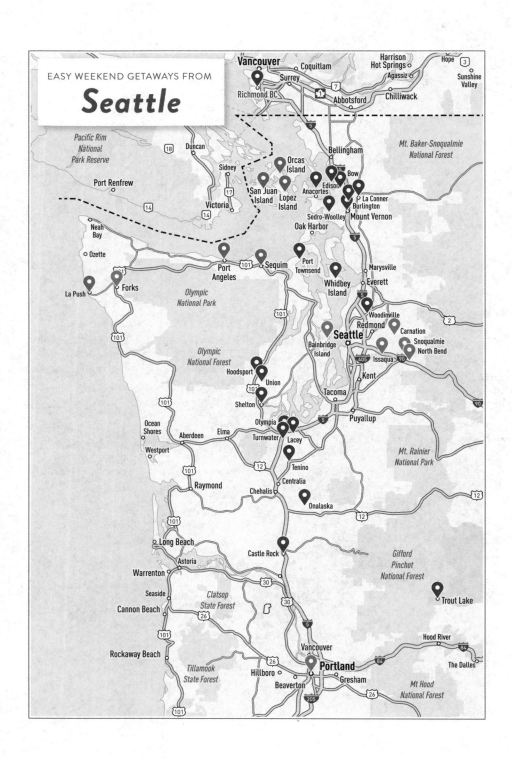

EASY WEEKEND GETAWAYS FROM

Seattle

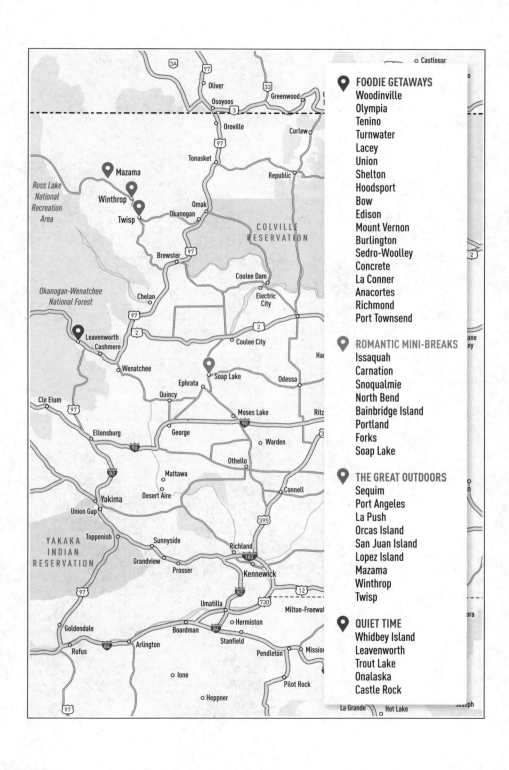

FOODIE GETAWAYS
Woodinville
Olympia
Tenino
Turnwater
Lacey
Union
Shelton
Hoodsport
Bow
Edison
Mount Vernon
Burlington
Sedro-Woolley
Concrete
La Conner
Anacortes
Richmond
Port Townsend

ROMANTIC MINI-BREAKS
Issaquah
Carnation
Snoqualmie
North Bend
Bainbridge Island
Portland
Forks
Soap Lake

THE GREAT OUTDOORS
Sequim
Port Angeles
La Push
Orcas Island
San Juan Island
Lopez Island
Mazama
Winthrop
Twisp

QUIET TIME
Whidbey Island
Leavenworth
Trout Lake
Onalaska
Castle Rock

Top 10 Experiences

1 • Swim in Lake Crescent *(page 182)*.

2 • Drink your way through the Skagit Farm to Pint Ale Trail *(page 51)*.

3 • Go kayaking in the Salish Sea, where you might just see a whale or two *(page 205)*.

4 • Ski the trails of Methow Valley *(page 231)*.

5 • Get some of the best Chinese food in the world *(page 75)*.

6 • Unplug at Trout Lake Abbey *(page 276)*.

7 • Live the #vanlife in Bainbridge and beyond *(page 127)*.

8 • Eat your food cart fill at Cartlandia, Portland *(page 149)*.

9 • Sleep in a tree at TreeHouse Point *(page 107)*.

10 • Soak in Soap Lake *(page 168)*.

Part One
Foodie Getaways

Wine in Woodinville

FROM SEATTLE: APPROXIMATELY 27 MILES · DAYS HERE: 1

DO	EAT	DRINK	BUY
wine tasting	prime dip sandwich at the Cut Shop	wine	wine

If you've voiced the opinion that good wine only comes from across the pond, in the distant lands of Italy and France, where a noble people wander their ancient fields under a golden European sun, then maybe it's time you examine your biases. Wines in Washington are great, so quit being a snob and start drinking.

From Puget Sound in the northwest to Walla Walla (that's two Wallas) on the southeast, next to the Washington–Oregon border, Washington has 14 American Viticultural Areas. Many of the 55,000-plus acres of vineyards were established by Europeans and Australians who were looking for more space and less smugness. There's a distinct climate difference between the western part and eastern part of Washington State, which can be attributed to the Olympic Mountains and Cascade Mountains, which run south to north and block precipitation moving east from the Pacific Ocean. The wee Puget Sound viticultural area is the only wine-growing region to the west of the Cascades, living the rain forest life under the rain shadow. The temperate maritime climate makes for some stellar pinot noir and riesling.

Eastern Washington has a much dryer climate, so dry in fact that it's categorized as a semi-desert. That, in combination with it being so far north, equals 300 days of sun per year, which makes grapes happy (until they get sunburn, that is). Much of the wine in Woodinville comes from grapes grown in the Columbia Valley. These nearby wineries have done Seattlelites the favor of bringing Walla Walla's and Yakima's flavors close to home. It is highly recommended, however, that you make the longer trek—approximately five hours, or 260 miles—to **Walla Walla** for wine tasting at the source.

According to the marketing website woodinvillewinecountry.com, Woodenville has 118 tasting rooms; 14 microbreweries, distilleries, and cideries; and 30 restaurants and eateries. All that epicurean mayhem is located just 30 miles northeast of Seattle, and it's easy to get to by car or bike. The Burke–Gilman Trail ride from Seattle to Woodinville is a popular one, and many people make the trek come summer for some good drinking sans car. Plan to either stay overnight or hire a shuttle to get you home.

Getting There

BY CAR | Take I-5 N, or take either 520 or I-90 to I-405 N for approximately 27 miles. Travel time: approximately 40 minutes.

BY BIKE | Ride the Burke–Gilman Trail. It starts in Ballard and runs approximately 19 miles. Get the full route (plus itinerary if you want to make it a thing) at www.traillink.com.

SHUTTLE | Hire a shuttle so you don't have to worry about getting to and from (woodinvillewinecountry.com/play/book-a-tour).

>> Bikers, take a right at the Aurora Avenue Bridge and stop for a photo op with the **Fremont Troll** at his residence under a bridge, 3404 Troll Avenue N, Fremont.

Highlight Reel

PASSPORT TO WOODINVILLE

woodinvillewinecountry.com/passport

Get a "free" tasting at more than 50 wineries, plus a dozen or so breweries and distilleries, with the Passport to Woodinville. This hotcake goes up for sale at Costco on Black Friday and, at $99.99 for a two-pack, sells out quickly. Passports are valid for one year, from January 1 to December 31, and are valued at $600.

WOODINVILLE DISTRICTS

woodinvillewinecountry.com/woodinville-districts

The city is divided into four districts, each of which, the PR folks at Woodinville Wine Country claim, has a distinct flavor. The **Warehouse District** is made up of around 20 wineries and a brewery packed into a few industrial parks, qualifying it as the home of more boutique wineries per square foot than anywhere else in the world; the **West Valley District** has more space and fewer wineries, giving it a more relaxed vibe; the **Downtown District** has the amazing plant store and restaurant Molbak's Garden & Home and other businesses along with the wineries; and the **Hollywood District** sits in the Sammamish River Valley and is home to some super foodie and wine-geek establishments. Try them all.

CHATEAU STE. MICHELLE

14111 NE 145th Street, Woodinville • www.ste-michelle.com • 425-488-1133 • Open daily
10 a.m.–5 p.m.

One of Chateau Ste. Michelle's claims to fame is that it's the oldest winery in Washington. The estate was initially owned by a rich logging magnate. Later on, some other dudes who were super jazzed about the repeal of Prohibition bought it, and thus Ste. Michelle the winery was born. The Chateau didn't come until later, in 1976.

The vineyards that supply Chateau Ste. Michelle are located in Eastern Washington's AVA of Horse Heaven Hill. Cold Creek Vineyard, established in 1972, is one of the state's historic vineyards, and younger sibling Canoe Ridge Estate came along in 1991. Together they grow cabernet franc, cabernet sauvignon, chardonnay, merlot, and riesling, and syrah varietals.

Walk the grounds, do a tasting, eat some cheese. Talk about mouthfeel or whatever. Take a class and tour, such as the unique offerings of Sensory Sojourn or Champagne and Sparkling Literacy.

// Chateau Ste. Michelle

JM CELLARS

14404 137th Place NE, Woodinville • jmcellars.com • 425-485-6508 • Tasting room open Friday–
Sunday 11 a.m.–4 p.m.

JM Cellar's Margaret's Vineyard in Walla Walla features cabernet sauvignon, merlot, cabernet
franc, malbec, petit verdot, and carménère grapes from France's Bordeaux region. The winery
is located on seven acres on a hill called "Bramble Bump," which used to be a dairy farm and
has since become, along with a winery, a private arboretum with over 400 rare conifers, 120
Japanese maples, and other rare specimens. Try the Tre Fanciulli, $15, waived with purchase.

PATTERSON CELLARS

Warehouse District Winery and Tasting Room • 19501 144th Avenue NE, D-600, Woodinville •
www.pattersoncellars.com • 425-483-8600 • Tasting room open Friday 3–7 p.m., Saturday noon–6 p.m.,
and Sunday noon–5 p.m.

Hollywood Hill Tasting Room • 14505 148th Avenue NE • 425-892-2964 • Tasting room open
Monday–Thursday noon–7 p.m., Friday and Saturday noon–9 p.m., Sunday noon–6 p.m.

A visit to Patterson Cellars is like visiting your wine-loving uncle—the pours are generous,
and you can tell just how much the owner/winemaker enjoys what he does. See some of the
actual winemaking at the Warehouse District location, or see live music on Friday and Satur-

// JM Cellars

day nights and admire the view from the outdoor patio of the Hollywood Hill location. Flights include a sample of five or six wines. $25, waived with purchase.

>>   For more Patterson Cellars, visit the Sodo Tasting Room, the Leavenworth Wine Cellar, or go to the website for a schedule of Seattle-area events.

GORMAN WINERY

14505 148th Avenue NE, Woodinville • www.gormanwinery.com • 206-351-0719 • Open Monday–Thursday noon–7 p.m., Friday and Saturday noon–9 p.m., Sunday noon–6 p.m.

A small-batch winery that is committed to the idea that Washington State makes some of the finest wines in the world. Eclectic bands provide summer weekend entertainment, and you can enjoy glass pour specials at the tasting room along with or instead of a flight. Afterward, step over to Vivi Pizzeria (page 21), a fabulous Italian restaurant next door.

DELILLE CELLARS

Carriage House Tasting Room • 14421 Woodinville-Redmond Road NE, Woodinville • www.delillecellars.com • 425-489-0544 • Tasting room hours: Sunday–Thursday noon–5 p.m., Friday noon–7 p.m., Saturday 11 a.m.–5 p.m.

Listed as a *Wine & Spirits* Top 100 Winery and featured in local, national, international, and wine-geek publications, the Carriage House Tasting Room is located a quarter mile north of DeLille Cellars' Chateau, their beautiful event venue in Redmond. Wines are from grapes grown in Eastern Washington's American Viticultural Areas and are delicious. $20, waived with two-bottle purchase.

Plan Around

SUMMER CONCERTS AT CHATEAU STE. MICHELLE

14111 NE 145th Street, Woodinville • www.ste-michelle.com/visit-us/summer-concerts • 425-488-1133

During the summer, Chateau Ste. Michelle hosts a series of music concerts that's known far and wide for its A-listers and A-list adjacents who come to perform on the sprawling green lawn of the outdoor amphitheater. Bring your own picnic, or buy dinner from the food vendors and wine from Chateau Ste. Michelle's wine shop and enjoy the amazing blues, jazz, or rock performance.

≡ *Eat & Drink*

Get Caffeinated

MERCURYS COFFEE CO.

17641 Garden Way NE, Woodinville • 425-286-2518 • www.mercuryscoffee.com • Open Monday–Friday 4:30 a.m.–8 p.m., Saturday and Sunday 5 a.m.–8 p.m.

15608 NE Woodinville Duvall Road, Woodinville • 425-487-8747 • Open Monday–Friday 4:30 a.m.–7 p.m., Saturday and Sunday 5 a.m.–7 p.m.

A local coffee shop chain serving the cities of Woodinville, Redmond, Kirkland, Sammamish, Bellevue, and Fall City, and featuring classic and signature coffee drinks, teas, hot chocolates, smoothies, and daily specials. Try the Blonde Hawaiian.

WOODINVILLE BAGEL BAKERY

14126 NE Woodinville Duvall Road, Woodinville • woodinvillebagel.com • 425-488-9899 • Open Monday–Friday 6:30 a.m.–4 p.m., Saturday and Sunday 7:30 a.m.–4 p.m.

Absorb last night's wine with an organic steam-baked bagel and house-made cream cheese or bagel sandwich, plus a standard coffee or a frozen blend, fruit smoothie, tea, or Italian soda.

GROUNDS COFFEE CO.

14575 148th Avenue NE, Woodinville • 425-483-3002 • Open Monday–Friday 6 a.m.–6 p.m., Saturday 7 a.m.–6:30 p.m., Sunday 7 a.m.–5 p.m.

A cute little coffee stand with a drive-thru and some outdoor seating, fresh-baked goods, coffee drinks, teas, and friendly service.

Farm Fresh

TONNEMAKER VALLEY FARM & WOODINVILLE FARM STAND

16211 140th Place NE, Woodinville • tonnemaker.com/woodinville-farm-stand • 206-930-1565

21 ACRES

13701 NE 171st Street, Woodinville • 21acres.org • 425-481-1500 • Open Friday 11 a.m.–6 p.m., Saturday 10 a.m.–4 p.m.

A center for sustainable agricultural education and collective action, with a farmers' market that brings in produce from their own organic farm and the best of other local and organic ranches and farms for grocery shopping and healthy food-to-go at the deli. 21 Acres also offers a wide range of activities, such as farm walks, plant sales, and cooking classes.

OFF THE BRANCH FARM

13404 Woodinville-Redmond Road, Redmond • www.pugetsoundfresh.org/farm/minea-farm-branch
-farm • 425-883-1286 • Open year-round, Friday 4–7 p.m., Saturday 10 a.m.–5 p.m., Sunday noon–
5 p.m., weekdays by appointment

Come for the fresh-pressed apple cider, and pick up apples, local canned fruit and vegetables,
chicken and duck eggs, organic cheeses and yogurts, raw local honey, and aged vinegars.

Dining

THE COMMONS

14481 Woodinville-Redmond Road, Woodinville • www.thecommonscafe.com • 425-892-7012 • Open
Sunday–Thursday 8 a.m.–9 p.m., Friday and Saturday 8 a.m.–10 p.m.

Definitely the best breakfast in town, with fresh-baked pastries, hangover-defeating egg
dishes, and eye-opening coffee drinks. Lunch and dinner feature high-end comfort food, such
as the BLTA with spicy aioli on multigrain bread, the kale Caesar, and the grain bowl alongside
chicken and dumplings or the lamb burger. Long list of wines, too, and great cocktails—try the
Beer's Knees or the Netflix and Chill.

VIVI PIZZERIA

14505 148th Avenue NE, Woodinville • www.vivipizzeria.com • 425-408-0711 • Open Sunday–
Thursday 11 a.m.–9 p.m., Friday and Saturday 11 a.m.–10 p.m.

Delicious bruschetta, handmade pizza and pasta, and carne and pesce entrées. Anything with
Brussels sprouts is highly recommended, as is anything with meatballs. Definitely try the
pasta, served al dente.

CUT SHOP

12081 NE 175th Street, Woodinville • www.woodinvillecutshop.com • 425-408-1173 • Open Tuesday–
Thursday 4 p.m.–12 a.m., Friday and Saturday 11 a.m.–2 a.m., Sunday 11 a.m.–9 p.m.

A stellar roadhouse decor committed to '70s rock; a small, no-frills menu featuring burgers,
sandwiches, and picnic-style sides; and an outdoor lounge area.

HOLLYWOOD TAVERN

14501 Woodinville-Redmond Road, Woodinville • www.thehollywoodtavern.com • 425-481-7703
• Open Sunday–Thursday 11 a.m.–9 p.m., Friday–Saturday 11 a.m.–10 p.m.

A casual pub with inspired comfort foods such as Cajun wings and Tavern cornbread, juicy
burgers and sandwiches, and a decent selection of creative salads. Get a signature Woodinville
Whiskey milkshake.

Booze and Beyond

WOODINVILLE WHISKEY CO.

14509 Woodinville-Redmond Road NE, Woodinville • www.woodinvillewhiskeyco.com • 425-486-1199 • Tasting room hours: daily 11 a.m.–5 p.m. • Complimentary tours: Friday 4 p.m., Saturday and Sunday 1 p.m. and 3 p.m.

Award-winning Kentucky-meets-Washington handcrafted small-batch whisky, made with time-honored tradition mixed with the latest distilling technology. All grains are single-sourced from a family farm in Quincy, Washington. $10, waived with purchase.

PURPLE CAFÉ AND WINE BAR

14459 Woodinville-Redmond Road, Woodinville • www.purplecafe.com • 425-483-7129 • Open Monday–Thursday 11 a.m.–9 p.m., Friday 11 a.m.–10 p.m., and Saturday 10 a.m.–10 p.m.

A high-end wine bar with seasonal brunch, lunch, happy hour, and dinner menus and a long list of wines. Get a flight—they offer a variety of white trios such as Citrus and Spice and The Local, red trios such as Rustic and Teethstainer, and mixed trios such as Under the Radar and Postcards from Italy.

VILLAGE WINES

14450 Woodinville-Redmond Road NE, Ste 111 • www.myvillagewines.com • 425-485-3536 • Open Sunday–Wednesday 11 a.m.–9 p.m., Thursday–Saturday 11 a.m.–10 p.m.

A wine bar with an enormous wine library, local beers, tapas, flatbread pizza, salads, sandwiches, and live music on the weekends. Get the cheese fondue, smoked salmon, or charcuterie platter to share. Be prepared for a line.

 *Stay Over*

WILLOWS LODGE

14580 NE 145th Street, Woodinville • www.willowslodge.com • 425-424-3900

Just down the street from Chateau Ste. Michelle, Willows Lodge is a good spot to hunker down post-wine tasting. The lodge itself is built from timber of a reclaimed pier in Oregon, and each of the 84 guest rooms is well appointed, with two-person soaking tubs, stone fireplaces, and access to the heated pool. The spa offers lovely massage and facial treatments, and the concierge is happy to help you plan your wine-tasting tour. Off the main lobby is the Fireside Lounge, which has signature cocktails, a daily "Happier Hour" menu, and, of course, a long list of great wines, with the Barking Frog's fine dining just up the road. Pet-friendly accommodations available.

MCMENAMINS ANDERSON SCHOOL

18607 Bothell Way NE, Bothell • www.mcmenamins.com/anderson-school • 425-398-0122

If only all junior high schools could have a swimming pool, a music venue, a movie theater, a game room/sports bar/pub, three restaurants, a brewery, and a bar. McMenamins Anderson School has replaced all those dumb books and stuff with everything an adult with a little cash to spend would want. Get sober in Woodinville so that you can drive halfway home, stop in Bothell, and start drinking again! The grounds are lush and well tended, and all restaurants have outdoor seating come bloom season. Be sure to eat at the North Shore Lagoon, a tiki-themed restaurant above the pool. Add a little romance by getting the Add a Little Romance Package. Pet friendly. $135–270.

COTTAGE LAKE B&B

17324 185th Avenue NE, Woodinville • www.cottagelakebedandbreakfast.com • 425-236-9146

A private tree house above Cottage Lake, built by the same folks who built TreeHouse Point in Issaquah, located on a quiet cul-de-sac yet close to Woodinville Wine Country. Sit in the outdoor hot tub and watch the waters of Cottage Lake ripple, or go on down for a swim. Enjoy the view from the outdoor deck while you uncork your bottle. $195–250.

>> There are plenty of chain hotels—the inns of Westin, Marriott, Hilton, Hyatt, Holiday, and Hampton—in the area if you find yourself too inebriated to get yourself home. Remember, you can get a DUI on a bicycle, so whether you biked over or drove, if you're feeling at all wobbly, be safe and rent a room.

≡ While You're Here

ADVENTURA

14300 NE 145th Street, Woodinville • adventuraplay.com • 1-866-892-5632

Go to Adventura, an adult-size giant outdoor rope course jungle gym. You will be safely strapped in, but there's a good chance you'll have some fears to face as you cross swaying loop bridges, swing on the Tarzan rope, and hop across tires, all suspended 40 feet above the ground. By the time you get to the zip line exit, you'll feel much more sure-footed and kind of like a kid on a playground having the best darn recess of their life. Save the wine tasting for afterward. $100.

SEE A CIRCUS SHOW AT TEATRO ZINZANNI

14200 NE 145th Street, Woodinville • zinzanni.com • 206-802-0015

See a crazy mix of cabaret, body-bending cirque, and fine dining in this former Red Hook Brewery. The dinner menu is designed by a James Beard Award–winning chef, and acrobats, clowns, circus artists, and comedians will entertain the socks off you while you eat and drink.

HOT-AIR BALLOON WITH LET'S GO BALLOONING

letsgoballooning.com • 425-487-8611

During the summer, you can take a sunrise or sunset hot-air balloon flight over Sammamish Valley. At the high point, you'll be able to see Mount Rainier and Mount Baker, the Puget Sound, Lake Washington, Lake Union, and the Seattle skyline. Morning fliers get champagne and fruit juice upon landing, while evening fliers get a wine tasting and appetizers at Matthew's Estate. $199-plus.

>> **The Balloonist Prayer**
May the winds welcome you with softness
May the sun bless you with its warm hands
May you fly so high and so well that God
Joins you in laughter and sets you gently
Back again into the loving arms of Mother Earth.

RENT CUSTOM COSTUMES AT BARNPLACE

www.barnplace.com/costumes.htm • 425-213-9426

These days, it's hard to find authentic period dress. Thank goodness for BarnPlace, where not only can you find farm-fresh eggs but also frills and thrills from medieval to Roaring Twenties, Victorian to black tie! Call ahead to schedule an appointment.

1   Adventura
2   Teatro ZinZanni

ABOVE & BEYOND

Dogs | If you're driving in from Seattle on WA-520 just for a sip, bring your pup along and stop by **Marymoor Park** (6046 W Lake Sammamish Parkway, NE, Redmond; 206-205-3661), the area's beloved Doggy Disneyland. This 40 acres of off-leash fun times, including water access, is located approximately 7 miles south of Woodinville.

Not Ready to Go Home | Make the trek to the wine's source in Walla Walla, approximately 270 miles to the southeast.

Good to Know | Since 1980, the number of wineries in Washington State has increased 45 times, from 19 to over 900.

Been There, Done That | Head southeast to Issaquah and Snoqualmie Valley (page 105).

2

Shellfish in South Puget Sound and Hood Canal

FROM SEATTLE: 1 TO 2 HOURS · DAYS HERE: 0.5-PLUS

DO	EAT	DRINK
watch the West Coast Oyster Shucking Championships	fresh-caught oysters	artesian well beer

"It's the water!" was the slogan for now-defunct Olympia Beer Company, a brewery founded in 1896 and a business that was pivotal in the development of the city of Olympia and Thurston County—which includes the cities of Tenino, Tumwater, Yelm, Rainier, and Lacey—as a whole. There used to be many artesian wells throughout the city, though the number of wells in use has dwindled since the 1940s.

But it's not just about well water—it's about saltwater, too, and all the places shellfish can be harvested in the South Puget Sound and Hood Canal. Brewing beer is a relatively new pastime, compared to the shellfish harvesting that has been going on in the area for thousands of years. These days, shellfish farms dot the shores, and some public beaches are open year-round for u-pick harvesting. There are best times of the year to come down for this hybrid hunting and gathering, and some beaches are better for oysters than clams, or vice

// Oyster vista

versa. All are susceptible to the whims of weather and the spills of humanity, so check the Department of Health for important information about the water quality; for beach maps, visit the Washington Department of Fish and Wildlife at wdfw.wa.gov and www.explore hoodcanal.com.

The area is also a hub of agriculture and the artisan farm-to-fork cuisine that such proximity generates. So even if you aren't the world's #1 best shucker, you're guaranteed to find something that will spark your appetite.

☰ *Getting There*

BY CAR | To Olympia, drive on I-5 South for approximately 60 miles. To get to Hood Canal, continue on N Highway 101.

BY BUS | Take Sound Transit #594 to Lakewood Station, then take Intercity Transit #620. Approximate travel time: 2.5 hours.

BY TRAIN | To Olympia, take Amtrak Cascades Coast Starlight to Centennial Station, then take Intercity Transit #94. Approximate travel time: 2.5 hours.

BY BIKE | To Olympia, bike the Interurban Trail. Approximate distance: 78 miles; approximate travel time: 7 hours.

☰ *Highlight Reel*

#shuckyeah

SHELLFISH WEEK

April • www.explorehoodcanal.com

For a week in April, the area's shellfish farms, lodgings, and restaurants come together to shell-ebrate the bivalves they love to eat with farm visits, u-pick activities, and shellfish-centric eats and drinks. Around the solstice, Hama Hama Company (35846 N Highway 101, Lilliwaup; www.hamahamaoysters.com; 360-877-5811) hosts **Hama Hama Oyster Rama,** which includes a "tideflat ho-down" on the beach of Hood Canal and a range of fun arthropod-inspired activities, including u-pick oysters and clams, and intertidal tours with oyster growers and ecologists. Sign up to compete in the Shuckathalon, which is a totally made-up sport involving cluster picking, clam digging, single picking, and, of course, shucking. Competition to win the title of World Champion of oyster sports is fierce, so you better start practicing now. There's also live music, a raffle, cooking classes, and lots of non-oyster food and drink, including locally crafted beer, cider, and ice cream. Proceeds go to local environmental and marine education charities, and tickets sell out every year, so get yours early. $15.

SLURP: SHELLFISH LOVERS ULTIMATE REJUVENATION PARTY

May • Olympia • pcsga.org/slurp

For the past 20-plus years, Olympia has celebrated shellfish, local restaurants, and Washington wines and beer at SLURP. It features live music, a grand oyster bar, a celebrity slurp-off, and a live auction. All proceeds go to the Pacific Coast Shellfish Growers Association's Shellfish Habitat Restoration Fund. $65 in advance, $80 at the door.

// Oysters, Hood Canal

ALLYN DAYS & GEODUCK FESTIVAL

July • Allyn Waterfront Park, 18560 E State Route 3, Allyn • www.allynwa.org

Ever wanted to pet a geoduck (pronounced "gooey-duck")? Then come to the Allyn Days & Geoduck Festival on three days in July, where you can not only pet these oversize clams but eat them, too! Friday night kicks off the event with Open Mic Night, so come ready to perform or be embarrassed yet supportive of other amateurs. Booze it up in the wine and beer garden, then eat an alder-smoked salmon dinner or the shellfish delicacies from the 100 other vendors. They make you wait until Sunday for the geoduck unveiling. It's family friendly, so expect kids. Free.

TASTE OF HOOD CANAL

August • Belfair State Park, 3151 WA-300, Belfair • tasteofhoodcanal.com

Listen to live music, drink beers, and eat a boatload of shellfish. Check out the blinged-out custom and classic autos and motorcycles in the Car and Bike Show—you can even weigh in on your favorites for the People's Choice Award. $5.

OYSTER FEST

October • Port of Shelton, 21 W Sanderson Way, Shelton • www.oysterfest.org

For one weekend in October, 100 nonprofits gather to celebrate shellfish and raise money for Mason County efforts in environmental stewardship and education. These nonprofits are the real deal when it comes to good oyster eating, and you'll be able to sample oysters in all their iterations. There's a beer garden (they're fancy and call it a "Microbrew Garden") and a whole lot of Washington wines to go with your bivalves, along with live music, live touch tanks, art, and exhibits on the sea and its life. Be sure to attend the Cook-Off and the West Coast Oyster Shucking Championships. $5.

TAKE THE BOUNTIFUL BYWAY

thurstonbountifulbyway.com • 1-877-704-7500

From Olympia south through Tumwater, Littlerock, and Rochester, then east through Tenino, Rainier, and Yelm, and north up to Lacey and Billy Frank Nisqually National Wildlife Refuge (or vice versa), drive, bike, or walk along this 60-mile scenic byway to visit the many craft breweries, wineries, distilleries, farms, and farmers' markets.

>> Use a bicycle for free through **Tenino Yellow Bicycle Project**. Pick up a key at The Iron Works Boutique (224 Sussex Avenue W, Tenino; www.ironworksandhomedecor.com; 360-264-5228), sign a waiver, and then go out to the bike corral and match a key up with its lock. This is the honor system, so a) don't be an asshole, and b) feel free to take the bike as long as you want. People usually return the bike that same day, though every now and then someone keeps one overnight. If you get back late, simply lock up the bike and put the key in the boutique's front door mail slot.

1 Canal cookout, Hood Canal
2 South Sound Coffee Trail, Olympia
3 Thurston Bountiful Byway, Thurston County

TAKE THE SOUTH SOUND COFFEE TRAIL

www.southsoundcoffeetrail.com

Get fully caffeinated on the South Sound Coffee Trail, which features the committed coffee roasters of the "local specialty coffee roaster movement" through events and cuppings. Fair and environmentally friendly sourcing is a big deal for all, as is making the perfect cup of joe. Are you a sophisticated connoisseur, a minimalist, or a coffee conversationalist? Go online to the South Sound Coffee Trail to find out!

OLYMPIA COFFEE ROASTING CO. 600 4th Avenue NE, Olympia • olympiacoffee .com • 360-753-0066 • Open Monday–Friday 6:30 a.m.–7 p.m., Saturday 7 a.m.–7 p.m., Sunday 7 a.m.–6 p.m. Dedicated to Fair for All and awarded the Micro Roaster of the Year by *Roast Magazine*, Olympia Coffee Roasting has a few locations in Olympia, one in Tacoma, and one in West Seattle. Offers complimentary coffee cuppings on Fridays at 10 a.m.

BATDORF & BRONSON COFFEE ROASTERS 200 Market Street NE, Olympia • batdorfcoffee.com • 360-786-6717 • Open Wednesday–Sunday 9 a.m.–4 p.m. Locals credit Batdorf & Bronson for launching Olympia's specialty coffee movement in 1986, when the flagship location (516 S Capitol Way) opened its doors. The tasting room on Market Street is located in the roastery—come by to try coffee from Africa, Indonesia, and Latin America. Register for a two-hour to two-day class to really go deep.

OLYMPIC CREST COFFEE ROASTERS 4211 Pacific Avenue SE, Lacey • olycrest.com • 360-923-0973 • Open Monday–Saturday 6 a.m.–5:30 p.m., Sunday 7 a.m.–3 p.m.; drive-thru daily 6 a.m.–6 p.m. Watch the roasting process using a state-of-the-art Diedrich IR-12 roaster while you sip in Lacey's only full-service coffee company, where everything except the actual growing of beans is done on-site. Get breakfast or lunch. Or go through the drive-thru.

GO ON THE SOUTH SOUND CRAFT CRAWL www.experienceolympia.com Get your Craft Crawl passport stamped at 15 of the 21 locations in order to claim your prize: a 32-ounce mini-growler, along with the opportunity to drink a bunch of great beer and cider crafted in Thurston County and Pierce County. Pick up a map at Olympia's visitor center (103 Sid Snyder Avenue SW, Olympia; 360-704-7544) and then get ready for some drunken crawling.

SOUTH SOUND WINE TRAIL

www.southsoundwinetrail.com

Visit these five award-winning wineries located throughout Lacey, Olympia, Tenino, and Shelton. Like most Washington wines, the grapes are grown in the eastern part of the state, then delivered to their western counterparts for fermentation, bottling, and all the other necessary processes that turn fruit into a liquid that will give you a happy head buzz. These wineries offer a range of settings in which to enjoy a tasting, from grand farm homestead to in-town, barrel-side taproom.

MEDICINE CREEK WINERY 947 Old Pacific Highway, Olympia • www.medicinecreekwinery .com • 360-701-6284 • Open mid-February–mid-December, Saturday and Sunday noon–5 p.m.

STOTTLE WINERY 2641 Willamette Drive NE, Suite E, Lacey • www.stottlewinery.com • 360-515-0356 • Open March–October, Wednesday–Sunday noon–6 p.m.; November–February, Wednesday–Sunday noon–5 p.m.

MADSEN FAMILY CELLARS 2625 Reinhardt Lane NE, Suite D, Lacey • www.madsen familycellars.com • 360-438-1286 • Open Wednesday–Sunday 11 a.m.–5 p.m.

SCATTER CREEK WINERY 237 Sussex Avenue W, Tenino • www.scattercreekwinery.com • 360-264-9463 • Open Monday–Friday 3–9 p.m., Saturday 1–9 p.m., and Sunday 1–7 p.m.

WALTER DACON 50 SE Skookum Inlet Road, Shelton • www.walterdaconwines.com • 360-426-5913 • Open Wednesday–Sunday noon–6 p.m.

SOUTH PUGET SOUND: OLYMPIA, TENINO, TUMWATER, LACEY

FROM SEATTLE: 1 TO 2 HOURS · DAYS HERE: 0.5-PLUS

EAT	DRINK	DO	BUY
cheese at The Mouse Trap	absinthe at Cryptatropa Bar	see wolves at Wolf Haven	a book at Browser's Bookshop

Getting There

BY CAR | Drive south on I-5 for 60 miles. Travel time: approximately 1 hour.

BY BUS | Take the Greyhound Bus to Olympia. Travel time: approximately 1 hour, 35 minutes. $15-plus

BY TRAIN | From the King Street Station, take Amtrak Cascades #501 to Olympia. Travel time: approximately 1 hour, 20 minutes. $18-plus

Plan Around

YELM UFO FESTIVAL

July • 201 Prairie Park Lane SE, Yelm • www.thetriadartstheater.com

Everyone knows it's all a conspiracy, they just don't want *you* to know that *they* know. For one glorious weekend in July, however, the truth will be out there in the form of a UFO festival and symposium. Hear from UFO experts, drink alien pale ale in the beer garden, wear a tinfoil hat. Free.

>> **Good to Know:** People have been reporting **UFO sightings** around Mount Rainier since 1896. A married couple spotted some unidentifiable fast-moving lights, and 50 years later, in 1947, a local pilot reported the same, though by then the term "flying saucer" had entered the lingo. This just so happened to be a couple weeks before a flying saucer crashed in Roswell, New Mexico. Coincidence? Certainly not!

SCARY-NIGHTS AT BOO-CODA

October • 403 N Nenant Street, Bucoda • www.scary-nights.com • Open October, Friday and Saturday 7–11 p.m., plus Halloween

Get your pants scared off in the town of Bucoda ("Boo-coda"), 20 miles south of Olympia. Scary-Nights is a legit haunted house held in the haunted town gym, which is apparently known for its paranormal activity. You will be frightened.

Eat & Drink

Get Caffeinated

HAWLEY'S GELATO AND COFFEE

511 Washington Street SE, Olympia • www.hawleysgelato.com • 360-489-1801 • Open Monday–Thursday noon–9:30 p.m., Friday–Saturday noon–10 p.m., and Sunday noon–7 p.m.

Have Italian ice cream for breakfast with your coffee, then get a Miss Moffett's Mystical cupcake to go. For more coffee options, see South Sound Coffee Trail on page 31.

Farm Fresh

OLYMPIA FARMERS' MARKET

700 N Capitol Way, Olympia • www.olympiafarmersmarket.com • 360-352-9096 • Open January–March, Saturday 10 a.m.–3 p.m.; April–October, Thursday–Sunday 10 a.m.–3 p.m.; November–December, Saturday and Sunday 10 a.m.–3 p.m.

This farmers' market is probably older than you are. Open year-round, it's been doing local/artisan/groovy for more than 40 years. Pick up some fresh groceries for your own home cooking or sample the delicious fare from food vendors and local restaurants' farm stands.

WEST OLYMPIA FARMERS' MARKET

West Central Park, Harrison Avenue and Division Street • www.wolyfarmersmarket.org • 360-972-8379 • Open mid-May–mid-October Tuesday 4–7 p.m.

The baby sister of the Olympia Farmers' Market, located on the west side of Olympia and mostly hyperlocal to that little area. Many of the vendors are new or just starting out—you can support these small-scale upstarts by buying their local produce, prepared foods, baked goods, and pretty flowers.

THE MOUSE TRAP

408 Washington Street SE, Olympia • www.olymousetrap.com • 360-489-0678 • Open Tuesday–
Saturday 11 a.m.–6 p.m., two Sunday brunch sittings at 9 a.m. and 11 a.m.

There are no two more beautiful words in the English language than "cheese bar." Tastings
feature curated, mostly local cheese—twelve hard cheeses, eight soft—charcuterie from
Seattle-based Salumi, and other specialty sweets and savories, plus cider, beer, and cocktails.
Come for Sunday brunch and pop-up dinners, too, then leave with a gift basket. Reservations
required.

OUR TABLE

Brick and Mortar Restaurant: 406 4th Avenue E • Open daily 9 a.m.–3 p.m.
Farmers' market: 700 N Capital Way • Open Thursday–Sunday 10 a.m.–3 p.m.
www.ourtableolympia.com • 360-932-6030

Home cooking, with ingredients sourced from a ton of local farms and Olympia Farmers' Market vendors. Along with getting the homestyle breakfasts and lunches at Our Table's farmers'
market stand and brick-and-mortar restaurant, you can order food from Our Table through a
window at the Eastside Club Tavern to go with your beer.

Dining

HOTSTONE AUTHENTIC KOREAN CUISINE

119 5th Avenue SW, Olympia • 360-596-9332 • Open Monday–Saturday 11 a.m.–9 p.m.

Like the name says, it's authentic Korean cuisine, served in a cozy setting. Yes, "cozy" can be a
euphemism for small, and sometimes the place does get crowded. But that's because the food
is good. Start with the kimchi pancake and the Soon Do Boo (tofu soup), then get the bi bim
bap and spicy pork bulgogi.

RICARDO'S KITCHEN + BAR

676 Woodland Square Loop SE, Lacey • chefricardo.com • 360-413-9995

Carnivores, this is your spot. Specializing in custom dry-aged beef steaks, with a long wine list,
organic salads, and other drool-inducing entrées made from locally sourced ingredients, Ricar-
do's is worth the 10-minute drive from Olympia proper to Lacey.

Find them with the hashtag #sexybeef101.

222 MARKET

222 Capitol Way N, Olympia • www.222market.com

Everything is delicious in this artisanal market. Hang out all day, or come back again and again for breakfast, lunch, happy hour, dinner, and spirits tasting at the following locales. Don't forget to stop by Fleurae (open Tuesday–Saturday 10 a.m.–5 p.m., Sunday 10 a.m.–4 p.m.) for flowers and other gifty items before you leave. Below are some of the best spots in the market.

THE BREAD PEDDLER, PEDDLER BISTRO, AND THE CREPERIE

breadpeddler.com and www.222market.com/creperie • Open daily 7 a.m.–5 p.m. This sister bake-shop, café, and French crêperie each serve breakfast and lunch made from scratch and have an open, modern ambiance. Get the *kouign amann*, a salty/sweet French pastry, and the *oeufs en meurette*, two poached eggs topped with red wine and herb sauce, with lardons and a whole bunch of goodies served with toasted challah. The Peddler Bistro offers good beer and wine for classy day drinking, while The Creperie offers sweet and savory, with options for the bread-phobic, and antiques to purchase after your meal.

SOFIE'S SCOOPS GELATERIA
www.sofiesscoops.com • Open Tuesday–Sunday noon–9 p.m. Fresh gelato made with milk from Tunawerth Creamery, located in nearby Tenino. Flavors rotate—past favorites have included salty B (butterscotch), earl gray with lavender and, always, the chocolate. The waffle-ato, a hot handmade Belgium liege waffle topped with Oly-Fog gelato (black tea with rose petals and vanilla), is killer.

DOS HERMANOS MEXICAN KITCHEN
Open Tuesday–Saturday 11 a.m.–8 p.m., Sunday 11 a.m.–5 p.m. Family-owned Mexican restaurant, with highlights including handmade tortillas, homemade salsas, stellar chips and guac, and Cadillac margarita.

CHELSEA FARM OYSTER BAR
www.chelseafarms.net • Open Tuesday–Friday 11 a.m.–9 p.m., Saturday 10 a.m.–10 p.m., Sunday 10 a.m.–9 p.m. Eat raw or cooked oysters and clams straight from Chelsea Farm in the Eld Inlet, shellfish from other Washington and Oregon farms, as well as beautifully prepared apps and entrées. Good happy hour Tuesday through Sunday from 3 to 5 p.m.

SHOEBOX SPIRITS
www.shoeboxspirits.com • Tastings Tuesday–Saturday 11 a.m.–8 p.m., Sunday noon–5 p.m. Booze it up at this in-house craft distillery and tasting room. Everything is made in small batches and mostly from Washington-grown malted barley, and you can sign up for "Make Your Own," a three-hour class on how to make moonshine. Register in advance, $165.

Booze and Beyond

CRYPTATROPA BAR

421 4th Avenue E, Olympia • 360-754-3867 • Open daily 4 p.m.–2 a.m.

It's a vampire bar. What's a vampire bar, you ask? Well, it's a bar that's mostly black and red, with a vintage embalming table, organ music and other goth tunes on the jukebox, a life-size gold demon, church pews, and tabletops made out of the lids of coffins from, rumor has it, Transylvania. Gargoyles stand by to watch you drink absinthe. Give a bartender the freedom to make something of their choice and you will get a highly boozy and delicious cocktail. Oddly enough, the bartenders are known for their friendliness, and they swear there's no blood in the beer.

THE BROTHERHOOD LOUNGE

119 Capitol Way N, Olympia • thebrotherhoodlounge.com • 360-352-4153 • Open daily 3 p.m.–2 a.m.

Originally a union workers' bar, The Brotherhood is the oldest bar in Olympia. It's done its best to maintain that blue-collar vibe—even the fanciest drink won't cost you more than $12, and during the 3 p.m. to 7 p.m. daily happy hour, well drinks and Budweiser pints are only $2.50. Micro-brew pints are $3. Sunday night is movie night, vintage Japanese movie posters and paintings of bulls and matadors grace the walls, and at all times you can hear billiards click-clacking away. Is it haunted, as some claim? Probably.

>> Coming or going, stop by **Bob's Java Jive** in Tacoma (2102 S Tacoma Way, Tacoma; 253-475-9843; daily 8 p.m.–2 a.m.). The establishment is a giant coffee pot, built in 1927, a former speakeasy and music club, and now a dive bar. Cheap beer and wine and karaoke.

THREE MAGNETS BREWING CO. AND THE MAGNET

600 Franklin Street SE, Suite 105, Olympia • www.threemagnetsbrewing.com • 360-972-2481 • The Magnet menu available daily 8 a.m.–2 p.m.; Three Magnets Pubhouse menu available Sunday–Thursday 11 a.m.–10 p.m., Friday and Saturday 11 a.m.–midnight

Nighttime is for beer and fancy, vegan-friendly pub food (get the vegan queso dip, the blackened rockfish sliders, or the Cuban mojo). Morning through midafternoon is for hair-of-the-dog drinks and The Magnet menu, with a traditional and creative assortment of breakfast and lunch food. (Say yes to the butter pecan waffle.) Look for the special beer release dinners and random pop-ups.

WELL 80 BREWHOUSE

514 4th Avenue E, Olympia • well80.com • 360-915-6653 • Open Sunday–Thursday 11:30 a.m.–
10 p.m., Friday and Saturday 11:30 a.m.–11 p.m.

A new brew pub sits atop Well 80, one of the functional artesian wells for which Olympia is
known. Using water directly from that source, brewers craft well-made beer for the tap and
the bottle. Come for the refreshments and get a hand-tossed pizza, burger or sandwich, or
other brewhouse faves.

DILLINGER'S

406 Washington Street SE, Olympia • www.dillingerscocktailsandkitchen.com • 360-515-0650 •
Open Monday–Thursday 4–10 p.m., Friday and Saturday 4 p.m.–midnight, Sunday Suppers 4–8 p.m.ish

A Prohibition-themed craft bar, housed in a former Securities Building built during the sad-
times teetotaling era. One of the rooms is an actual bank vault. They don't use mixers in their
cocktails, instead doing it the old-fashioned way and juicing fresh every day. The bartenders
know what they're doing, and they're happy to have a chat about the whats and whys of the
cocktail they're making you. The drink menu is long, with a ton of fantastic cocktail options
plus flights. The happy hour (opening until 6 p.m. daily), and the Friday and Saturday late-
night happy hour (10 p.m. to midnight) have great noshes and $6 drinks. Get any of the
classics, including the gold rush (bourbon, lemon, and honey) and the boilermaker (a shot
of bourbon and pacific ale). Later on, try one of their originals, such as Konjo Bunna (pisco,
angostura amaro, cynar, lemon, blueberry hill syrup) or This is Shroberry (mezcal, tequila,
strawberry, lemon, Kümmel). Or, for the courageous, pick your base spirit and let the bartender make something up on the spot. You could get a great wine, but why? The fresh and
locally sourced dinner will make foodies, picky eaters, and food allergists happy. Free live
music every Monday.

Good to Know: Olympia Brewery (originally
The Capital Brewing Company) was founded
in 1906 at the base of Tumwater Falls in
nearby Tumwater. Credit goes to Olympia's
founder, Leopold Schmidt, and the brewery,
of which he owned a portion, for coining the
phrase "It's the Water." They were referring
to the high-quality beer.

// South Sound Craft Crawl, South Sound

WHITE WOOD CIDER CO.

728 4th Avenue E, Olympia • whitewoodcider.com • 360-890-1852 • Open Monday, Wednesday, and Thursday 3–9 p.m., Friday–Sunday noon–9 p.m.

It's an acclaimed "teeny tiny" tasting room and taproom featuring heirloom apples grown in the South Puget Sound and Washington State. They pick and press apples in autumn, when they're ripe and ready to go, then ferment the juice through the winter.

 Stay Over

SWANTOWN INN AND SPA

1431 11th Avenue SE, Olympia • www.swantowninn.com • 360-753-9123

A four-bedroom, one-suite "bed & breakfast retreat" in a Queen/Anne Eastlake Victorian mansion built in 1887. Get a massage while you're there and enjoy the three-course gourmet breakfast. $129-plus.

THE INN AT MALLARD COVE

5025 Meridian Road NE, Olympia • www.theinnatmallardcove.com • 360-491-9795

Located on 14 forested acres, this English Tudor–style three-bedroom B&B is quiet, with views of Puget Sound and Anderson Island, nature trails, gardens, and a private beach. Each of the bedrooms has a private bath, sitting area, terrace, and fireplace. $199.

GROUND INN

417 Union Avenue SE, Olympia • www.groundinn.com • 360-539-8300

A hostel in walking distance to downtown Olympia and the Capitol, this "green lodging" features organic continental breakfasts, organic linens and towels, and musical instruments. There's room for 14 people, with three private rooms and two dorm rooms with bunks, divided by gender. $40-plus.

OLYBUNGALOWS

1232 5th Avenue SE, Olympia • www.olybungalows.com • 360-999-6961

Two little guest houses and a cottage, custom renovated using local wood, built by craftspeople, and surrounded by a garden full of herbs, fruits, berries, and native plants. Within walking distance of downtown and the Capitol. Cottage $125, bungalow $145.

Camping

TENINO CITY PARK

Park Avenue E, Tenino

Stay at the park within the city for ease of access to the Stone Quarry swimming pool, many bike trails, and nice small-town vibes. Only $8/night.

MILLERSYLVANIA STATE PARK

12245 Tilley Road S, Olympia • 360-753-1519

An 842-acre camping park, with 3,300 feet of freshwater shoreline on Deep Lake, two swimming beaches, miles of hiking and biking trails, and watercraft rental. Reserve a site at washington.goingtocamp.com.

OFFUT LAKE RESORT

4005 120th Avenue SE, Tenino • offutlakeresort.com • 360-264-2438

A family-owned campground with cabins, tent sites, the lakefront, and historic Public House Restaurant, open for fishing and lodging year-round.

☰ *While You're Here*

SWIM IN THE QUARRY POOL

City Park, 319 Park Avenue E, Tenino • www.ci.tenino.wa.us • 360-264-2368 • Open end of June–early September, Wednesday–Sunday noon–6 p.m.

In its heyday, the city of Tenino was home to a booming sandstone quarry. (That's why it's called Stone City. They even had their own wooden currency.) The sandstone quarry has long been closed for production, after some guy accidentally struck a spring and the pit filled with water, drowning all the quarrymen's machinery and equipment. Now it's a pool with shallow and deep ends, two diving boards, and a waterfall. This is 15 miles south of Olympia and truly has a small-town vibe, so call ahead to confirm times. $5.

>> If you're down for some more stone-related entertainment, visit the Tenino Stove Carvers (147 Olympia Street N, Tenino; 360-280-9098; teninostonecarvers.com) on Friday or Saturday between 9 a.m. and 4 p.m. to see the professional stone artists at work.

// Tenino Stone Quarry, Tenino

RUN WITH WOLVES AT WOLF HAVEN INTERNATIONAL

3111 Offut Lake Road SE, Tenino • wolfhaven.org • 360-264-4695

Since 1982, Wolf Haven International has taken in displaced and captive-born animals. Take a 50-minute guided walking tour of the sanctuary, where you might see a wolf. You also might not see a wolf because humans have probably screwed them over and now they are scared of you. Proceeds go to conservation efforts and the care of these endangered animals. Reservations required. $13.

>> Instead of crying over the state of the world and how humans ruin everything, **"adopt" a wolf**. For $125 you will get a biography and matted photo of your wolf, biannual updates, a window cling, an adoption certificate, as well as a one-year subscription to *Wolf Tracks* magazine!

☰ *Take a Tour*

COFFEE IN THE MORNING, BEER IN THE AFTERNOON BIKE TOUR

Start/end: Tumwater Historical Park, 802 Deschutes Way SW, Tumwater • southsoundadventures .com • 360-970-9619 • March–November, coffee tour 9:30 a.m., beer tour 1 p.m.

Ride rain or shine, stopping for three servings of coffee or beer, depending on the tour, along the way. During the 3.5-hour, 12-mile tour, you'll also pull over to experience some scenic locations, such as Priest Point Park and Governor's Mansion. $45 includes bike and helmet, $40 if you bring your own. Super fun time and awesome day are included on all tours.

WASHINGTON STATE CAPITOL TOURS

Legislative Building, 416 Sid Snyder Avenue SW, Olympia • des.wa.gov • 360-407-2200 • Monday– Friday tours start 10 a.m., with last tour at 3 p.m.; Saturday and Sunday tours start 11 a.m., with last tour at 3 p.m.

See where the sausage gets made, because if you stop paying attention for even a second you open a door to fascism. Free public tours of the Legislative Building, a.k.a. the Capitol, start on the hour and run 50 minutes in length, though you can make an appointment for a botanical tour of the Capitol Campus grounds or a tour of the Governor's Mansion. You can also get a map online or at the north entrance or visitor's office of the building for a self-guided tour.

KAYAK NISQUALLY TOURS

Luhr Beach, 4949 D Milluhr Road NE, Olympia • www.kayaknisqually.com • 360-453-7135

Go on an eco-tour of Nisqually Reach, a small bay of the Puget Sound approximately 11 miles east of Olympia. See sea lions and seals, porpoises, all kinds of birds, and maybe even orcas or gray whales, all while learning the history of the Puget Sound Basin! The porpoise tour meets not at Luhr Beach but at the Steilacoom Ferry dock and continues on to a porpoise and whale-seeking adventure. For you morning people, the Predawn & Sunrise tour puts you in the run-ning for seeing bioluminescent plankton. Tours are three- to five-hours long. You can also go on two- and three-day camping expeditions. Tours: $69–89; Camping: $299–$499.

ABOVE & BEYOND

Olympia is a town full of bibliophiles, with specialty stores featuring comics, multicultural books, and cheap, rare finds along with the more standard literary fare. It also has a couple nice dog parks and a couple nice skate parks for your fresh-air needs.

Dogs | Dogs roam free at **Sunrise Park** (505 Bing Street NW, Olympia), which includes separate fenced-off areas for big and small dogs and water stations for humans and canines. Lacey's **Off-Leash Dog Park** (2418 Hogum Bay Road NE, Lacey; 360-867-2491) is open daily from 7 a.m. to dusk and has separate fenced-off areas for big and small dogs, sand and gravel areas for digging, obstacles and trick structures for playing on, a dog-shaped patio, and a big field.

Skates | At 11,500 square feet, **Friendly Grove Skate Court** (2316 Friendly Grove Road NE, Olympia) has enough space to spread out, plus a snake run, a mini-bowl, and lots of other fun features. **Yelm Skate Park** (203 1st Street NE, Yelm) has a lot of flat surface to work with, plus a small clover bowl, a small handrail, and some other small features. For photos and more information, go to www.northwestskater.com.

Books | Since the founding of **Browsers Bookshop** (107 Capitol Way N, Olympia; www.browsersolympia.com; 360-357-7462) 80 years ago, this bookstore has been under the ownership of four badass book-loving ladies. Today it carries a range of fiction and nonfiction and hosts author and literary events regularly.

Orca Books (509 4th Avenue E, Olympia; www.orcabooks.com; 360-352-0123) is the largest indie bookstore in Olympia. They will take your used books but not your used VHS.

Half Price Books Outlet (1520 Cooper Point Road SW, Olympia; www.hpb.com; 360-705-0236) is a national chain of used bookstores, with used books under $1 to rare books and first editions in the $1,000s. They also take, buy, and sell movies. Open daily 10 a.m.–8 p.m.

The claim to fame of **De Colores Books** (507 Washington Street SE, Olympia; 360-357-9400) is that it's a multicultural bookstore with books in many languages and from cultures around the world.

Last Word Books (111 Cherry Street NE, Olympia; www.lastwordbooks.org; 360-786-9673) wants you to know, "If books are your drug of choice, Last Word has your fix!" Across the street from Olympia Coffee Roasters. Open Monday–Saturday 11 a.m.–7 p.m.

Danger Room Comics (201 4th Avenue W, Olympia; www.dangerroomoly.com; 360-705-3050) is a comic book store with a wide selection of superhero and indie comics. Lasers have been deactivated.

Not Ready to Go Home | Head east to **Mount Rainier National Park** (www.nps.gov/mora) for a day trip or longer of wilderness hiking, biking, or camping. $30 single vehicle.

SOUTH HOOD CANAL: UNION, SHELTON, HOODSPORT

FROM SEATTLE: 1.5 TO 2.5 HOURS · DAYS HERE: 0.5-PLUS

EAT	DRINK	DO	BUY
oysters	a margarita at 2 Margaritas	scuba	air for your scuba tank

Plan Around

OYSTER MONTH AT ALDERBROOK RESORT & SPA

April · www.alderbrookresort.com

Watch oyster-harvesting demos, eat barbecued and fresh oysters prepared by the executive chef on the resort's dock, take local beach tours, and watch guest shucker demonstrations.

Eat & Drink

Get Caffeinated

UNION SQUARE DELI

310 E Dalby Road, Union · www.unionsquaredeli.com · 360-898-DELI · Open Saturday–Thursday 7 a.m.–9 p.m.

Nummy brick-oven pizzas, breakfasts, sandwiches, paninis, wraps, and salads. Also something called "breakfast pizzas," which seem to be pizzas with eggs on top. Coffee, too.

URRACO COFFEE CO.

628 Cota Street, Shelton · www.urracocoffee.com · 360-462-5258 · Open Monday–Friday 6 a.m.–7 p.m., Saturday 7 a.m.–7 p.m., Sunday 7 a.m.–5 p.m.

Fair-trade and organic coffee is roasted on-site, and even though they hate the phrase "gourmet coffee," the label does apply. Get your coffee to go via the drive-thru window, or stop in for a cinnamon roll and a chat.

BLONDIE'S FAMILY RESTAURANT

628 W Railroad Avenue, Shelton • 360-432-2777 • Open daily 6 a.m.–7:30 p.m.

Good ol' American home cooking and small-town vibes for old-fashioned prices. Stop in for a big breakfast and get a piece of pie, made from scratch just like moms of legend used to do.

Farm Fresh

HUNTER FARMS

1921 E State Route 106, Union • hunter-farms.com • 360-898-2222 • Open daily 9 a.m.–5 p.m.

The farm has been in the family since the 1880s. Pick up a Christmas tree and wreaths; potatoes, berries, asparagus, and other produce; and greenhouse plants, hay, and pumpkins, depending on the season.

UNION CITY MARKET

5101 WA-106, Union • www.unioncitymarket.com • 360-898-3500 • Open Thursday–Monday 10 a.m.–6 p.m.

A community gathering space where locals present their food and drink, gifts, and art for public consumption. Come for the Canal Cookouts on every third Thursday of the month to get the freshest local culinary delights.

// Oysters at Alderbrook

TAYLOR SHELLFISH MARKET

130 SE Lynch Road, Shelton • www.taylorshellfishfarms.com • 360-432-3300 • Open daily
10 a.m.–6 p.m.

High-quality, sustainable shellfish in Puget Sound since the 1890s. That's a long-ass time ago, and people have been obsessed over it for the duration. Pour some Tabasco on that fresh-out-of-the-ocean oyster and slurp it down with a cold beer.

SOUND FRESH CLAMS & OYSTERS

www.skookumpoint.com

Located on Skookum Point, where the inlets of Totten and Little Skookum meet. Sound Fresh Clams & Oysters has been in the Evans family since the 1930s, and today they grow Manila clams and Kumamoto, Olympia, and Skookum Point Pacific oysters. You can find them at the Olympia Farmers' Market (see page 34) and at restaurants throughout the area.

Dining and Booze

SMOKING MO'S

203 W Railroad Avenue, Shelton • www.smokingmos.com • 360-462-0163 • Open Tuesday–Saturday
11:30 a.m.–close

Another former bank, which makes you think about the lifespan of banks. (The plaque, from 1915, still adorns the brick building.) Smoking Mo's—after owner/chef Monica—serves award-winning Carolina-style hickory-smoked BBQ, fresh salads, and Southern specials and sides. Get the pork rinds fried to order, the loaded mac & cheese, and a BBQ plate. This being the Hood Canal, you can go to the upstairs Oyster Bar starting at 3 p.m. Tuesday through Saturday, or go downstairs to The Palmetto for craft beers. Pick up a shaker of one of Mo's Signature Spices before you head out.

2 MARGARITAS

5121 E State Route 106, Union • www.2margaritasunion.com • 360-898-2462 • Open Sunday–Thursday 11 a.m.–10 p.m., Friday and Saturday 11 a.m.–11 p.m.

Mexican with a big menu, a big selection of margaritas, and bottomless chips and salsa. Get the seafood enchiladas and the carne asada burrito, and expect to take home leftovers. For more **2 Margaritas**, check out the location in Allyn (18321 WA-3, Allyn).

HOODSPORT WINERY

23501 Highway 101, Hoodsport • www.hoodsport.com • 360-877-9894 • Open daily 10 a.m.–6 p.m.

Founded in 1978, Hoodsport Winery is one of Washington State's early trendsetters. Taste award-winning wines while looking out over the Hood Canal and the Olympic Mountains.

☰ *Stay Over*

Resorts

ALDERBROOK RESORT & SPA

10 E WA-106, Union • www.alderbrookresort.com • 360-898-2200

This resort is of the hardcore variety in that you never have to leave it. Everything's curated and the devil is in the details in terms of luxurious amenities. Stay in one of 77 guest rooms, or in one of the 16 cottages, each with a fully equipped kitchen, TV and DVD player, and nice linens. Everything you could ever want is right there: a Creativity on the Canal program for the artistically inclined, a day spa for the rejuvenation inclined, a pool and a marina with boat rentals for the water sports inclined, 5 miles of nature trails for the hiking inclined . . . the list goes on. Get any and all foods at the resort's restaurant, including a big selection of locally sourced oysters. Pet-friendly accommodations available. $190-plus.

ROBIN HOOD VILLAGE RESORT

6780 E State Route 106, Union • www.robinhoodvillageresort.com • 360-898-2163

In 1934, the Hollywood set designer for the original *Robin Hood* movie built, or had built, this resort. Beyond being a forest, it doesn't look like Sherwood Forest or anything, so take this factoid however you want. The 16 wood-paneled cottages have been updated since both the 16th century and the 1930s. Some have flat-screen TVs, some have WiFi, and some have private hot tubs, just as the heroic outlaw of yore would have wanted it. You can walk down to the water and take out one of the resort's complimentary kayaks or, at low tide, harvest some oysters and then gulp them raw right there or take them back to your cottage's kitchenette and cook them up. The gazebos along the canal provide a great spot for reading a book and drinking a glass of wine while the water rolls by. For romantic times, the on-site restaurant has legit candlelit dining with lots of good wine. Pet-friendly accommodations available for $20–50, depending on your pet's size. $140-plus per night.

MIKES BEACH RESORT

38470 N US 101, Lilliwaup • www.mikesbeachresort.com • 360-877-5324

There are four waterfront options: a cabin, a honeymoon cabin, an RV named *The Franklin*, and "glamping"—one waterview cabin across the road from tent and RV campsites. You can harvest oysters and clams from the private beach or launch directly from there for some good beginner to advanced scuba diving. Fill your scuba tank at their fill station after. Pet-friendly accommodations available. $35-plus.

SUNRISE MOTEL AND DIVE RESORT

24520 Highway 101, Hoodsport • myweb.hcc.net/sunrise/index • 360-877-5301

Not fancy in the least, but the owner is nice and it's right on the water, ideal for the many divers who use this spot as a launch point on the regular. Seasonal fishers and crabbers can harvest right off the dock, and you can moor your boat. $69.50-plus.

Caboose

PIRATE'S COVE CABOOSE

3571 Kamilche Point Road, Shelton • greatgetaways.com/pirate-s-cove-caboose.html • 360-462-6278

A fully restored eight-sleeper Great Northern Railway caboose on 3 acres of beach with a private hot tub, flat-screen TV, gas fireplace, equipped kitchen, beachside charcoal grill, fire pit, picnic table, and two kayaks free to use. Pet friendly.

ABOVE & BEYOND

Books | Perhaps you noticed that the one kind of book Olympia was missing was the metaphysical variety. Fortunately, there's **Brilliant Moon** (221 W Railroad Avenue, Suite A, Shelton; 360-868-2190), where you can get books, teas, and gifts for all your metaphysical needs. Stop by for Tea & Tarot Reading Tuesdays.

Not Ready to Go Home | Visit the other five locations on the Washington Shellfish Trail (www.shellfishtrail.org), including **Port Angeles** (page 192) and **the San Juan Islands** (page 203).

Good to Know |

- An earthquake in 1949 rocked Olympia's downtown, and many buildings were damaged or destroyed.
- Evergreen State College was authorized by the state legislature in 1967.
- Hama Hama Oyster Company is owned by the descendants of ship captain G. K. Robbins, one of Hoodsport's first settlers.

Been There, Done That |

- Head northwest to the Olympic Peninsula (page 175) and northeast to Port Townsend (page 91).
- Head northeast to the Kitsap Peninsula for Bainbridge Island (page 125) and Whidbey Island (page 249).

SHELLFISH IN SOUTH PUGET SOUND AND HOOD CANAL   49

Camping

POTLATCH STATE PARK

21020 N Highway 101, Shelton • parks.state.wa.us/569/Potlatch • 1-888-CAMPOUT

An 84-acre camping park with 5,700 feet of saltwater shoreline. This state park is not about the hiking trails—it's about the water.

☰ *While You're Here*

SCUBA

The Hood Canal is well known in the scuba community as an ideal place to dive with giant Pacific octopuses and wolf eels because of its relatively gentle currents. Visit **Octopus Hole**, located between Lilliwaup and Hoodsport; **Sund Rock**, with access at Hoodsport 'N Dive; **Jorsted Creek** (37941 Highway 101, Lilliwaup); or **Mikes Beach Resort** (page 47). Get scuba gear and training at **Hoodsport 'N Dive** (24080 Highway 101, Hoodsport; hoodsportndive .com; 360-877-6818).

SKYDIVE

141 W Airview Way, Shelton • www.skydivekapowsin.com • 360-432-8000

Jump out of a plane tandem or solo to fall at 120 miles per hour for 13,000 or 18,000 feet, only to land softly on a grass field in Shelton. Pay a little extra for the professionally edited video and digital photos of your face peeling back. $205-plus.

3

Beer and Beyond in Skagit Valley

FROM SEATTLE: 1.5 HOURS · DAYS HERE: 1 TO 2

DO	EAT	DRINK	BUY
the Skagit Farm to Pint Ale Trail	blueberries	beer	tulip bulbs

If it's been a while since you left the hilly, skyscraper-dense city, the expansive big-skyness of the Skagit Valley is going to be a welcome change. The area is known for the Skagit Valley Tulip Festival, which starts according to Mother Nature sometime in April. During that time, hundreds of thousands of tourists from near and far come to gawk at the rows upon rows of glorious flowers lifting their skirts. It's a big deal, and busy—locals caution about the intense traffic and recommend you visit during the week if you want to avoid the chaos. The surrounding towns of Bow and Edison (called "**Bow Edison**" colloquially because Edison is so tiny) in the north, **Mount Vernon** and **La Conner** to the south, **Anacortes** to the west on the **Salish Sea**, **Concrete** off to the east, and **Burlington** and **Sedro-Woolley** in the middle are happy to hop on the tourism train. The same month kicks off an extravaganza of springtime festivals, such as Skagit Beer Week and the Kiwanis Salmon Bake.

Although it's famous for the tulips and the Tulip Festival, most of the year Skagit County is pretty quiet, and its primary industry is agriculture. You can assume that whatever restaurant at which you're eating leans organic and is sourcing locally. Restaurants partner with local farms, many of which operate farm stands that are open to the public all year-round, though of course the spring through fall is when the harvest is most bountiful. With Skagit Bay and the Salish Sea to the west, you can also find plenty of fresh catch. Most notably, the Skagit Valley is one of the few places in the world that does the seed-to-stein **trifecta of brewing**: growing the barley varietals on Skagit Valley fields, malting it locally at Skagit Valley Malting, and brewing it in town at the 11 local breweries. That's where you come in.

Getting There

BY CAR OR SHUTTLE | Take I-5 N for 60 miles

BY TRAIN OR BUS | From King Street Station to Skagit Transportation Center (105 E Kincaid Street, Mount Vernon), take Amtrak Cascades #516 or #518, or the 5622 Thruway Bus. Travel time: approximately 1.5 hours. Cost: $13–31.

Highlight Reel

SKAGIT FARM TO PINT ALE TRAIL

skagitfarmtopint.com

Download the Skagit Farm to Pint passport at skagitfarmtopint.com to take yourself on a tour of Skagit Valley's breweries, from Anacortes Brewing Company in the west to Skagit River Brewery in the east. If you get all 11 stamps, you win a free pint glass! You also win the experience of drinking 11 beers.

LA CONNER BREWERY

117 S 1st Street, La Conner • www.laconnerbrewery.com • 360-466-1415 • Open Sunday–Thursday 11:30 a.m.–9 p.m., Friday and Saturday 11:30 a.m.–9:30 p.m.

Using Skagit Valley malts and hops from Yakima, La Conner Brewery makes rotating and seasonal brews. The food menu is a mishmash of PNW and cuisines from elsewhere (a.k.a. American), with tacos and enchiladas, burgers and sandwiches, salads, and wood-fired pizza.

ANACORTES BREWERY AND ROCKFISH GRILL

320 Commercial Avenue, Anacortes • www.anacortesrockfish.com/brewery.cfm • 360-588-1720

So nuts about local sourcing, they even sourced the vessels from Ripley Stainless in British Columbia! Sit down at the Rockfish Grill and order a red ale or an American IPA to go with the Hefeweizen cheese dip, ghost pepper fish tacos, and their Caesar salad with wood-fired garlic cheese croutons.

BASTION BREWING COMPANY

12529 Christianson Road, Anacortes • www.bastionbrewery.com • 360-399-1614 • Open Sunday and Tuesday 11:30 a.m.–8 p.m.; Monday 4–7 p.m., Wednesday and Thursday 11:30 a.m.–9 p.m.; Friday and Saturday 11:30 a.m.–10 p.m.

Its location makes it an ideal spot to stop by after biking or frolicking along the beach. The selection of ales, IPAs, and a stout or two rotates seasonally, and you can get a range of dipping sauces with your wings, which come in medium, hot, or "hellfire." We recommend getting a flight of beer and the mango curry dipping sauce. Or the spicy garlic Parmesan. Also the KC BBQ, because why not.

CHUCKANUT BREWERY AND TAP ROOM

South Nut: 11937 Higgins Airport Way, Burlington • chuckanutbreweryandkitchen.com • 360-752-3377 • Open Monday–Friday 3–7 p.m., Saturday and Sunday 12–7 p.m.

Established by the founders of one of the first craft breweries in the Northwest, Chuckanut Brewery approaches brewing as the competitive sport that it is, medaling in the Great American Beer Festival, the World Beer Cup, the North American Beer Awards, Washington Beer Awards, and more. Along with the award-winning beers, they serve noshes and hard cider, plus they welcome food trucks from other local restaurants. **Chuckanut Brewery's North Nut** is located in Bellingham at 601 W Holly Street.

FLYERS RESTAURANT & BREWHOUSE

15426 Suite B Airport Drive, Burlington • www.eatatflyers.com • 360-899-1025 • Open Sunday 11–5 p.m., Monday 11 a.m.–3 p.m., Tuesday–Thursday 11 a.m.–8 p.m., Friday and Saturday 11 a.m.–9 p.m.

In this aviation-themed brewery and restaurant at Skagit Airport, watch planes and helicopters land and take off as you eat pub fare, sandwiches and burgers, and some aggressive-sounding and award-winning ales, porters, hefes, pilsners, and porters. They don't have to stretch their pun-making muscles in naming the "test flight," which includes a 5-ounce sampling of six brews.

>> Always dreamed of being a pilot? Before drinking a brew, take a pilot training course with Cascade Aviation. The introductory class includes 30 minutes on the ground and 30 minutes in the air for only $99 and can go toward the 40 hours of flight time required for a private pilot certification. You can also rent an aircraft if you're already certified. www.flycascade.com, 360-707-2838.

SKAGIT VALLEY CARDINAL CRAFT BREWING ACADEMY TAPROOM

15579 Peterson Road, Burlington • 360-416-2537 • Open Fridays 4–8 p.m.

Skagit Valley College offers a craft-brewing certificate program in which, for one year, aspiring brewers study the culture, biochemistry, wort production, maintenance, flavor productions, and business of brewing. Of course, all that time in the brew lab yields more than just know-how—it yields beer. Come drink some at the Cardinal Craft Taproom. Bring your own food and snacks.

GARDEN PATH FERMENTATION

11653 Higgins Airport Way, Burlington • gardenpathwa.com • Open Wednesday–Monday noon–8 p.m.

Garden Path Fermentation's goal is to let people see the production of brew, cider, mead, and wine from seed to glass. By sharing brewing space with local breweries, they are able to focus on fermentation, mixing native yeast from flowers and fruits with the air of Skagit Valley and somehow turning that into beer, and you get to taste the results of this process.

NORTH SOUND BREWING

17406 State Route 536, Unit A, Mount Vernon • www.northsoundbrewing.com • 360-982-2057 • Tasting room open Monday–Thursday 3–7:30 p.m., Friday 1–8:30 p.m., Saturday noon–8:30 p.m., Sunday noon–6:30 p.m.

An ambience of sunporch meets garage, brews of the United Kingdom meet the Northwest. They serve snacks such as nachos and Costco burgers, and you're welcome to bring your own food or order a pizza or Mexican from nearby restaurants. It's an adults-only oasis; dogs welcome.

SKAGIT RIVER BREWERY

404 S 3rd Street, Mount Vernon • www.skagitbrew.com • 360-336-2884 • Open Sunday–Thursday 11 a.m.–8 p.m., Friday and Saturday 11 a.m.–9 p.m.

For more than 20 years, Skagit River Brewery has been wood-firing pizza, barbecuing meats, and brewing craft beer. They stick by kindergarten's number one most important lesson—sharing is caring—and so feature beers from other regional breweries on their tap. Get the fried pickles.

FARMSTRONG BREWING CO.

110 Stewart Road, Mount Vernon • www.farmstrongbrewing.com • 360-873-8852 • Open Monday 3–9 p.m., Tuesday–Thursday noon–9 p.m., Friday and Saturday noon–10 p.m., Sunday noon–9 p.m. (open 30 minutes prior to 10 a.m. Seahawks game kickoffs)

Tall windows, the gleaming wood bar, and an updated version of bar furnishings (green glass, maroon walls, but fancy) make the La Raza Ambar and Stackin' Hay IPA taste even better. Outside you can get food from the food truck, which is usually Sushi by Chin, though every now and then there's a pop-up oyster bar. Bring your own home-brew in during Skagit Beer Week for the Wort Challenge and enter a photo of your dog for the Dog of the Month Competition.

BIRDSVIEW BREWING COMPANY

38302 WA-20, Concrete • www.birdsviewbrewingcompany.com • 360-826-3406 • Open Tuesday– Thursday noon–7 p.m., Friday and Saturday noon–8 p.m., Sunday noon–6 p.m.

Pull over on WA-20 on your way back from North Cascades National Park to stretch your legs, refuel with a burger or sandwich, and drink some Ditsy Blonde, SasScotch Ale, or any of the beers brewed on the premises—look for their beer crossing signs. Voted the Best Brewery in Skagit County in 2014, this family-owned business is small and adorable, with bragging rights to its father-daughter brewing team.

>> Looking for another epicurean-focused trail? Check out the **Bow Edison Food Trail**, a self-guided road-trip tour of Bow Edison's artisan spirits, produce, meat, and seafood. To download the map, go to bowedisonfoodtrail.tumblr.com or visitskagitvalley.com.

// Birdsview Brewing Company, Concrete

Beer and Beyond Festivals

There are many Skagit celebrations of inebriation and local farm-fresh bounty during the year. There are also a few Skagit Valley–wide events that don't involve beer but that are absolutely essential to know about. You can, of course, see tulips and then drink beer, or drink beer and then see the tulips. Same goes for birds during the Birds of Winter. You won't need to be drunk to fall off your chair when you see those bald eagles or the fields of flowers.

SKAGIT FARM TO PINT FESTIVAL AND SKAGIT BEER WEEK

March • www.skagitbeerweek.com

A weeklong celebration featuring the 11 breweries of the Skagit Farm to Pint Ale Trail.

BIER ON THE PIER

One weekend in October • Port of Anacortes Events Center, 100 Commercial Avenue, Anacortes • anacortes.org/bier-on-the-pier • 360-293-7911 • $25–35, or $7–12 for designated drivers.

BREW ON THE SLOUGH

One Saturday in October • Maple Hall, 104 Commercial Avenue, Anacortes • lovelaconner.com/la-conner-beer-festival • $30

SKAGIT BEER AND WINE FEST

One Saturday in November • Eaglemont, 4800 Eaglemont Drive, Mount Vernon • www.mountvernonchamber.com • 360-428-8547 • $55–100

SKAGIT VALLEY TULIP FESTIVAL

April • @skagitvalleytulipfestival • tulipfestival.org

In the 1630s, a tulip craze took over Holland. According to legend, a single bulb could cost as much as a house. Like, a fancy house. But like any bubble, eventually it popped and people lost their fortunes. Fortunately, you don't have to take out a second mortgage on your condo to enjoy the incredible beauty of these perennial herbaceous bulbiferous geophytes. Just head up to Mount Vernon in Skagit Valley for the annual Tulip Festival. Over a million tulips are planted in fields around the Skagit Valley every year, and the festival marks the colorful culmination of all that planting. From the end of March through the beginning of May—depending on the weather—visitors can enjoy trolley rides and strolls through glorious petal-plush fields. Warning: Leave your drones at home.

Self-Guided

ROOZENGAARDE

15867 Beaver Marsh Road, Mount Vernon • www.tulips.com • 1-866-488-5477

In preparation for the springtime festival, the 3-acre show garden is planted with 300,000 bulbs. You can check bloom status at www.tulips.com/bloommap. The business is open year-round, and you can buy tulip, hyacinth, daffodils, muscari, and crocus bulbs from their website to make a little tulip festival in your backyard. Entrance fee: $7.

TULIP TOWN

15002 Bradshaw Road, Mount Vernon • www.tuliptown.com/wordpress • 360-424-8152

Check out the Prater Homestead, where new-to-the-US tulips are showcased. If you're feeling foot sore, take the Blue Trolley through the fields (cost: $2), or visit Tulip Town's Pot Shop (sorry, pots are referring to those cylindrical things that hold plants). Professional kite flyers come to Tulip Town weekends to show off their skills; you can buy kites in the art shop. Entrance fee: $7.

 *Tours*

SHUTTER TOURS

www.shuttertours.com • 425-516-8838

Get picked up in downtown Seattle or Lynwood, then take an all-day tour through tulips fields in Mount Vernon, with a stop for lunch in La Conner. $99.

ROADS2TULIPS

www.roads2tulips.com • 425-493-4555

Pickup at the La Conner Channel Lodge (205 N 1st Street, La Conner; www.laconnerlodging .com; 360-466-1500). Includes all-day tour through tulip fields, lunch in La Conner, a tulip exhibit at Skagit Valley Museum, or take the Tulips-Only tour.

SKAGIT GUIDED ADVENTURES

www.skagitguidedadventures.com • 360-474-7479

Pickup at Mount Vernon's Amtrak station and local hotels. All-day tour includes visit to tulip fields with expert (and friendly) guide. $96.

TULIP COUNTRY BIKE TOURS

www.countrycycling.com • 360-424-7461

Self-guided tour includes bike rental, maps, and festival tips/information. $40.

BIRDS OF WINTER

birdsofwinter.org • 360-421-8423

From early November to April, you can find 15,000 trumpeter swans scattered throughout Skagit Valley farmland. That's in addition to the 100,000 noisy snow geese who trek 3,000 miles from Wrangel Island, Russia, to get here, making them the only migratory birds who come all the way from the other side of the international date line. Early in the winter, hundreds of bald eagles feed upriver on salmon near Concrete, Rockport, and Marblemount, where a special festival is held in their honor. When the spawning season ends, they congregate in huge numbers on Fir Island near La Conner and the Samish Flats near Edison.

The valley is renowned for wintertime birds of prey, and it's one of the only places in North America where you can see all five species of falcons that regularly inhabit the United States, plus many other kinds of raptors that head south from colder climes to visit the Skagit River to hunt ducks, geese, moles, and voles. If you're lucky, you might even see some owls, including snowy owls that, in seemingly random irruption years, come down from the Arctic to patrol the dikes and shorelines along Padilla Bay.

You don't have to be a binocular-obsessed birder to be amazed by the sheer number and beauty of these birds. And you don't need to take a hallucinogen to get seriously tripped out by murmurations, when a dozen or a hundred or 20,000 birds do some synchronized flying.

Come to Skagit Valley's Birds of Winter to see the birds, the bird-inspired art (put a bird on it), and exhibitions, or take a class, workshop, or guided tour.

>>   There aren't too many hotels or B&Bs in the Skagit Valley, but there are a ton of campgrounds and state parks, plus lots of places on Airbnb and VRBO.

// Snow Geese

BOW–EDISON

FROM SEATTLE: 1 TO 1.5 HOURS • DAYS HERE: 0.5-PLUS

EAT	DO
Bow Hill u-pick blueberries	Bow Edison Food Trail

 ## Eat & Drink

Get Caffeinated

TWEETS

5800 Cains Court, Bow • tweetscafe.com • 360-820-9912 • Open Friday–Sunday 9 a.m.–6 p.m.

An artisan cafe and eatery near Samish Bay. Get a breve and an ice cream scoop or something snacky from the weekly menu.

EDISON CAFÉ

5797 Main Street, Bow • 360-766-6960 • Open Tuesday–Saturday 7 a.m.–3 p.m., Sunday 8 a.m.–2 p.m.

A converted gas station and local favorite, Edison Café serves American-style breakfast and lunch. Small-town vibes with good coffee and French toast.

Farm Fresh

BOW HILL U-PICK

15628 Bow Hill Road, Bow • www.bowhillblueberries.com • 360-399-1006 • U-pick open mid-July–mid September Friday and Saturday 10 a.m.–5 p.m., Sunday 11 a.m.–5 p.m. • Farm store open Wednesday–Saturday 10 a.m.–5 p.m., Sunday 11 a.m.–5 p.m.

Get the $5 Grazing Pass and turn your tongue purple at Bow Hill U-Pick, open for self-service when blueberries bloom. Eat some blueberry ice cream, made from the farm's heirloom Jersey berries and Lopez Island Creamery milk, and take a hard-earned flat of blueberries home.

SAMISH BAY CHEESE

15115 Bow Hill Road, Bow • www.samishbaycheese.com • 360-766-6707 • Open Monday–Thursday 10 a.m.–4 p.m., Friday and Saturday 10 a.m.–5 p.m., Sunday 11 a.m.–4 p.m.

Come down to the retail shop and tasting room to learn about this certified organic farm's cheese-making processes, get a cheese board with a sampling practically straight out of the cows, and enjoy a glass of beer, wine, or cider. Take some cheese to go, plus some yogurt, kefir, and some pork and grass-fed beef from animals raised on the farm.

BLANCHARD MOUNTAIN FARM

15404 Estes Road, Bow • www.blanchardmountainfarm.com • 360-399-1495 • Open seasonally, daily 10 a.m.–6 p.m.

Stop by the farm stand for a variety of greens, beans, eggplants, squash, and heirloom toma-toes still warm from the sun.

TAYLOR SHELLFISH SAMISH OYSTER BAR AND SHELLFISH MARKET

2182 Chuckanut Drive, Bow • www.taylorshellfishfarms.com • 360-766-6002 • Open 9 a.m.–5 p.m.

High-quality, sustainable shellfish in Skagit Valley since the 1890s. That's a long time ago, and people have been obsessed with it ever since. Pour some Tabasco on that fresh-out-of-the-ocean oyster and slurp it all down with a cold beer.

GOTHBERG FARMS

15203 Sunset Road, Bow • gothbergfarms.com • 360-202-2436 • Open 9 a.m.–5 p.m.-ish; call ahead or look for the "Open Today" sign

Gothberg Farms' purebred LaMancha goats breathe only the freshest air, eat only the most delectable grasses, and are milked twice daily. Basically, if you were going to be a milk goat, you'd want to live here. Stop by the self-service refrigerator to pick up a bunch of fresh, semi-soft, and aged cheeses and leave some money in the honor box.

GOLDEN GLEN CREAMERY

15014 Field Road, Bow • www.goldenglencreamery.com • 360-766-6455 • Open Monday–Friday 10 a.m.–4 p.m.

Get cheeses and butter from the happy Holstein, Guernsey, and Jersey cows of Golden Glen Creamery, est. 2004.

Dining

BREADFARM

5766 Cains Court, Edison • www.breadfarm.com • 360-766-4065 • Open 8 a.m.–6 p.m.

The smell of baked goods will tickle your nose from down the street. The bakers are a bunch of bread geeks and small-batch pastry and cookie nerds. Take a loaf of sourdough, a bag of whiskey pecan cookies, and a Danish with you to go. Please don't grumble about them not taking cards and be sure to bring cash.

SLOUGH FOOD

5766 Cains Court, Suite B, Edison • www.sloughfood.com • 360-766-4458 • Open Wednesday–Saturday 11 a.m.–6 p.m., Sunday 11 a.m.–5 p.m.

Slough Food's menu is small because it really can get away with it. Get a nibble of local and European cheese or artisan meats (or both) and a glass of wine from that day's offerings. They know their wine, so take a few recommended bottles—or a case—with you.

// Slough Food, Edison

MARIPOSA

14003 Gilmore Avenue, Bow • 360-820-9912 • Open Friday–Monday 11 a.m.–5 p.m.

Giant tacos made with fresh ingredients and a dollop of creativity. Ever had fresh fruit as garnish on your taco? It's delightful.

THE OLD EDISON INN

5829 Cains Court, Bow • theoldedison.com • 360-766-6266 • Open Sunday–Thursday 11:30 a.m.–11 p.m., Friday and Saturday 11:30 a.m.–12 a.m.

A local favorite watering hole, The Old Edison Inn has gone by a bunch of different names and operated out of four different locations since its founding in 1900 or so. They claim that their fried oysters are simply the best, and they have 15 beers on tap, both local microbrews and the regional or national kind. Play some shuffleboard, see live music, and eat anything oyster, the Bow burger or classic sandwich, and a big salad.

☰ *Stay Over*

BLANCHARD MOUNTAIN FARM

15404 Estes Road, Bow • www.blanchardmountainfarm.com •360-399-1495

One-bedroom furnished guest house with fully stocked kitchen on 20-acre organic produce farm in the Samish Flats outside Edison.

ORGANIC FARM COTTAGE: BOW-EDISON

Climb down the ladder of the bedroom loft and step outside the private cottage to visit sheep, donkeys, and ducks, and watch veggies and culinary and medicinal herbs grow. Available on Airbnb.

DECEPTION PASS STATE PARK

41229 State Route 20, Oak Harbor • parks.state.wa.us/497/Deception-Pass • 360-675-3767

Almost 4,000 acres, with 172 tent sites and both saltwater shoreline along Bowman Bay and freshwater shoreline on Pass Lake, Cranberry Lake, and Quarry Pond. To park at Deception Pass State Park and in other state parks and recreational lands in Washington, you need a Discover Pass. Buy an annual pass or a one-day pass at discoverpass.wa.gov.

☰ *While You're Here*

HIKE TO OYSTER DOME

5 miles round-trip • Elevation gain: 1,050 feet • Trailhead: 48.6096, -122.4264

The trailhead starts at the Pacific Northwest Trail on Blanchard Mountain in Bow—from I-5, take Exit 240 and drive west on Lake Samish Road. Turn left onto Barrel Springs Road, then right onto a dirt road at the sign for Blanchard Forest Block. After 1.8 miles, turn left at the sign for Samish Overlook and pass through the yellow gate. Drive 2.2 miles to the Samish Overlook Day Use Area. From the Pacific Northwest Trail, walk up and up through second-growth forest, over creeks, and around the giant stumps left over from the mountain's logging days. You can turn right at the junction for Lizard Lake and Lily Lake, or keep going to the left up a steep climb. The rocky Oyster Dome will give you an incredible view of Samish Bay, with Anacortes and the Skagit River flats to your left, Orcas Island and Lummi Island to your right, with the hulk of Vancouver Island beyond that. To park at Pacific Northwest Trail trailhead and in other state parks and recreational lands in Washington, you need a Discover Pass. Buy an annual pass or a one-day pass at discoverpass.wa.gov.

MOUNT VERNON, BURLINGTON, SEDRO-WOOLLEY, CONCRETE

FROM SEATTLE: 1 TO 2 HOURS · DAYS HERE: 0.5-PLUS

EAT	DRINK	DO	BUY
salmon	limoncello	birding	antiques

 ## Plan Around

KIWANIS SALMON BARBECUE

End of March–End of April • Hillcrest Park Lodge, 1717 S 13th Street, Mount Vernon • www.kiwanisbbq.com

Get a plateful of wild king salmon barbecued over alder, a baked potato, slaw, and garlic bread. Ice cream for dessert. Proceeds donated to youth and community programs in Skagit Valley. Cost: $15.

GARAGE SALE, ANTIQUES & MORE

April • Skagit County Fairgrounds, 479 W Taylor Street, Mount Vernon • www.skagitcounty.net/departments/fairgrounds/GS.htm • 360-416-1350

With over 150 vendors, who knows what treasures are waiting to be discovered? There's food and live music, too. Admission: $3.

TULIP RUN

April • Skagit Regional Airport, 12035 Higgins Airport Way, Burlington • www.tuliprun.com • 207-610-0532

Run/walk a 2- or 5-mile course on scenic, flat, gravel-packed trails. If you're used to running in the city, then this will be a delight. Cost: $20.

SHOP BOOKS AT ANNUAL USED BOOK SALE AT MOUNT VERNON LIBRARY

April • 315 Snoqualmie Street, Mount Vernon • www.mountvernonwa.gov •360-336-6209

Buy the brain spill of the gods (a.k.a. books) plus CDs and DVDs at deep discount prices.

≡ *Eat & Drink*

Get Caffeinated

RISTRETTO COFFEE AND LOUNGE BAR

416 S 1st Street, Mount Vernon • www.ristrettocoffeelounge.com • 360-336-0951 • Open Monday–Saturday 7 a.m.–6 p.m., Sunday 8 a.m.–5 p.m.

Voted *Cascadia Weekly*'s Best of Skagit in 2018, Ristretto serves Victrola coffee and craft beers, as well as all-day breakfast, salads, paninis and wraps, and shakes. On a warm day, get a frozen latte or mocha or a fruit smoothie.

DARREN'S DONUTS

1800 Riverside Drive, Mount Vernon • 360-424-4085 • Open Monday–Friday 5 a.m.–6 p.m., Saturday and Sunday 6 a.m.–6 p.m.

The kind of warm doughy donut that melts in your mouth and leaves a divine trace of sweetness on your tongue. Many claim that these donuts have changed their lives forever.

ESPRESSO CONNECTION

1701 Continental Place, Mount Vernon • 360-848-1554 • Open Monday–Friday 4 a.m.–7 p.m., Saturday and Sunday 7 a.m.–6 p.m.

A little coffee stand with quick drive-thru service, great coffee, and excellent chai options, including the famous chai milkshake.

CALICO CUPBOARD CAFÉ AND BAKERY

www.calicocupboardcafe.com • Hours vary by location

720 1st Street, La Conner • 360-466-4451

901 Commercial Avenue, Anacortes • 360-293-7315

121-B Freeway Drive, Mount Vernon • 360-336-3107

Known for local sourcing and their specialty hash, such as local favorite Brussels sprout hash, Calico Cupboard Café and Bakery is a three-part chain that offers classic all-day breakfast and salads, sandwiches made with bread fresh out of the oven, and homemade soups, some of which you can get in a bread bowl.

.m Fresh

MOUNT VERNON FARMERS' MARKET

mountvernonfarmersmarket.org

Riverwalk Plaza • May–October, Saturday 9 a.m.–2 p.m.

Skagit Valley Hospital • June–September, Wednesday 11 a.m.–4pm

SNOW GOOSE PRODUCE

15170 Fir Island Road, Mount Vernon • www.snowgooseproducemarket.com • 360-445-6908 • Open March–October, daily 8 a.m.–6 p.m.

Known for their "immodest" ice cream cones, this produce stand is open seasonally, with offerings beyond straight flora to locally produced or caught cheese, seafood, bread, beer, and wine.

HEDLIN FARMS

12275 Valley Road, Mount Vernon • www.hedlinfarms.com • 360-466-3977 • Open May–October, daily 10 a.m.–6 p.m.

Just outside the town of La Conner, this third- and fourth-generation farm produces more than 40 crops. Stop by on a summer's day for beets and carrots straight out of the ground, beefsteak tomatoes, blueberries, broccoli, cucumbers, and more.

SCUH FARMS

15565 Memorial Highway, Mount Vernon • 360-424-6982 • Open April-December 9 a.m.-6 p.m.

Pick a pumpkin, get lost in a corn maze, take a tour of this 5-acre homestead. Warning: There will be kids.

FROM THE FARM

18561 Josh Wilson Road, Burlington • www.fromthefarmtreats.com • 360-661-4252

During berry season, farmer Tami brings strawberries, blueberries, raspberries, tayberries, and more straight from the field, while baker Susan supplies the shortcake. Eat some in-house handcrafted strawberry shortcake, then buy the ingredients plus a pie or two to take home.

PERKINS VARIETY APPLES

8243 Sims Road, Sedro-Woolley • www.perkinsvarietyapples.com • 360-856-6248 • Open Friday–Sunday 9 a.m.–6 p.m.

Perkins's Apple Store (the kind with actual apples) is open from the end of August through November and sells apples and pears as they come into season. You can find varietals with familiar grocery-store names, such as Gravensteins, Gala, Braeburn, and Honeycrisp, as well as less well-knowns such as Sweetheart, Akane, Tsugaru, and Mutsu. Check the website for dates, and pick up orchard honey and cider, too.

SEDRO-WOOLLEY FARMERS' MARKET

Hammer Heritage Square, 810 Central Avenue, Sedro-Woolley • sedrowoolleyfarmersmarket.com • Open May–October, Wednesdays 3–7 p.m.

Find locally grown produce and sweet treats while listening to live music, then attend a cooking or home-brew demo. You can also pick up some landscape plants and unique products, such as homemade essential oils or handcrafted wood puzzles, to take home.

Dining

LORENZO'S MEXICAN RESTAURANT

lorenzosmexicanrestaurant.com

2121 E College Way, Mount Vernon • 360-848-7793

902 WA-20, Sedro-Woolley • 360-856-6810

For 30 years, before opening their own family Mexican restaurant, Lorenzo and Laura Velasco worked as dishwasher, cook, buser, waiter, and manager in other people's restaurants. Lorenzo's food is authentic Mexican for the American palate, served in huge portions. Get the tortilla soup, a macho de carne asado burrito, and two to 10 orders of the guacamole fresca.

RACHAWADEE THAI CAFE

410 W Gates Street, Mount Vernon • www.rachawadeethaicafe.com • 360-336-6699 • Lunch Monday–Friday 11 a.m.–3 p.m., dinner Monday–Friday 5–8 p.m.

An itty-bitty place that lends itself to to-go orders, though the bar stools are A-OK. They claim the secret is in the sauce, and it's true—there's a spicy kick to it. Get your curry spicy.

Booze and Beyond

VALLEY SHINE DISTILLERY

320 S 1st Street, Mount Vernon • www.valleyshinedistillery.com • 360-588-4086 • Open Tuesday–Thursday 11 a.m.–8:30 p.m.; Friday and Saturday 11 a.m.–9:30 p.m.; Sunday 11 a.m.–6 p.m.

Vodka, bourbon, gin, rum, unique liqueurs, and limoncello made by the grandson of an (alleged) bootlegger with—according to legend—ties to Al Capone. Good eats, too, such as the lemon yogurt marinated chicken skewers and warm cured pastrami sandwich, plus wine and beer from local wineries and breweries. Tours daily.

EAGLE HAVEN WINERY

8243 Sims Road, Sedro-Woolley • www.eaglehavenwinery.com • 360-856-6248 • Open Friday 11 a.m.–7 p.m.; Saturday and Sunday 11 a.m.–6 p.m.

The estate-grown pinor noir, Siegerrebe, and Madeleine Angevine are a farm-to-glass experience, and you can do a tasting or get a glass and relax in their cushy fireside chairs. Or take yourself on a tour through the wine garden and orchard to see how the sausage gets made. In the summer, they host concerts that tend to feature bluegrass, traditional country, and rock.

Stay Over

#farmlife

THE GOOSEROSA

18225 Best Road, Mount Vernon • www.thegooserosa.com • 206-359-0810

A few miles away from La Conner, the Nest Condo in Mount Vernon has a view of the farm and Mount Baker beyond, and guests are welcome to help themselves to whatever vegetables are in season. (If you're chicken savvy, venture into the chicken coop for fresh eggs.) And there's a goat!

SINGING DOG FARM

Sedro-Woolley • www.singingdogfarm.com

Do you like doggies, horsies, and kitties? You're not a monster, so of course you do. Singing Dog Farm, a small "hobby farm" 10 minutes away from Mount Vernon, hosts three of the world's happiest animal, a.k.a. golden retrievers, Friesian horses, and a couple of cats. The dogs are so happy it's stupid, and they're available for romping through green grass fields or taking a nap under a tree in the yard. Sometimes puppies are around for some rough and tumble and cuddles, too, depending on whether the big dogs have been feeling sexy. The pampered Friesians—those big black horses with the long, flowing manes—are uniquely friendly and

// Singing Dog Farm, Sedro-Woolley

interactive, and once you pet the cats, you are basically signing a lifetime contract of friendship. The cottage itself is situated by the owners' house (the owners are also friendly), a mile and change from the tiny town of Clear Lake. You can see one other house way off in the distance and that's it as far as other humans go. It has a full kitchen, two full baths, a couple TVs with cable, and two bedrooms. The master bedroom has a Jacuzzi tub with a skylight over it. $120 per night. There are enough animals already, so leave your dogs at home.

HOEHN BEND FARM

26923 Hoehn Road, Sedro-Woolley • farmstayskagit.com • 360-466-0135

Three-bedroom guest house situated on 30 acres a few miles east of Sedro-Woolley. Pet the pig or gently caress a chick, or lead a "dinkey"—a dinky donkey—around the field. Setting is quiet and all animals are cute.

OVENELL'S HERITAGE INN LOG CABINS, GUEST HOUSES & HISTORIC RANCH

46276 Concrete Sauk Valley Road, Concrete • www.ovenells-inn.com • 360-853-8494;

Book a fully equipped cabin on this working farm in February and you might just get to see a calf born. If bovine effluvia aren't your jam, stay other times of year (or just don't watch the farm animals giving birth). On the forested and riverside trails near the farm you might spot an elk or deer out of the corner of your eye, birds swooping and soaring above, or bear and cougar scat left behind. The inn provides grills and sells their beef on-site so you can whip up a beef-tastic meal. Two dog-friendly units are available

☰ *While You're Here*

OUTLET SHOPPING AT THE OUTLET SHOPPES AT BURLINGTON

448 Fashion Way, Burlington • www.theoutletshoppesatburlington.com • 360-757-3548 • Open Monday–Saturday 9:30 a.m.–8:30 p.m.; Sunday 10 a.m.–7 p.m.

They put an "e" in "shoppes," so you know it's fancy. Save 25 to 60 percent on designer outlets, including Coach, Nike, Coleman Outdoor, Helly Hansen, Gap, Eddie Bauer, Justice, Pendleton, and more.

T NORTHERN STATE DISC GOLF COURSE

26032 Helmick Road, Sedro-Woolley

A well-designed course with lots of ravines and hills, tons of holes, and space for long shots. Depending on the season, there are some natural motivators for throwing straight—blackberry bushes, brush, tall grass—and during the wet season you'll likely run into soggy ground. Pick up a map at the kiosk.

HIKE TO NORTHERN STATE GHOST TOWN

5 miles round-trip • Elevation gain: 180 feet • North State Recreation Area, 25625 Helmick Road, Sedro-Woolley • www.wta.org

Formerly Northern State Hospital, this now-defunct facility for the mentally ill opened in 1912. It reached full capacity in the 1950s, at about 2,700 patients, and was closed down in 1976. Many of the buildings have since been torn down, but you can still explore the old barns of this self-sustaining 700-acre farm, milking shed, cannery, and the cemetery where 1,500 people eternally slumber.

WATCH EAGLES FROM A BOAT

1-888-675-2448; www.skagiteagles.com

Take a three-hour tour through the Skagit River's bald eagle sanctuary. This length of river east of Concrete, from Rockport to Marblemount, has the most eagle visitors in mainland United States. Tours run from <u>mid-November to late-February</u>. Although the heated boats will thoroughly heat your bunsies, wear a heavy coat, hat, and mittens, and bring your camera. $75 per person.

ABOVE & BEYOND

Dogs | Let your dog be a dog at **Bakerview Park** (3101 E Fir Street, Mount Vernon; 360-336-6215) or **Bark Park** (710 Front Street, Sedro-Woolley; 360-855-1661). Both are large fenced areas with some grass and shade.

Skates | **Bakerview Park** (3101 E Fir Street, Mount Vernon; 360-336-6215) also has a decent skatepark and a BMX bike track. **Sedro-Woolley Skate Park** (324 Metcalf Street, Sedro-Woolley) has a nice big bowl, and **Burlington Skate Park** (729 S Section Street, Burlington) has enough space and interesting elements to make it worth your while. For more information and photos, go to northwestskater.com.

Books | Used paperbacks and hardbacks, books that are out of print, and collectibles are available at **Easton's Books** (701 S 1st Street, Mount Vernon; eastonbooks.com; 360-336-2066). It's open Monday–Saturday 10:30 a.m.–5:30 p.m., and Sunday noon–5 p.m.

LA CONNER & ANACORTES

FROM SEATTLE: 1.25 TO 2 HOURS • DAYS HERE: 0.5 PLUS

EAT	DRINK	DO
a cream puff from Seeds Bistro and Bar and BBQ sauce from Vagabond Station	blueberry apple moonshine from Deception Distilling	visit Guemes Island

 *Plan Around*

LA CONNER DAFFODIL FESTIVAL

March • lovelaconner.com

Not up to weathering the crowds of the Skagit Valley Tulip Festival? Then plan to come to La Conner one month earlier for its daffodil festival, where your seasonal affective disorder will be cured by sunshine in plant form, a.k.a. happy yellow daffodils. Go online to lovelaconner.com to check the bloom map.

TULIP PEDAL

April • La Conner Elementary School Complex, 512 N 6th Street, La Conner • 360-661-7417 • www.safekidsnorthwest.org

Pick the 20-, 40-, or 60-mile routes. Or ride all three! Course begins near tulip fields and gives you all kinds of epic views along the way. Preregistration: $35. Day-of: $40.

ANACORTES SPRING WINE FESTIVAL

April • Port Warehouse Center, 100 Commercial Avenue, Anacortes • anacortes.org/spring-wine-festival • 360-293-7911

Sample the fares of 30 regional vintners and local restaurants. VIP tickets ($88) give you access to a special VIP section and all the goodies from noon to 5 p.m., so you can start your day drinking early. General admission tickets ($55) get you in the door at 1:30 p.m. Everyone gets all the unlimited wine and bites.

SKAGIT RIVER POETRY FESTIVAL

May • www.skagitriverpoetry.org

Attend readings, learn at workshops, and meet your fellow poets for a three-day celebration of poetry.

≡ *Eat & Drink*

Get Caffeinated

CALICO CUPBOARD CAFE AND BAKERY

www.calicocupboardcafe.com • Hours vary by location

720 S 1st Street, La Conner • 360-466-4451

901 Commercial Avenue, Anacortes • 360-293-7315

121-B Freeway Drive, Mount Vernon • 360-336-3107

Known for local sourcing and their specialty hash, such as local favorite Brussels sprout hash, Calico Cupboard Cafe and Bakery is a three-part chain that offers classic all-day breakfast and salads, sandwiches made with bread fresh out of the oven, and homemade soups, some of which you can get in a bread bowl.

Farm Fresh

ANACORTES FARMERS' MARKET

Depot Arts Center, 611 R Avenue, Anacortes • anacortesfarmersmarket.org • 360-293-7922 • Winter Market: second Saturday January–April, 9 a.m.–2 p.m.; Summer Market: Saturday May–October, 9 a.m.–2 p.m.

QUILTING: IT'S NOT JUST FOR OLD PEOPLE!

Check out the Anacortes Quilt Walk and Fidalgo Island Quilters Show in April. For the entire month, businesses in town display quilted items made by locals. The event culminates in the Quilts in Bloom Quilt Show, in which quilters compete for top rankings in appliqués, art pictorial, art abstract, wearable, and other quilting categories. www.fidalgoislandquilters.com

Dining

SEEDS BISTRO AND BAR

623 Morris Street, La Conner • www.seedsbistro.com • 360-466-3280 • Open Sunday–Thursday 11 a.m.–8 p.m.; Friday and Saturday 11 a.m.–9 p.m.; Happy hour daily 3–6 p.m.

Using Skagit Valley produce, meat, beer, and Northwest wines, Seeds Bistro has created a hippy's dream menu, with a wide range of "weeds" (a.k.a salads), burgers and sandwiches, seafood, and big plates. Get the Hands Down the Best Veggie Burger and an enormous cream puff. Sit under Washington State's oldest beech tree with your doggo.

NELL THORN WATERFRONT BISTRO & BAR

116 S 1st Street, La Conner • www.nellthorn.com • 360-466-4261 • Open Tuesday–Sunday 11:30 a.m.–9 p.m.; Happy hour Tuesday–Friday 3–6 p.m.

Fresh-caught and local seafood up the wazoo, steaks, and fabulous salads. For dessert, order the Skagit Mud, a hazelnut brownie with caramel and hand-whipped cream, and stare out wistfully at the Swinomish Channel passing by.

ADRIFT

510 Commercial Avenue, Anacortes • www.adriftrestaurant.com • 360-588-0653 • Open Monday–Thursday 8 a.m.–9 p.m.; Friday and Saturday 8 a.m.–10 p.m.

Hearty breakfasts, burgers and sandwiches, salads, tacos, seafood, and steaks made fresh in downtown Anacortes. Lots of delectable veggie options to choose from alongside carnivorous fare, and the vegan chocolate coconut mousse will wipe the memory of dairy-based mousse from your hard drive. The tables have sails like sailboats.

VAGABOND STATION

2120 Commercial Avenue, Anacortes • vagabondtrailerfood.com • 360-421-4227

Burgers, chicken on waffles, chicken on biscuits (a.k.a. the Yard Bird), biscuits cooked like waffles (a.k.a. the Wiscuit). Lots of sauces to choose from. Everyone freaks out over the maple barbecue sauce, FYI.

Booze and Beyond

DECEPTION DISTILLING

9946 Padilla Heights Road, Anacortes • deceptiondistilling.com • 360-588-1000 • Open Monday–Friday 10 a.m.–4:30 p.m.

Come in for a free tasting of handcrafted, small-batch vodka, gin, and bourbon. Try the blueberry apple pie moonshine, made from 100 percent locally grown blueberries.

Stay Over

Lodge

LA CONNER CHANNEL LODGE

205 N 1st Street, La Conner • www.laconnerlodging.com • 360-466-1500

La Conner Channel Lodge holds bragging rights for being the only waterfront hotel in town. And for good reason: the Swinomish Channel sure is pretty. Get the Bed and Brew package, which comes with nuts and snacks, two bottles of beer, and water, or drop in next door at Hellman's Wine Shop for a complimentary tasting March through September. $139 and up.

SKAGIT BAY HIDEAWAY

17430 Golden View Avenue, La Conner • skagitbay.com • 360-466-2262

Each of the two suites has a separate entrance for privacy, a two-headed walk-in shower, a living room fireplace, a skylight over the queen-size bed, and a private rooftop deck overlooking Skagit Bay. Featured in *Sunset Magazine* and *Coastal Living.*

Camping and Glamping

LA CONNER RV & CAMPING RESORT

16362 Snee Oosh Road, La Conner • www.thousandtrails.com • 360-466-3112 • Open year-round

A 111-acre campground five minutes away from town, with a half mile of saltwater beach. Rent a six-person beach cabin, park your RV, or pitch a tent, all near resort-style amenities. Pet friendly.

>> If you're cruising to La Conner via the Swinomish Channel in your yacht or whatever, then park at the **La Conner Marina** for only $3 a day (lovelaconner.com/la-conner-marina; 360-466-3118).

ABOVE & BEYOND

Great skating, big dog park, quaint bookstores.

Dogs | Your dog will have a grand time at **Ace of Hearts Rotary Dog Park** (3901 H Avenue, Anacortes; 360-293-3832), where they will have 1.5 acres to run around on, with separate fenced-in areas for large and small dogs, and a gazebo for the humans.

Skate | The **La Conner Skate Park** (311–399 N 6th Street, La Conner) is a hybrid of clover and kidney bowls, and **Anacortes Skate Park** (R Avenue at 22nd Street, Anacortes) features a bunch of ramps and rails for perfecting your slides and grinds. For more information and photos, go to northwestskater.com.

Books | With a curated selection of fiction, nonfiction, children's books, and poetry, **Seaport Books** (106 1st Street, La Conner; seaportbooks.com; 360-399-1800) is a small bookstore specializing in topics of interest in the Pacific Northwest. It's open Wednesday–Monday 10 a.m.–6 p.m.

Get a latte, a sea-salt biscuit, and a book at **Pelican Bay Books & Coffeehouse** (520 Commercial Avenue, Anacortes; www.pelicanbaybooks.com; 360-293-1852). It's open Monday–Saturday 9 a.m.–5:30 p.m.

The Watermark Book Co. (612 Commerical Avenue, Anacortes; www.watermark bookcompany.com; 360-293-4277) is a warm and friendly mom-and-pop bookshop, open Monday–Saturday 9:30 a.m.–5:30 p.m. and Sunday 11 a.m.–4 p.m.

Not Ready to Go Home | Take a day trip or longer to Mount Baker-Snoqualmie National Forest (www.fs.usda.gov/mbs), located approximately 40 miles northeast.

Good to Know |

· *Another Roadside Attraction*, written by best-selling author and La Conner eccentric Tom Robbins, is set in Skagit County.

· Trumpeter swans weigh over 20 pounds, making them one of the heaviest flying birds in the world, second to the Andean condor in South America.

· Swans and geese consume tens of millions of pounds of grass, leftover corn, and potatoes on Skagit farmland.

· During the winter, the Skagit Valley sees a dozen or more of the fastest birds in the world.

Been There, Done That | Head north to go on the Dumpling Trail in Richmond, BC (page 77).

☰ *While You're Here*

VISIT GUEMES ISLAND

Guemes Island is a teeny island at 5,505 acres, 540 acres of which are protected. Take the Guemes Ferry from the Guemes Island Ferry Terminal (500 I Avenue, Anacortes; www.guemesislandferry.com; $4–20)—it's only a five-minute trip.

HIKE the 2.5-mile round-trip route up Guemes Mountain, where you'll be able to see the San Juan Islands and the Skagit Valley flats. Dogs on leash welcome. Or walk through the prairies, forests, beaches, and wetlands of this quiet island.

EAT at Guemes Island General Store (7885 Guemes Island Road, Guemes Island; www .guemesislandgeneralstore.com; 360-293-4548). Come for a cup of coffee or a chilled bev, a fresh salad, sandwich or entrée, and a big cookie.

STAY at the Guemes Island Resort, established 1947 (4268 Guemes Island Road, Anacortes; www.guemesislandresort.com; 360-293-6643) on the island's North Beach. It's a collection of yurts, tiny cabins, and big beach houses. Use the boats and buoys for free, and give the owners a heads-up and they'll prep the sauna for you. No TVs, no phones, limited WiFi. $120–635 per night. Pets allowed for a $14 daily fee.

DRIVE CHUCKANUT DRIVE

www.bellingham.org

From Burlington, take WA-11, a.k.a. Chuckanut Drive, which runs along the shoreline of Samish Bay and Bellingham Bay up to the Fairhaven neighborhood of Bellingham, the quietish college town of Western Washington University. The route is scenic, with places to stop along the way for a hike or an amazing vista, including Larrabee State Park at milepost 14.

>>   While in Fairhaven, consider doing a **cocktail or pub crawl** (as long as you aren't going to be driving or biking any time soon). Like Skagit Valley, Whatcom County is all about the brews and booze (www.bellingham.org/eat/wine-spirits).

4

Chinese Delights in Richmond, British Columbia, Canada

FROM SEATTLE: 2 TO 3 HOURS · DAYS HERE: 2 TO 3

DO	EAT	DRINK	BUY	BRING
eat and drink	Xiao Long Bao soup dumplings	sake	frozen dim sum, curry	your passport

In Chinese foodie communities (and in the *New York Times*), an epic battle is being waged over where to get the best Chinese food: Is it in the economically thriving, densely populated Hong Kong, separated from mainland China by a mere river or two? Or is it in Richmond, British Columbia, a hiccup of a city in the Pacific Northwest?

The super-duper short version of this story is that Hong Kong was colonized by the British when the British had a bee in their bonnet regarding global expansion after China lost the First Opium War. After a brief stint under Japanese control during World War II, Hong Kong returned to its colony status under the British. Then this thing called communism happened, and a bunch of Chinese people fled the mainland for Hong Kong, where they could buy and sell stuff and also not get killed. The colony was open to the world, and the economy and tourism boomed, meaning good food-making boomed, too. In the late '90s, however, Britain and China negotiated for the return of Hong Kong to Chinese rule, which led to another panic and resulted in a brain drain or, more relevant to this controversy, a chef drain. Multitudes of talented chefs moved to Canada, Vancouver and Richmond in particular. Today, 74 percent of Richmond's citizens come from an Asian background.

OK, so back to the controversy: Proponents of the argument that Chinese food is better in Hong Kong claim that it's because . . . it's Hong Kong. Fair enough. Those who take Richmond's side point out that real estate is too valuable in Hong Kong proper to be used for agriculture and, since China has a bit of a pollution problem, the mainland produce isn't ideal. In addition, Richmond's nickname, Ditchland, is well earned, based on its lush farmlands. The produce in Richmond, they posit, is the best you can get, as is the seafood, which swims in the relatively clean waters of the Pacific Ocean to the west. The final answer? You'll have to visit both locales and decide for yourself.

☰ *Getting There*

BY CAR | Get on I-5 N and drive approximately 160 miles. The trip takes roughly two to three hours, depending on the wait at the Canada-US border crossing. You will be going to a foreign land, so be sure to leave the contraband at home and bring your passport.

BY TRAIN | Take Amtrak #516 from Seattle's King Street Station to Vancouver, BC, Pacific Central Station. Travel time: approximately four hours. From Waterfront Station, take the TransLink Canada line to the Richmond–Brighouse Station ($2.95). Or get a cab.

BY BUS | Take a Greyhound bus from Seattle to Vancouver, BC, Pacific Central Station ($19–62). All passengers will get off the bus at the border for passport check, then reboard and continue on to their destination. At the Greyhound Station, transfer to TransLink Canada Line.

BY FERRY | Take the Clipper Ferry to Victoria on Vancouver Island ($99–125) and then take the BC Transit #72 ($2.50), or drive approximately 32 miles north to Swartz Bay and take the BC Ferry to Tsawwassen, Vancouver Harbour ($17.20 per on-foot passenger), then take TransLink Bus #620 to Richmond. Or, from Vancouver Island, take a Helijet helicopter from Victoria Harbour to Vancouver Harbour ($189–230). This is not the cheapest or fastest way to go, but it sure is pretty.

BY BIKE | There are bike trails that connect from Seattle to Vancouver. It's a 160-mile, 15-hour ride. If you're that hard core, check out *Cycling the Pacific Coast: The Complete Guide from Canada to Mexico* by Bill Thorness.

≡ *Highlight Reel*

NIGHT MARKET

8351 River Road, Richmond, BC • richmondnightmarket.com • Open May–October Friday and Saturday 7 p.m.–12 a.m.; Sunday 7–11 p.m.

A seasonal smorgasbord of Richmond cuisine and culture, with a sea of red tents extending as far as the eye can see. The number of food options is impressive. Add to that the incredibly creative edible creations, such as butterfly pea milk tea served in baby bottles or the pho fries, which are french fries topped with beef, bean sprouts, sriracha, and other classic pho ingredients. There are also carnival games to be played and random retail, such as clothing decorated with the prime minister's face, glitzy cell phone covers, and marijuana paraphernalia, to be purchased. Get lost here for an evening. For some reason, there's also a Magical Dino Park, with giant animated replicas. Dogs on leashes OK. The market is mostly cash-only, so skip the long line at the ATM by withdrawing Canadian cash ahead of time. $4.25 CAN.

// Night Market, Richmond, BC

THE DUMPLING TRAIL

www.visitrichmondbc.com/food-and-drink/dumpling-trail

The brilliant minds at Richmond Tourism put together the Dumpling Trail, a self-guided tour of Richmond restaurants organized by type of dumpling, which CNN named among 12 of the world's most enticing food and drink trails.

Dumplings for Days

Back in the day, dim sum was a lunchtime/teatime thing. That's mostly still the case, but due to popular demand, you can sometimes order these darling dumplings at dinnertime, too.

// Dumplings, Richmond, BC

Restaurants sometimes try to prove their authenticity by displaying an elderly grandmother-like woman in a glass enclosure, handmaking dumplings to prove they're handmade, much like those abuelitas rolling tortillas in Mexican restaurants. Whether they're old-lady crafted, the dim sum is awe sum. The following list of great eateries could be a hundred miles long, but suffice it to say that if you throw a stone in Richmond, you're likely to hit some amazing cuisine.

MAMA'S DUMPLING AND COFFEE

103-11782 Hammersmith Way, Richmond, BC • www.mamasdumpling.com • 778-297-1618 • Open Monday–Saturday 11:30 a.m.–8 p.m.

If you've never had pork and kimchi dumplings with your macchiato, it's worth a try. Mama's has a full menu, with nummy veg entrées, seafood entrées, rice and noodles, and a long list of made-from-scratch dumplings.

TYPES OF DUMPLINGS

Chiu Chow Fun Gor: thick wrapping stuffed with peanuts, pork, and dried radish
Wu Gok: taro pastry stuffed with shrimp, pork, and scallions
Ham Sui Gok: Cantonese-style croquettes stuffed with minced pork
Jian Dui: sweet rice flour pastry stuffed with lotus or red bean paste
Siu Mai: thick wrapping stuffed with pork, shrimp, and salmon roe or prawn
Har Gow: tapioca starch pastry filled with shrimp
Gyoza: pan-fried and filled with pork or seafood
Mandu: Korean dumplings filled with meat and vegetables, served with kimchi
Wonton: a versatile dumpling stuffed with meat or vegetables
Guo Tie: pan-fried, usually filled with pork
Shui Jiao: boiled dumplings stuffed with meat, seafood, or vegetables
Xiao Long Bao: classic Shanghainese soup dumpling

KIRIN

200 Three West Centre, 7900 Westminster Highway (at No. 3 Road), Richmond, BC •
www.kirinrestaurants.com • 604-303-8833 • Open daily 10 a.m.–2:30 p.m., 5–10 p.m.

Kirin is well known as the area's go-to Cantonese and seafood restaurant. Cantonese cuisine
encompasses a wide range of flavors and styles, with a real emphasis on freshness, and Kirin is
a thriving, popular place. They have amazing dim sum, and their homemade XO sauce is to die
for. If you forgot to make a reservation and the wait at the location in Richmond is too long, go
to one of the two in Vancouver or the one in New Westminster.

CHEF TONY SEAFOOD RESTAURANT

101-4600 No. 3 Road, Richmond, BC • cheftonycanada.com • 604-279-0083 • Weekday dim sum:
10:30 a.m.–3 p.m.; weekend dim sum: 10 a.m.–3 p.m.; daily dinner: 5–10 p.m.

Winner of "Best Dim Sum" and "Best Upscale Chinese," this restaurant goes for the unique
take. The beef noodle soup is the saliva-generating epitome of savory. Try the spike sea
cucumber or the squid ink custard bun. Make a reservation.

FISHERMAN'S TERRACE SEAFOOD RESTAURANT

Aberdeen Centre Mall, 4151 Hazelbridge Way, Richmond, BC • 604-303-9739 • Daily dim sum:
10 a.m.–2:30 p.m.; Dinner: 5:30–9 p.m.

A favorite among locals, visitors from Hong Kong, and tourists from the United States, Fisherman's Terrace Seafood Restaurant serves great traditional dim sum on the top floor of the
Aberdeen Centre Mall. People go bananas for anything on the menu that has shrimp. Try the
chicken's feet. Make a reservation.

SHANGHAI RIVER RESTAURANT

7831 Westminser Highway, Richmond, BC • 604-233-8885 • Open daily 11 a.m.–2:30 p.m., 5–9:30 p.m.

The Shanghai River Restaurant is one of the most popular Shanghainese restaurants in Richmond, famous for their xiao long bao, a.k.a soup dumplings. For brunch, get the salty soy milk
soup. Reservations recommended.

// Dumplings, Richmond, BC

DINESTY DUMPLING HOUSE

160-8111 Ackroyd Road, Richmond, BC • dinesty.ca • 604-303-7772 • Dim sum: daily 11 a.m.–3 p.m.;
dinner: Monday–Friday 5:30–10 p.m.; Saturday and Sunday 4:30–10 p.m.

Another award winner: "Diner's Choice," "Best Dining Environment," "Best Shanghainese
Restaurant," and "Best Xiao Long Bao." The all-picture menu makes it easy for those who don't
speak the language. Get the soup dumplings, then get some more. Reservations recommended.

>> **Dinesty Richmond Continental** (1168-3779 Sexsmith Road, Richmond, BC; 604-279-9927;
   open daily 11 a.m.–7 p.m.) is a retail store that sells handcrafted, frozen, packaged dumplings,
   buns, and other goodies directly to hungry consumers. Stop by on your way home to stock up
   for many meals to come. If you have a favorite, call ahead—they sell out fast.

≡ *Plan Around*

CANADA DAY

July • www.richmondcanadaday.com

Celebrate Canada Day—or, as they like to say in Steveston Village, "Canada's Biggest Little
Birthday Party since 1945"—as the Canadians do, with a maple syrupy pancake breakfast,
parade, and festivities. They even shoot off fireworks, just like their more warmongering neigh-

bors to the south! Join your fellow 70,000 revelers for the world-famous salmon barbecue, $16 CAN. per plate.

>> Check the Minor League Baseball schedule to see if the Vancouver Canadians (that's their real name, honest) are playing in Vancouver's Nat Bailey Stadium (www.milb.com/vancouver).

CHINESE NEW YEAR

February • lunar-festival.squarespace.com

For two weeks in February, it's party time in Richmond (and all over the world, wherever Chinese people live). Come for the parades, the traditional lion and dance performances, the cool pop-ups, and, per usual, epic food. The International Buddhist Temple hosts a big to-do, with a flower market and bonus Taste of Zen snacks, and the Tibetan Thrangu Monastery offers some quieter prayer and meditation services. The Aberdeen Centre hosts a flower and gift fair, a cultural showcase, a golden dragon and lion dance, and a New Year's countdown, as does the Yaohan Centre. Find more festivals at Lansdowne Centre, Bodhi Meditation, Parker Place Mall, and more. Go to Vancouver's Chinatown for the huge New Year parade.

RICHMOND CHERRY BLOSSOM FESTIVAL

April • Garry Point Park, 12011 7th Avenue, Richmond, BC

In April, the 255 Akebono cherry blossom trees in Garry Point Park bloom. For two weeks, their delicate pink glory is a sight to behold, before they lose their petals and we all get sad about impermanence. The one-day festival includes traditional bento boxes and food from other local favorites, sado tea ceremonies, the performances of Japanese dancers and taiko drummers, and demonstrations of shodo Japanese calligraphy and sakura origami. Free.

 Eat & Drink

Get Caffeinated

FRESH PRESS COFFEE BAR

4940 No 3 Road #121, Richmond, BC • www.freshpresscoffeebar.com • 604-787-3028 • Open Monday–Thursday 8 a.m.–5 p.m., Friday 8 a.m.–7 p.m.,Saturday 9 a.m.–7 p.m., Sunday9 a.m.–5 p.m.

Vinyl records, cakes and pies, and, of course, fresh-pressed coffee. Espressos are good, and the environment is all white and shiny in the Seattle-Portlandia style, with organic dairy and great baked goods.

WAVES COFFEE HOUSE

5951 No 3 Road #18, Richmond, BC • wavescoffee.com • 604-273-9283

Coffee with a yenta-like mission. Like, they really want you to "connect," at least that's the case on the website. In person, it's chill (they won't make you introduce yourself to the person sitting next to you or hug you or anything). They purchase their beans from small farmers and real Belgian chocolate for mochas and their many other chocolaty beverages. Also with the soups, sandwiches and wraps, and fresh pastries. They also have a bitcoin ATM.

CAFE SAVOUREUX

8368 Capstan Way #1326, Richmond, BC • www.cafesavoureux.com • 604-207-2589 • Open Sunday–Thursday 1–8 p.m., Friday and Saturday 1–11 p.m.

Stop in for an afternoon pick-me-up with coffee made from fresh Arabica coffee beans, some of which come from the top of the world (grown at an altitude of over 1,000 meters). The atmosphere is cute, and their dishware is the kind of china that Queen Victoria herself would love. Try the specialty iced drip coffee and a slice of one of their many kinds of cakes.

Markets

All you have to do is stop by a market and buy a jar or bag of something you've never tried before and–voila!–you have yourself an adventure. In Osaka—which is a Chinese market with a Japanese name—you can find a wide range of Japanese cookies, including Manju, a delightful confection reminiscent of mochi, with a gooey flour rice outside and sweetened red bean paste inside. In the candy section, you'll find sweets with bright colors, exotic flavors, and unique shapes. There is usually a hot section and a cold section of the deli, plus a station where you can get food made fresh. In the produce section, get some lychees and galangal, a rhizome similar to ginger. Before buying some fresh-baked tarts at the bakery, do the **Cocktail Bun Test**: If the cocktail buns are good, then you can bet the other treats are good, too.

>> If you see a grandmother-type person browsing the grocery aisles, respectfully watch her. An inside source revealed that these matriarchs are renowned for their shopping discernment— for example, if you see an elderly Asian woman examine a fish in the seafood section and toss it back, then you should know to steer clear.

T&T MARKET

351-5511 Hollybridge Way, Richmond, BC • 604-303-8633 • Open Sunday–Thursday 10 a.m.–
9:30 p.m.; Friday and Saturday 10 a.m.–10 p.m.

OSAKA

3700 No. 3 Road, Richmond, BC • www.tnt-supermarket.com/bc • 604-276-8808 • Open daily
8:30 a.m.–11 p.m.

T&T Market and Osaka are part of the same chain, which was purchased by Loblaws, one of
the largest mainstream Canadian supermarkets. This means that some crossover has developed, and you can find cool things sold in T&T and also in Loblaws. But for the best of Asian
grocery, go to the source. Osaka has more focus on Japanese products, including a huge
selection of packaged foods, as well as sushi and sashimi.

>> South Korea has a booming skin-care industry, and they have established a complicated skin-
care regimen that people swear by. Be sure to stop by the health and wellness aisle for some
K-Beauty products.

BKH JERKY

3201 Fraser Street, Vancouver, BC • www.bkhjerky.com • Open Tuesday–Sunday 10 a.m.–6 p.m.,
Monday and holidays 11 a.m.–5 p.m.

This is not your average Slim Jim. This is the real deal, a Singapore-style jerky, with the choice
of original or spicy. They don't use preservatives, so you can't put it in your glovebox and
expect it to be good 10 years hence. Stock up on fresh beef or pork jerky, or pork floss—they
don't ship outside of Canada.

STEVESTON FARMERS' AND ARTISANS MARKET

Steveston Community Centre, 4111 Moncton Street, Richmond, BC • sfam.ca • Open two Sundays
per month, May–September, 10:30 a.m.–3:30 p.m.

Come to the historic seaside village of Steveston to see all that produce and seafood you've
been enjoying cooked up in its fresh form, straight from the farmers of British Columbia,
along with wine, baked goods, chocolates, jewelry, home furnishings, and other artisan crafts.
Stop by Furry Munchies to get your pups a treat.

CANNERY'S FARMERS' MARKET

Gulf of Georgia Cannery National Historic Site, 12138 4th Avenue, Richmond, BC • Open two Sundays per month, October–April, 10 a.m.–3 p.m.

Richmond's fall and winter farmers' market goes on, rain, shine, or snow. Wear a scarf.

>> You are allowed to bring packaged foods across the border. Same goes for most produce, though be prepared to declare your purchases for inspection. For more information on rules and regulation at the US-Canadian border, visit the Washington State Department of Transportation at www.wsdot.wa.gov.

Malls

When you think of mall food courts in the US, usually watered-down fast food chains such as Sbarro or Panda Express come to mind. But the malls in Richmond are worth a self-guided culinary tour. Not every restaurant is amazing, of course, and many are part of a ho-hum chain. But the court certainly offers a variety to choose from, and many will be good verging on great.

ABERDEEN CENTRE MALL

4151 Hazelbridge Way, Richmond, BC • www.aberdeencentre.com/en/home.php • 604-270-1234 • Open Monday–Wednesday and Sunday 11 a.m.–7 p.m.; Thursday–Saturday 11 a.m.–9 p.m.

YAOHAN CENTRE AND OSAKA MARKET

3700 No. 3 Road, Richmond, BC • 604-231-0601 • First floor open daily 9 a.m.–9 p.m.; second floor open daily 11 a.m.–7 p.m.

Dining
CURRY HOUSE

Yaohan Centre, 3700 No. 3 Road, Richmond, BC • 604-721-2426

This Yaohan Centre food court restaurant is worth the 160-mile trip from Seattle. The Hainese Chicken Rice is phenomenal, and the reputation of having the best curry in town is well earned. You might feel the urge to drink this secret-recipe sauce, but instead get it on everything. Also get anything with chicken.

ANNA'S CAKE HOUSE

Lansdowne Centre, 828-5300 No. 3 Road, Richmond, BC • www.annascakehouse.com • 604-273-ANNA • Open Monday and Tuesday 10 a.m.–6 p.m.; Wednesday–Friday 10 a.m.–9 p.m.; Saturday 9:30 a.m.–6 p.m.; Sunday 11 a.m–6 p.m.

Tired of dim sum? Then visit this bakery beloved by Vancouverites. Anna's Cake House has multiple locations around the city. Their desserts are a main feature at locals' birthday parties. The fresh cream cake, with its topping of fresh fruit, is a staple, as is pastry made out of chestnut cream. The cakes are super light, not as dense or heavy compared to their French counterparts. They're not as sweet either, and less dairy-centric (perhaps this has something to do with a higher percentage of lactose intolerance among the Asian population). Frosting is a light whipped cream, and the cake tends to be very airy and spongy. Come early to get the good stuff—they often sell out of their bestsellers by noon. Definitely try the peanut butter cream cake.

Go Veg

4 STONES VEGETARIAN CUISINE

160-7771 Westminster Highway, Richmond, BC • www.fourstonesvegetarian.com • 604-278-0852 • Open Tuesday–Sunday, dim sum 11 a.m.–2:30 p.m.; dinner 5–8:30 p.m.

Fake meat is an example of human ingenuity at its best. Take a break from all that delish pork and shellfish and stop by this restaurant for some Kung Pao "chicken," BBQ "pork," and steamed gyozas.

TASTE OF ZEN AT INTERNATIONAL BUDDHIST TEMPLE

9160 Steveston Highway, Richmond, BC • buddhisttemple.ca • 604-274-2822 • Taste of Zen available daily 11:30 a.m.–3 p.m.

For a taste of Zen, come to this international Buddhist temple. All offerings are vegetarian and vegan, and every meal is tasty Chinese cuisine with a slight Western flair. While you're there,

// Soup, Richmond, BC

walk the grounds—the temple is extraordinary, constructed in traditional Chinese imperial style, with ornate carvings, intricate roof ridges, and lots of gold and red. The garden is full of bonsai, water features, and other landscaping delights. Come on a Saturday for the meditation and Dharma talk from 9 to 11 a.m., then stay for lunch. $18 CAN. per person.

Poutine

Though the focus is on Richmond's stellar Chinese cuisine, you can't forget about poutine, a Quebec delicacy comprising fries, gravy, and cheese curds.

SMOKE'S POUTINERIE

942 Granville Street, Vancouver, BC, and 3700 Willingdon Avenue, Burnaby, BC • 604-434-5734 • Open Monday–Thursday 10 a.m.–3 p.m., Friday 10 a.m.–2 p.m.

A dual-national chain that specializes in poutine with a bunch of crazy fixings.

CHEF'S PLAYGROUND EATERY

170-12420 No. 1 Road, Richmond, BC • chefsplayground.ca • 604-285-8079 • Open Monday 11 a.m.–2 p.m.; Wednesday–Friday 11 a.m.–8 p.m.; Saturday and Sunday 10 a.m.–8 p.m.

Fresh, crafty food such as Chef's Healthy Salad and the Big Boss Burger, with Canadian brisket poutine and other fries options as starts.

THE CANADIAN BREWHOUSE

4755 McClelland Road, #1305, Richmond, BC • thecanadianbrewhouse.com • 778-732-0766 • Open Monday–Friday 11 a.m.–2 a.m.; Saturday and Sunday 10 a.m.–2 a.m.

A Canada-only chain with a selection of Oh Canada Poutine (try the donair), plus enough entrée options to make your eyes cross.

BEEN THERE, DONE THAT

Eaten your way through Richmond but still want more? Then visit **Vancouver's Chinatown**, where you can go for round two of great eating and shopping (106 Keefer Street, Vancouver, BC; vancouver-chinatown.com; 604-632-3808).

Booze and Beyond

LULU ISLAND WINERY

16880 Westminster Highway, Richmond, BC • www.luluislandwinery.com • 604-232-9839

This is the rare winery dedicated to table wines and fruit wines, using grapes from Okanagan and berries from Frasier Valley. And it produces Canada's own icewine, which is a concoction made by picking grapes only after temperatures reach below freezing and then pressing them before they thaw. This process creates a rich, sweet dessert wine. Call ahead to reserve a tour or tasting.

YK3 SAKE

Unit 23, 11151 Horseshoe Way, Richmond, BC • www.yk3sake.com • 604-821-0539

Winner of the 2004 Sake Technical Competition in Nagano, sake master Yoshiaki Kasugai has been brewing sake for more than 20 years, using traditional methodology to cook up small batches. You can find bottles of the junmai sake all over Richmond and beyond, but stop by the sakery to pick some up at its source.

☰ *Stay Over*

Of the airport hotel variety, there are a ton of places to stay in Vancouver and Victoria. In Richmond, staying over is more of a do-it-yourself situation. Find listings on Airbnb, VRBO, bedandbreakfast.eu, and booking.com.

THE STONE HEDGE BED & BREAKFAST

5511 Cathay Road, Richmond, BC • www.thestonehedge.ca • 604-274-1070

Featuring an outdoor pool for those six glorious weeks of intermittent hot weather, the Stone Hedge B&B is 2.4 kilometers from Richmond's city center. Bathrobe and slippers are provided, plus complimentary brandy!

THE SEABREEZE GUEST HOUSE

3111 Springside Place, Richmond, BC • www.theseabreeze.net • 778-686-1248

Each suite has a jacuzzi tub. Two of the rooms have an ocean view of the Strait of Georgia, and the third overlooks a private patio that leads out to the W Dyke Trail. Rates include a continental breakfast, which you can take out onto the large ocean-facing deck.

ABOVE & BEYOND

You can't bring your dog across the US-Canada border without the proper permits. Take the time you'd usually spend at the dog park to peruse the following bookstores.

Books | **Indigospirit** (Richmond Centre, 6551 No. 3 Road #1516a, Richmond, BC; www .chapters.indigo.ca; 604-273-7114) is Canada's biggest bookstore and has it all. Buy the latest bestseller and, while you're at it, a "Yay for rosé!" insulated wine glass or an inflatable peacock pool float. It's open Tuesday–Saturday 10 a.m.–9 p.m., Sunday and Monday 11 a.m.–7 p.m.

The Chinese-language **SUP Bookstore** (4151 Hazelbridge Way, Richmond, BC; 604-821-9875) has novels, comics, and more.

Good coffee and a great selection of used books creates nirvana at **Village Books and Coffee House** (12031 First Avenue, Richmond, BC; 604-272-660).

For books about British Columbia come to the **Steveston Book Store** (3760 Moncton Street, Richmond, BC; 604-274-3604).

At **Serendipity's Backyard** (12111 1st Avenue, Richmond, BC; www.serendipitysbackyard .ca; 604-275-1683), a metaphysical giftshop, you can buy books, crystals, sacred gem jewelry, oracle cards, and get an aura or tarot reading from one of their mediums. Open daily 10 a.m.–5:30 p.m.

Good to Know |
- Lulu Island, on which Richmond is located, was named after Lulu Sweet, a young actress who performed with the traveling Potter Dramatic Troupe in New Westminster in 1861. Colonel Moody (not a Clue character) thought she was a hottie and so, in an impulsive outburst probably motivated by the rugged area's lack of elegant ladies, promised to name the island after her.
- A massive dike system has been built to protect Richmond—which is only 1 meter above sea level—from flooding. For the same reason, houses in the city do not have basements.
- The ABC series *Once Upon a Time* was filmed in Richmond.

Been There, Done That | On your way to or from Richmond, spend some time eat and drinking in Skagit Valley (page 50).

BEST HOME INN

10660 Westminster Highway, Richmond, BC • www.besthomeinn.ca • 778-892-9888

A cul-de-sac–style inn, with shiny wood floors, fast WiFi, and flat-screen TVs.

LOVELY HARMONY HOUSE

6011 Alta Court, Richmond, BC • lovelyharmonyhouse.wordpress.com • 778-886-1107

Near Minoru Park, the Lovely Harmony House has three rooms and is decorated in a style that inspires thoughts of both the 1980s and the Queen of England. It's quiet, cozy, and about 20 minutes from the city center by public transit. Includes continental breakfast and, in season, a backyard hammock.

☰ *While You're Here*

SHOP AT DAISO

Aberdeen Centre, 4151 Hazelbridge Way, Richmond, BC • www.daisocanada.com • 604-295-6601 • Open daily 9:30 a.m.–9 p.m.

Any doodad or thingy you could possibly want—say, a specialty brush for washing plastic water bottles or a spatula with a cover for cleaning under the microwave—can be found here, at the "Japanese dollar store." Though the store has the same name as the one in Seattle, the inventory is different. And it's huge.

WALK THE HIGHWAY TO HEAVEN

Along No. 5 Road there are 20 places of worship, from mosques to monasteries, synagogues to temples to churches. With ornate architecture, fruit orchards, and serene gardens, these are worth a visit. Some give tours to visitors, some serve lunch, some host events or spiritual practices. Calling ahead is recommended.

INTERNATIONAL BUDDHIST TEMPLE (9160 Steveston Highway, Richmond, BC; buddhisttemple.ca; 604-274-2822)

THRANGU MONASTERY (8140 No. 5 Road, Richmond, BC; www.thrangumonastery.org; 778-297-6010)

LINGYEN MOUNTAIN TEMPLE (10060 No. 5 Road, Richmond, BC; lymtcanada.com; 604-271-0009)

RAM KRISHNA MANDIR VEDIC CULTURAL CENTER (8200 No. 5 Road, Richmond, BC; vedicculturalsocietybc.com; 604-726-7002)

NANAKSAR GURDWARA GURSIKH TEMPLE (18691 Westminster Highway, Richmond, BC; 604-270-7369)

GET SIMULATED AT THE OLYMPIC OVAL

6111 River Road, Richmond, BC • richmondoval.ca • 778-296-1400 • Open daily 6 a.m.–11 p.m.

During or after eating your way through Richmond, come to the Olympic Oval to get your metabolism working. The options for what you can do are ridiculous: traverse a 44-foot climbing wall, express anger at the batting cages, strap blades to your feet and go skating, run some miles on the track, shoot some hoops, do some yoga. Then visit the Olympic Museum, where you can bobsled the 2010 Vancouver Olympics course, kayak the whitewater of the Chilliwack River, drive a Formula 1 race car, sit-ski in Alberta, and catch crazy air in ski jump, all from the safety of the state-of-the-art simulators.

DR. SUN YAT-SEN CLASSICAL CHINESE GARDEN

578 Carrall Street, Vancouver BC • vancouverchinesegarden.com • 604-662-3207 • Open October–April 10 a.m.–4:30 p.m.; May–mid-June 10 a.m.–6 p.m.; mid-June–August 9:30 a.m.–7 p.m.; September 10 a.m.–6 p.m.

Walk the grounds all by your lonesome or take a guided tour, during which you will learn all kinds of interesting factoids about the significance of each meticulously vetted plant and object. The pagoda overlooks the pond, while Vancouver's skyscrapers rise up just beyond the fence. $12–14.

>>   Looking for something similar in Seattle? Go to Kubota Garden.

5

Artisanal Eats in Port Townsend

FROM SEATTLE: 2 TO 3 HOURS · DAYS HERE: 2 TO 3

DO	EAT	DRINK	BUY
eat and drink	farm-fresh produce	heirloom apple cider	steampunk outfit

Self-proclaimed "New York of the West," Port Townsend is one of the three recognized Victorian seaports on the National Register of Historical Places. If that doesn't get your salivary glands all juiced up, then picture soft-ripened Mount Townsend cheese sourced from happy local cows, a cinnamon twist fresh from the oven of Pane d'Amore, or briny oysters straight out of Discovery Bay from Johnson and Gunstone Shellfish. Round out the fantasy with a homemade strawberry ice cream cone from Elevated Ice Cream Company and a Marc brandy from Admiralty Distillers.

You can get all the good eating your epicurean heart could desire by making the scenic two- or three-hour trek to Port Townsend on the northern tip of the Olympic Peninsula. Farmers and restaurateurs of the region work hard to maintain healthy relationships, and so the food you'll find there is, more often than not, locally sourced, organic, and sustainably grown. The fine Northwest dining can only be matched by the stunning water and mountain views. And the kayaking. Oh, and then there's the golf. Any way you swing it, Port Townsend is well worth the trip.

≡ *Getting There*

BY CAR | From Seattle proper, take either I-5 S to Tacoma, and then go around the southern tip of the Hood Canal into Kitsap County and up into Port Townsend. Compared to taking the ferry, it's roughly the same amount of time—a little over two hours, depending on traffic—but almost double the mileage for your car. Time: 2-plus hours.

BY FERRY | Walk, bike, or drive on the ferry for a beautiful Puget Sound crossing. If you're going during high season or rush hour, be prepared to wait. Ticket costs depend on the size of the vehicle and number of passengers, while bicycle and rider are a single fee. From the Seattle Ferry Terminal, take the Seattle–Bainbridge Ferry to Bainbridge Island, then drive north on WA-305 N, WA-3 N, WA-104 W, and WA-19 N to Port Townsend. Go to www.wsdot.wa.gov/ferries for more information. Click on VesselWatch to see ferry status and wait time. $15 standard vehicle, $1 bicycle, $8.35 per passenger.

From Seattle proper, drive north to Edmonds, where you will take the Edmonds–Kingston Ferry to Kingston. Follow WA-104 W and WA-19 N.

BY BUS | The Olympic Bus Lines have two daily three-hour trips between the Seattle area and the Olympic Peninsula. From Seattle, catch the Dungeness Line to Port Townsend. Ferry ride, WiFi, locally sourced chocolate chip cookies, and a bottle of water are included. Book online at olympicbuslines.com or call 360-416-0700. $69 round-trip.

≡ *Highlight Reel*

THE CIDER ROUTE

opciderroute.com

Visit Finnriver, Eaglemount, and Alpenfire, three cideries within 10 miles of one another and in or near Port Townsend.

FINNRIVER FARM & CIDERY 124 Center Road, Chimacum • 360-732-4337 • Summer cider tasting hours: daily noon–9 p.m. Just 12 miles south of Port Townsend proper, Finnriver is open daily year-round. Originally inhabited by the Chimakum, this area has a long history of farming. Today, Finnriver sits on 50 acres of lush farmland, which supports the cultivation of organic fruits, vegetables, grains, and, of course, apples for their cidery. Come by for the classics plus contemporary craft ciders such as the Habañero Cider and Black Currant Sparkling Cider, seasonal botanicals such as the Solstice Saffron and Cranberry Rosehip, or any of their delightful wines and brandies.

EAGLEMOUNT WINE & CIDER 1893 S Jacob Miller Road, Port Townsend • www .eaglemountwinery.com • 360-385-1992 • Tasting hours: Wednesday and Thursday 1–4 p.m., Friday and Sunday noon–5 p.m.; Friday after-hours with music 5–8 p.m. The words Gravenstein, Winter Banana, Jonathan, Roxbury Russet, Winesap, and Greening are music to Washingtonians' ears. And these heirlooms are featured in the hard cider and meads produced from hundred-year-old apple trees and supplemented by organic fruit from other nearby orchards, including honey from Sailing S Orchard in Sequim and quince from Willowrose Bay Orchard in the San Juan Islands. The wines are made with handpicked grapes from Eastern Washington. Try the rhubarb or the ginger peach cider if available.

ALPENFIRE CIDER 220 Pocket Lane, Port Townsend • www.alpenfirecider.com • 360-379-8915 • Tasting hours: Saturday and Sunday noon–5 p.m. These cider geeks looked to the cider regions of Europe when planting their trees, going for the apples that would provide European-style bittersweet and bitter-sharp flavors. Try the more familiar ciders, of course, as well as the Méthode Champenoise (sparkling rosé cider), pommeau (apple brandy mixed with apple juice), and the vinegars. Bring a picnic to enjoy in the orchard, too.

WINE, CIDER, AND CHEESE TOUR

End of April • www.olympicpeninsulawineries.org

To explore Port Townsend booze and beyond, meet nine award-winning wineries and cideries in Sequim, Port Angeles, Chimacum, and Nordland.

ANNUAL ARTISAN FOODS FESTIVAL

End of May • Jefferson County Farmers' Market, Tyler Street and Laurence Street

Featuring more than 70 vendors, live music, and demonstrations by local chefs and herbalists, this annual festival brings together the best that the Quimper Peninsula has to offer.

TASTE OF PORT TOWNSEND

Beginning of June • Northwest Maritime Center, 431 Water Street

For the price of a single meal, you can get a taste of PT's food, beer, wine, cider, and desserts, all while supporting the 501(c)(3) nonprofit Port Townsend Main Street Program and its mission to preserve the historic district.

≡ *Plan Around*

THE BRASS SCREW CONFEDERACY STEAMPUNK FESTIVAL

June • www.brassscrew.org

Come June, pack your petticoats and goggles and head over to the Brass Screw Confederacy Steampunk Festival for the Tactical Croquet Tournament, the Steampunk Scavenger Hunt, the Bodgers' Grand Exhibition Hall, the Bazaar of the Bizarre, and some tipsy gypsy at the Saturday Night Hootenanny.

>> Forgot your steampunk getup at home? Don't fret, because **World's End** has got you covered. Pick up your old-timey stripes and nautical-themed attire here (1020 Water Street, Port Townsend; worldsendporttownsend.com; 360-379-6906; open daily 10 a.m.–6 p.m.).

WOODEN BOAT FESTIVAL

September • nwmaritime.org/wooden-boat-festival/

Got a woody for wooden boats? Then get tickets to the Wooden Boat Festival, which features racing schooners, tall ships, and vintage and new boats of all kinds. There's live music, libations, exhibitions, and a boat-building competition.

PORT TOWNSEND BAY KINETIC SKULPTURE RACE

October • www.ptkineticrace.org

Can it traverse sand, crawl through mud, float on water, and make it over hills and dales? Is it a hodgepodge of duct tape, Styrofoam, and a hope and a prayer? If the answer to these questions is yes, then you have yourself a sculpture for the Kinetic Skuplture race. If not, stop by to watch the insanity and see the conferring of the highly prized Mediocrity Award.

≡ *Eat & Drink*

Get Caffeinated

VELOCITY COFFEE

431 Water Street, Port Townsend • 360-379-5383 • Open daily 6:30 a.m.–5 p.m.

Lots of coffee drinks, chai, bagels, and artwork on the walls. Get it to go and walk down to the water.

SUNRISE COFFEE COMPANY

308 10th Street, Port Townsend • www.sunrisecoffee.net • 360-385-4117 • Open Monday–Friday
6:30 a.m.–5 p.m., Saturday 8 a.m.–2 p.m.

Using a "super green" coffee roaster, Sunrise Coffee Company roasts fresh green coffee beans
that are fair trade, impact sourced, and organic. Plenty of room to hang out, pet friendly.

1012 COFFEE BAR

1012 Lawrence Street, Port Townsend • 360-379-1012 • Open Tuesday–Saturday 8 a.m.–3 p.m.

Wake up with some hip music playing on the RPM turntable, then get a fresh-baked cookie or
a Bob's bagel to go with your joe.

Farm Fresh

JEFFERSON COUNTY FARMERS' MARKET

jcfmarkets.org • 360-379-9098

Tyler Street and Laurence Street • Open Saturdays: April–October, 9 a.m.–1 p.m.; November–
December, 10 a.m.–2 p.m.

Landes Street and 12th Street • Open Wednesdays; June–September, 2 p.m.–6 p.m.

All year-round, you can get a sampling of the Northwest's ample bounty at the Jefferson
County Farmers' Market. There you can find just about everything: sauerkraut and kimchi,
grass-fed beef, shellfish straight from Discovery Bay, lavender, succulents, saffron, gourmet
mushrooms, meads, ciders, wine, wild-harvested herbal tinctures, organic vegetables, and berries of all kinds. Or get a cup of joe, a kebab, crêpes, paella made from local seafood, and more
at any of the many great artisan foods stands.

THE PORT TOWNSEND FOOD CO-OP

414 Kearney Street, Port Townsend • www.foodcoop.coop • 360-385-2883 • Open daily 8 a.m.–9 p.m.

You won't find any 365-brand products in the aisles of this local-centric co-op. Their mission is
to source produce and products from the nearby counties of Jefferson, Kitsap, Island, Mason,
and Clallam. Come in for a fresh scone from Uptown Catering, spicy lavender mustard from
Auntie Quaint's Lavender Pantry, some fresh raw goat cheese from Whiskey Hill Farm, and so
much more.

CHIMACUM CORNER FARM STAND

9122 Rhody Drive, Chimacum • chimacumcorner.com • 360-732-0107 • Open daily 8 a.m.–8 p.m.

If you're in Chimacum, 10 miles south of Port Townsend, then stop by this little grocery story
to get the best of local farmers and producers. What's on hand is local, organic, sustainable,

seasonal, and downright delish, with a greenhouse and community garden in the back that makes the distance from farm to table even shorter.

COLLINWOOD FARMSTEAD

1210 F Street, Port Townsend • 360-379-9610 • Open 24 hours

This is an actual farm stand. It offers whatever's in season, organic and fresh off the farm. It's the honor-system payment method, so bring cash and don't be an asshole.

MOUNT TOWNSEND CREAMERY

338 Sherman Street, Port Townsend • mttownsendcreamery.com • 360-379-0895 • Tasting room hours: Wednesday–Friday 11 a.m.–6 p.m., Saturday 11 a.m.–5 p.m., Sunday noon–4 p.m.; Turophile hour (25 percent off cheese): Thursday and Friday 1–6 p.m.

You don't have to take the long voyage to the French countryside for some très bon cheese. Just head over to the Olympic Peninsula, which has a microclimate similar to that distant locale and therefore makes it prime for the making of soft-ripened cheese. Since 1850, the area has been producing thousands of pounds of butter and cheese for Seattle's and Tacoma's turophilic citizens, and family-owned and operated Mount Townsend Creamery has continued this tradition. They use milk that comes from cows who live on a family-owned farm in nearby Sequim. You can buy their products in most grocery stores around Seattle, but to get to the source, visit the creamery during tasting hours for the season's Northwest flavor.

>> Download the Olympic Peninsula **farm tour map** in the Port Townsend Guide, updated every year (ptguide.com).

Dining

PANE D'AMORE ARTISAN BAKERY

617 Tyler Street, Port Townsend • www.panedamore.com • 360-385-1199 • Open Monday–Friday 7 a.m.–5 p.m., Saturday 7 a.m.–4 p.m., Sunday 8 a.m.–4 p.m.

From cheddar jalapeño scones to gluten-free chocolate walnut cookies, panini to caraway rye, this bakery has something savory, sweet, and everything in between. They source locally as much as possible, using wheat and rye from Nash Huber's farm in nearby Sequim, cheese from Mount Townsend Creamery, and apples grown in Washington. They make most of their goods fresh daily, but some of their specialty breads they make only on certain days of the week—you can check out the website for the baking schedule.

FINISTÈRE

1025 Lawrence Street, Port Townsend • www.restaurantfinistere.com • 360-344-8127 • Happy hour: Wednesday–Sunday 3–5 p.m.; dinner: Wednesday–Sunday 5–9 p.m.; brunch: Saturday–Sunday 10 a.m.–2 p.m.

When a foodie power couple falls in love with a town, you get a restaurant like Finistère. Chef Deborah Taylor has some big-time creds on her résumé, such as Seattle's fancy-shmancy Canlis and Ethan Stowell's Staple and Fancy. So does her romantic and business partner, Scott Ross, who also has some healthy creds, such as Seattle's Goldfinch Tavern and Tilth. Stop by on a Saturday or Sunday for brunch, where you can get Washington oysters and cider from nearby Finn River Farm and Cidery. They make their bread in-house and get their coffee from Port Townsend Coffee Company and beer from Port Townsend Brewing Company.

SILVERWATER CAFE

237 Taylor Street, Port Townsend • silverwatercafe.com • 360-385-6448 • Main floor: Monday–Sunday 11:30 a.m.–3 p.m. and 5 p.m.–9 p.m. • Mezzaluna Lounge: Sunday–Thursday 5 p.m.–10 p.m., Friday and Saturday 5 p.m.–11 p.m.

No longer a fish-and-chips shack on the ferry dock of yesteryear (yesteryear = 1989), the Silverwater Cafe offers American culinary crowdpleasers with a Northwest twist. Come for the Washington specialties such as apple salad, Cape Cleare coho, and blackberry pie, plus sandwiches, entrées, seafood aplenty, wines from near and far, and a long list of libations.

>> Next door to the Rose Theatre and above the Silverwater Cafe sits the **Starlight Room**, a 21-plus venue with a full bar, small plates, and big, cushy antique chairs from which to view the movie screen. Features classics, new releases, and "black and white" truffle fries made with white truffle oil and black sea salt (rosetheatre.com).

ELEVATED ICE CREAM COMPANY

627 & 631 Water Street, Port Townsend • elevatedicecream.com • 360-385-1156 • Open Friday–Saturday 10 a.m.–10 p.m., Sunday–Thursday 10 a.m.–9 p.m.

For over 40 years, Elevated Ice Cream Company has been making fresh, homemade ice cream, sherbet, and Italian ices, plus espressos and chocolates. Whenever possible, they source from local farms and they make their sweet treats on the premises.

Booze and Beyond

PORT TOWNSEND BREWING COMPANY

330 10th Street, Port Townsend • www.porttownsendbrewing.com • 360-385-9967 • Open daily noon–7 p.m. (Friday until 9 p.m.)

Port Townsend Brewing Company is all about the Northwest style, including beastmode brews honoring Seattle's beloved Seahawks. Come in to try the year-round and seasonal brews, including their popular IPAs, scotch ales, ambers, and porters. If you're going to be around on a summer Friday, check out their schedule of concerts and enjoy a pint in their beer garden.

ADMIRALTY DISTILLERS

820 Lake Street, Port Townsend • www.admiraltydistillers.com • 360-643-3530 • Tasting room open Saturday noon–5 p.m.

Take wine or cider, let it sit for a while in the hold of a ship, and what do you get? Brandy. With a focus on local sourcing and ethical business, Admiralty Distillers uses water from the Olympic Mountains and Orange Muscat grapes, locally grown lavender, and apples picked from their neighbors' trees to create their brandies and gins.

PORT TOWNSEND VINEYARDS

www.porttownsendvineyards.com • 360-344-8155

Winery tasting room: 2640 W Sims Way, Port Townsend • Open Sunday–Thursday noon–6 p.m., Friday and Saturday noon–8 p.m.

Downtown tasting room: 215 Taylor Street, Port Townsend • Open daily 3–9 p.m.

For the full rundown, visit all three locations: the vineyard on Portuguese Hill, where you can see the five-zone vineyard with varieties chosen for their ability to thrive in the coastal climate and have a sip or two; the winery facility in town, where you can see the newest sustainable, energy-efficient methods of winemaking; and the downtown tasting room, where you can sit back and savor a glass of Discovery White or a pinot noir with a snack.

>> Go to the **Olympic Peninsula Wineries** website for a full list of wineries on, duh, the Olympic Peninsula (opciderroute.com).

FAIRWINDS WINERY

1984 Hastings Avenue W, Port Townsend • www.fairwindswinery.com • 360-385-6899 • Tasting room open Memorial Day through Labor Day, daily noon–5 p.m.; September through May, Friday–Sunday noon–5 p.m.

This award-winning winery is the only one in Washington to produce Aligoté, a white wine originating from Burgundy, France. They've got cabs, sauv blancs, ports, and fireweed mead, too.

 *Stay Over*

Forts and Resorts

FORT WORDEN

200 Battery Way, Port Townsend • fortworden.org • 360-344-4400

No longer a military base in the coastal defense system nicknamed "Triangle of Fire," this 434-acre property is a one-stop vacation. With on-site restaurants (don't miss Whiskey Wednesdays at Taps at the Guardhouse), hiking trails, scenic overlooks, a sandy beach, defunct coastal defense batteries open for exploration, and the Port Townsend Marine Science Center, Fort Worden has something for history buffs and regular ol' vacationers. There are all kinds of accommodations, from cute little cottages to the multi-bedroom homes of Officers Row. You can camp, too, by reserving campsites through the Washington State Park's reservation system at washingtongoingtocamp.com. Includes dog-friendly suites.

FORT FLAGLER

10541 Flagler Road, Nordland • parks.state.wa.us/508/Fort-Flagler • 360-385-1259

Pitch a tent or park your RV at this 1,451-acre marine camping park on Marrowstone Island, to the south of Port Townsend across Port Townsend Bay. There are 59 standard sites, 55 full hook-up sites, two primitive sites, one dump station, and two restrooms—and many have easy access to the beach. Reserve a spot at washingtongoingtocamp.com.

>> The third point on this Triangle of Fire is Fort Casey, located across the Strait of Juan de Fuca on Whidbey Island. Why not visit all three?

CHEVY CHASE BEACH CABINS

3710 S Discovery Road, Port Townsend • chevychasebeachcabins.com • 360-385-1270

Failed forty-niner John Turkey and his wife, Linnie Chase, opened what was then called Saint's Rest in 1897. Back then, it seems, highfalutin urbanites were looking for a way to escape the city, just as we are today. Since then, the 500 sheep have left for better pastures and Discovery Bay Golf Course, a swimming pool, tennis court, a gazebo and BBQ area, shuffleboard court, and rope swing have taken their place. Named a Top 10 romantic cottage in *Sunset* magazine, an unforgettable cottage in *Seattle Met*, and best in the northwest in *Northwest Travel and Life*, the cabins aren't cheap, but the views are stellar and the private beach is perfect for Fido and Lucy. Dogs welcome for $20 per dog per night.

Feeling Royal

PALACE HOTEL

1004 Water Street, Port Townsend • palacehotelpt.com • 1-800-962-0741

Like most old buildings—retired Sea Captain Tibbals built this one in 1889—the Palace Hotel has been many things in its time, including a brothel. (FYI, just about everything in this area used to be a brothel.) Spend a little more for the Enchanted Evening Package featuring champagne, homemade chocolates, and an "adult board game," or rent a room overlooking Port Townsend Bay.

THE BISHOP VICTORIAN HOTEL

714 Washington Street, Port Townsend • bishopvictorian.com • 1-833-254-2469

Built in 1891, this hotel is ideal for those who like strolling along historic streets, Victorian period gardens and furniture, in-room breakfast service, and generally being charmed. Includes dog-friendly suites.

MANRESA CASTLE HOTEL

651 Cleveland Street, Port Townsend • manresacastle.com • 360-385-5750

Built by a rich dude in 1892, this castle has had a long and varied life, including 20 years of neglect and a long stint as a hangout for nuns and Jesuits. The rooms are surprisingly affordable, given the blueblood airs.

B&Bs and Inns

HUBER'S INN

1421 Landes Street, Port Townsend • hubersinn.com • 360-385-3904

Book a room at this "eco-friendly" downtown B&B, only a five-minute drive from the ferry. It's across the street from the Kah Tai Lagoon Park. To get a view of the park's bird sanctuary, reserve the Kah Tai suite.

THE COMMANDER'S BEACH HOUSE

400 Hudson Street, Port Townsend • commandersbeachhouse.com • 360-385-1778

Voted "Best B&B in Jefferson County" 2012–2015, the Commander's Beach House is within walking distance of the center of Port Townsend. Or, if you've had it up to here with shopping and eating, grab a book and lay a towel down on their 2,000-foot private beach on Admiralty Inlet.

5/13/2022 12:06:03 PM

SALISH LODGE & SPA

6351 RAILROAD AVE SE
SNOQUALMIE, WA 98065
P: 425-831-6525 F: 425-888-6375

SO#		Receipt #	466567
5/13/2022		Store:	001A
Assoc: Andrea		Cashier:	Andrea

ITEM	QTY	ORIG P	PRICE	EXT PRICE
9 BAG FEE	1	0.08	0.08	0.08 BAG
5650 EASY WEEKEND	1	22.95	22.95	22.95 SEA
6721 COMPENDIUM	1	3.99	3.99	3.99 STEP
15687 BO BIGFOOT	1	46.95	46.95	46.95
18357 PAINT BY STICKER	1	9.95	9.95	9.95 KIDS

	5 Unit(s)	Subtotal	83.92
	8.900 % WA Tax		7.47
	RECEIPT TOTAL:		**91.39**
	Tend:		91.39
CrCard 91.39 VISA			
			3451

Signature _____

THANK YOU

ALL SALES FINAL
NO REFUNDS

3% SLC Concession Fee on all
Concession Items

BLUE GULL INN

1310 Clay Street, Port Townsend • bluegullinn.com • 360-379-3241

When you imagine a B&B, this is exactly what comes up: floral wallpaper, wicker furniture, a feeling of general homeyness. The breakfasts are lovely—you can get a to-go bag if you need to leave early—and full of gluteny goodness.

QUIMPER INN

1306 Franklin Street, Port Townsend • www.quimperinn.com • 360-385-1060

At this inn, located in the Historic Uptown District, you can relax in an "embarrassing large private bath" in Michele's Room or browse your very own library in Harry & Gertie's Suite. Breakfast served at 8:30 a.m.

ROBIN'S NEST

1190 21st Street, Port Townsend • robinsnestpt.com • 208-390-5327

Innkeepers, they're just like us! Owned by a former stressed-out marketing professional, Robin's Nest is an intentional exercise in chill vibes. The rooms are reasonably priced, and the location is far enough from Port Townsend uptown and downtown to be quiet, but close enough to get there quickly.

#farmlife

SOLSTICE FARM BED & BREAKFAST

6503 Beaver Valley Road, Chimacum • solsticefarmstay.com • 360-732-0174

Make reservations early for this small two-bedroom B&B on a working farm in Chimacum. Breakfasts include farm-fresh eggs and fruit, and the large sunroom atrium is perfect for a cup of tea and a nice long afternoon with your book. If you're lucky, you'll get to pet a piglet.

THE COTTAGE AT TIBBALS LAKE

tibbalslakecottage.com; 360-379-0136

Think *Secret Garden*. Located on 60 acres of private land, this Craftsman-style cottage is fully equipped and has access to gorgeous flower and organic vegetable gardens, a private pond, and nearby hiking trails. The town of Port Townsend is reachable by a quick drive but feels far away.

☰ *While You're Here*

WHALE WATCHING WITH PUGET SOUND EXPRESS

227 Jackson Street, Port Townsend • www.pugetsoundexpress.com • 360-385-5288

All year long, you can go on this four-hour whale-watching cruise, operated by the Hanke family for more than 30 years. Includes a snack, a bathroom, and sightings of not just humpbacks, grays, minkes, and orcas—a.k.a. killer whales—but bald eagles, tufted puffins, sea lions, and seals.

KAYAK OR STANDUP PADDLEBOARD WITH PORT TOWNSEND PADDLESPORTS

For rentals or guided tours: Port Townsend Paddlesports • www.ptpaddlesports.com • 360-379-3608 • Season: late May–early September

Rent a kayak or SUP to explore the waters around Fort Worden State Park. Or you can take a guided kayak tour of the Victorian Seaport, Glass Beach, or Fort Worden. Either way, you'll get stunning, water-level views of the Northern Cascades, Mount Rainier, and Mount Baker.

HIKE MOUNT TOWNSEND

8.0 miles round-trip • GPS coordinates: 47.8564, -123.0359 • www.wta.org

Get your buns barstool-ready by hiking up Mount Townsend. Choose any of the four trails for a solid climb and a trek through old-growth forest and open meadow. To get there, take Highway 101 south to the Penny Creek Quarry, then turn left onto Forest Road 27. At 12.5 miles, you can follow signs for Mount Townsend to get to the Lower Trailhead. Or, to get to Upper Trailhead, continue 1 more mile and turn left onto FR27-190.

GHOST TOUR WITH TWISTED HISTORY TOURS

718 Washington Street, Studio E, Port Townsend • www.twistedhistorytours.com • 1-888-921-6562

According to the Twisted History Tours website, Port Townsend is one of the most haunted cities in the United States. Go on one of its many tours for some good homespun paranormal investigation. Murder, jealousy, tragic death . . . what more could you ask for?

BIKE WITH JEFFERSON COUNTY RECYCLERY

1925 Blaine Street, Port Townsend • ptrecyclery.org • 360-643-1755

Year-round you can rent a bike from the ReCyclery, a 501(c)(3) nonprofit that offers bike recycling services and promotes education around the health and environmental benefits of cycling. Rent a bike for cruising around town, or for one Saturday in June, join Tour de

Forts—you can choose from three loops ranging from 11 to 26 miles, or do them all! Check out the event's website for routes to scenic self-propelled tours around Jefferson County (www .tourdeforts.org).

>> **Everywhere is haunted**. To encounter ghosts of Seattle's past, take a tour with Seattle Underground (614 1st Avenue, Seattle; 206-682-4646; www.undergroundtour.com)

ABOVE & BEYOND

Dogs | Take your pup to **Chetzemoka Dog Park**, Jackson Street and Blaine Street, a couple blocks north of Chetzemoka City Park. It's on the small side, with a couple picnic tables and a decent field of turf.

Skate | **Jefferson Street and Monroe Street** is a good-size park with a ton of variety, featuring a couple bowls, some shallow ramps for beginners, and elements throughout. For more information and photos, go to northwestskater.com.

Books | Go to **William James Bookseller** (829 Water Street, Port Townsend; 360-385-7313; williamjamesbookseller.com) for fine-quality used and out-of-print vintage and collectible books. Open daily 11 a.m.–5 p.m. or later. **Imprint Bookstore and Writers' Workshoppe** (820 Water Street, Port Townsend; 360-379-2617; writersworkshoppe.com) calls itself an "eclectic general bookstore" and touts its dedication to providing a place for writers to gather for workshops and camaraderie. Open daily 10 a.m.–5:30 p.m. If it's weird, **Insatiables Books** (821 Washington Street, Port Townsend; 360-385-9262) has it, plus a unique collection of classic lit, children's books, and rarities. Though the competition is steep, **Phoenix Rising** (696 Water Street, Port Townsend; phoenixrisingpt.com; 360-385-4464; open daily 10 a.m.–6 p.m.) is one of the largest full-service metaphysical bookstores and shops in the Pacific Northwest. Along with books, you can get crystals, statues, and other odds and ends.

Good to Know

· For every place in the US, there's a white guy who named it after himself. Quimper Peninsula is named after Manuel Quimper, who sailed through what is now called the Strait of Juan de Fuca on his way to Alaska in 1790.

· One of Port Townsend's nicknames is "The City That Whiskey Built."

Been There, Done That

Head west to visit the rest of the Olympic Peninsula (page 175).

Head south to go to Bainbridge Island (page 125).

Head east to go to Whidbey Island (page 249).

Part Two
Romantic Mini-Breaks

In a Tree in Issaquah and Snoqualmie Valley

Come for the cherry pie, stay for the hiking. Or come for the hiking, stay for the giant doughnuts. Or come for the giant doughnuts, stay for the tree houses. Just a 30-minute drive from Seattle on I-90, Issaquah and the Snoqualmie Valley are little more than a stone's throw from the big city. David Lynch memorialized this tiny, fog-smothered area in his groundbreaking '90s show—recently brought back to life for a redux—and ever since the show's premiere, *Twin Peaks* fanatics have made the annual pilgrimage for the Twin Peaks Festival. But it's so much more than the site of poor Laura Palmer's murder. Hiking, biking, lovingly gazing into your sweetheart's eyes over a glass of sparkling wine in front of a roaring fire . . . these are the activities that have earned the Snoqualmie Valley the reputation of being *the* spot for a romantic getaway. If the term "the Niagara Falls of the Pacific Northwest" isn't a thing, then you heard it here first.

Enjoy a day trip to hiking in the Issaquah Alps, swimming in the tiny slice of public beach at Lake Joy, or taking a *Twin Peaks* tour. TreeHouse Point in Issaquah, a yurt at Tolt-MacDonald Park in Carnation, and Salish Lodge in Snoqualmie are excellent places to up the romance—the last offers a Romance Package, featuring a "Romance Concierge."

At first glance, **Issaquah** looks like just another suburb. And it's true that you can find cookie-cutter suburbia here, with its clean streets and perfectly manicured parks and quiet

// TreeHouse Point, Issaquah

nights. (That alone can be a draw for those who live in Belltown or Capitol Hill and want a break from the unceasing traffic and the 1 a.m. drunken ruckus happening in the alley below their windows.) But farther in, there are tree-enclosed homes and businesses that make it almost feel like country. Many people who work in Seattle believe that the commute to this forested suburban mecca is worth it. In fact, many of the coffee shops on the east side open earlier than other places (5:30 a.m.) to serve the motivated before they make the super early morning drive. For folks who live in Seattle's urban environs, Issaquah can serve as an easy landing point for some smoochie boochies or for some time outside.

Carnation, at just 27 miles from the big city, is a small farming community—population 2,000-ish—located at the convergence of the Tolt and Snoqualmie rivers, with lots of pastoral fields and pumpkin-related shenanigans. Farms and farm stands are open year-round, though the late fall months and berry season are when they really shine. Carnation is a famous cow town, the locale of Elbridge Amos Stuart's contented cows operation of Carnation Evaporated Milk Company. (The company was established at the turn of the 20th century in Kent and called Pacific Coast Condensed Milk Company, then renamed once Stuart established a farm hellbent on breeding productive and truly happy cows.) Carnation Farm continues the tradition to this day. It's also a motorcycle town and, surprisingly, a medieval cosplay town. It seems to also be a town that likes to keep its lakes private. But not everyone thinks water access should be reserved solely for the entrenched or the wealthy, and it is possible to find small slices of public beach if you know where to look. All in all, it's a great stopover for love-inspiring quiet time and farm-fresh vibes close to the city.

≡ *Getting There*

BY CAR | Get on I-90 E and drive.

BY BUS | To Issaquah, take the 554 Express to Issaquah Transit Center (an approximately one-hour ride). To North Bend, transfer to the 208 toward North Bend Snoqualmie Ridge or the 628 toward North Bend Snoqualmie (an approximately two-hour ride total).

BY BIKE | Bike the I-90 Trail to Sound Greenway Trail, or take the 520 Trail. Approximately 20 miles, 2.25 hours.

≡ *Highlight Reel*

TREEHOUSE POINT

6922 Preston–Fall City Road SE, Issaquah • www.treehousepoint.com • 425-441-8087

Spend the day forest bathing or building cairns along the Raging River, have a candlelit (or sloppy BBQ) dinner in town, and then sleep among the owls in one of TreeHouse Point's six private tree houses. Sunshine, rain, or snow—inside the tree house, it's quiet and warm, the perfect spot to curl up on the bed with your honey and look out upon the moonlight shining through the trees. Come morning, go to the central lodge, where you can find homemade breakfast, then take a yoga or tai chi class, get a massage, or have a hypnotherapy session. All it takes is a half-hour drive from Seattle to find this little fairyland.

>> Want a tree house in your own backyard? Contact TreeHouse Point's sister company, Nelson Treehouse and Supply (nelsontreehouse.com). To see what kind of crazy and creative construction they can do, go to the company's website or check out any of the episodes in the 11 seasons of *Treehouse Masters* on Animal Planet.

SALISH LODGE

6501 Railroad Avenue SE, Snoqualmie • www.salishlodge.com • 1-800-2-SALISH

Fans of *Twin Peaks* will recognize the iconic Salish Lodge, perched above the churning Snoqualmie Falls. A well-known wedding destination, this hotel has won such prominent awards as Best Place to Kiss, Best Place to Propose, and Best Place to Celebrate an Anniversary. Romantics and Peakies alike will go nuts over the Great Northern Escape package, which includes a map of *Twin Peaks* locations, cherry pie and damn good coffee for two, and Dale Cooper cocktails. Work up an appetite with the nearby hiking, biking, golfing, and horseback riding, then indulge in one of the many dining options—including a canine menu—to get a full-range taste of the Northwest. (Be sure to try the signature **Honey from Heaven**, in which the server drops a dollop of the lodge's very own honey from way up high onto your house-made

// TreeHouse Point, Issaquah

biscuits.) All of this will surely set the scene for some *brown chicken brown cow*, but if your love life really needs a kick in the pants, book the Romance Concierge, who will work with you to create a unique experience "on and off the menu." Dogs very welcome—book the It's a Dog's World package for the VIP treatment.

TWEDE'S CAFÉ

137 W North Bend Way, North Bend • www.twedescafe.com • 425-831-5511 • Open Monday–Friday 8 a.m.–8 p.m., Saturday and Sunday 6:30 a.m.–8 a.m.

There's a reason David Lynch chose this retro hometown spot to be the *Twin Peaks'* Double R Diner. Along with the famous *Twin Peaks* cherry pie, the café offers apple, boysenberry, banana, and chocolate cream pies, and most everything is made from scratch. (Call in advance to get a pie to go.) Servings are huge, so bring an appetite. It's *Twin Peaks* top to bottom, but be kind to your server and please refrain from ordering coffee "black as midnight on a moonless night."

ISSAQUAH

FROM SEATTLE: 30 MINUTES · DAYS HERE: 0.5 TO 2

EAT	DRINK	DO	BUY
BBQ	mezcal	get sexy in a tree	a grandfather clock

≡ *Getting There*

BY CAR | Drive on I-90 E for approximately 17 miles. Travel time: approximately 20 minutes.

BY BUS | Take Sound Transit #554 to Issaquah Highlands Park and Ride. Travel time: approximately 40 minutes.

≡ *Plan Around*

ANNUAL ZOMBIE WALK

October • downtownissaquah.com/zombie-walk

Zombies? Check. Flash mob to *Thriller*!? Check. Brews? Check. You are into zombies (that is not a question), so head to Issaquah in October for the Annual Zombie Walk on Front Street. If, for whatever strange reason, you don't have all the makeup necessities for getting your corpseface on, then show up early to get your makeup done by a professional makeup artist. At the end of the stagger/shuffle, you'll end up at Rogue Ales Issaquah Brewhouse, where you can drink up some Dead Guy Ale.

Mercer Island is roughly halfway between Issaquah and Seattle across the I-90 bridge, a thriving mini-city in its own right. Stop by the acclaimed Island Books (page 113), Luther Burbank Park and its waterfront dog park (page 113), the little skate park (page 113), or the **Mercer Island Farmers' Market**, which operates on Sunday, 10 a.m.–3 p.m., June through October (7700 SE 32nd Street, Mercer Island; www.mifarmersmarket.org), on the way there or back.

☰ *Eat & Drink*

Get Caffeinated

ISSAQUAH COFFEE COMPANY

Gilman Village, 317 NW Gilman Boulevard #46, Issaquah • issaquahcoffee.com • 425-677-7118 • Open Monday–Friday 6 a.m.–7 p.m., Saturday 7 a.m.–7 p.m., Sunday 7 a.m.–6 p.m.

A local favorite. Great classic and specialty coffee drinks using Stumptown coffee beans, along with smoothies and a selection of baked goods. Get the Cougar Mountain Latte.

KOFFEE SUTRA

102 Front Street S, Issaquah • 425-392-8646 • Open Monday–Friday 5:30 a.m.–6 p.m., Saturday 6:30 a.m.–6 p.m., Sunday 7 a.m.–6 p.m.

Cute drive-up coffee stand with friendly baristas and lovely lattes.

Farm Fresh

ISSAQUAH FARMERS' MARKET

Pickering Barn, 1730 10th Avenue NW, Issaquah • www.ci.issaquah.wa.us/market • 425-837-3321 • Open May–September, Saturday 9 a.m.–2 p.m.

// Artichokes from Carnation Farms, Carnation

Dining

RHODIES SMOKIN BBQ

30375 SE Highpoint Way, Preston • www.rhodiesbbq.com • 425-222-6428 • Open Monday–Friday 10 a.m.–8:30 p.m., Saturday and Sunday 11 a.m.–8:30 p.m.

The atmosphere is nothing fancy—the building used to house a Jack in the Box—but locals love the hootch sauce. If you're hungry, order the brisket platter and a big glass of ice-cold beer. For those on the move, grab a pulled beef or pulled pork sandwich to go. You will need napkins.

FLYING PIE PIZZERIA

30 Front Street S, Issaquah • flyingpiepizzeria.com • 425-391-2407 • Open Tuesday–Thursday 11 a.m.–9 p.m., Friday and Saturday 11 a.m.–10 p.m., Sunday 11 a.m.–9 p.m.

Family-owned and -operated since 1997, this pizza joint features fresh hand-rolled dough, strombolis and calzones, beers on tap, and pizza by the slice. This being Issaquah, vegan cheese or gluten-free crust is available on demand.

AJI SUSHI & GRILL

1052 NE Park Drive, Issaquah • ajisushiissaquah.com • 425-369-8445 • Open Monday–Thursday 11 a.m.–9:30 p.m., Friday and Saturday 11 a.m.–10:30 p.m., Sunday noon–9:30 p.m.

Sushi, sashimi, and other Japanese delicacies, as well as a couple Korean hot pots. Feeling spicy? Get the Heart Attack and the I Need a Bottle of Water, then geek out on the sake and its descriptive menu.

GILMAN VILLAGE

317 NW Gilman Boulevard, Issaquah • www.gilmanvillage.com • 425-392-6802

Outdoor shopping mall with a range of restaurants serving a range of everything from cold-pressed juices to dim sum, brunch to Tex-Mex, candy to tikka masala. Stop in at Aubrey's Clock Gallery (425-392-5200; www.aubreysclockgallery.com) after you eat. Hours depend on individual restaurant.

Booze and Beyond

AGAVE COCINA & TEQUILAS

1048 NE Park Drive, Issaquah • agavecocina.com • 425-369-8900 • Open Monday–Thursday 11 a.m.–10 p.m., Friday 11 a.m.–12 a.m., Saturday 10 a.m.–12 a.m., Sunday 10 a.m.–10 p.m.

Agave offers one of the most extensive lists of tequilas around, plus excellent Mexican fare. Get chips and guac (obviously), a scratch original margarita, any of the soft tacos made from in-house, hand-rolled corn tortillas, and a flight of tequila for dessert.

ROGUE ALES ISSAQUAH BREWHOUSE

35 W Sunset Way, Issaquah • www.rogue.com • 425-557-1911 • Open Sunday–Thursday 11 a.m.–12 a.m., Friday and Saturday 11 a.m.–2 a.m.

With breweries in California, Oregon, and Washington, Rogue is a West Coast booze empire. The Issaquah location is its most northerly, and it brews its own local favorites and cooks up some solid Northwesty pub fare. They also serve Rogue whiskey and gin distilled in Newport, Oregon. Check out the One Whiskey, One Scotch, One Beer dessert: It is simply delightful.

☰ *Stay Over*

TREEHOUSE POINT (page 107) is where it's at when it comes to staying over. If, however, you find yourself in need of a room, there are plenty of chain hotels—the inns of Marriott, Hilton, and Holiday.

☰ *While You're Here*

SEE A PLAY AT VILLAGE THEATRE

303 Front Street N, Issaquah • www.villagetheatre.org • 425-392-2202

From *Hairspray* to *Singin' in the Rain*, *Newsies* to *Billy Elliot*, there's always something good playing at the Village Theatre. If you see an evening performance, make sure you stop by Fins Bistro next door for some bread pudding.

HIKE POO POO POINT

Coordinates: 47.5195, -122.0299

This 7.2-mile round-trip hike on Tiger Mountain is close to the city but far enough out for you to get some peace and quiet with stellar views of the area. You may even see some paragliders launching. Dogs on leash. From I-90, take Exit 17 for Front Street. Head south through downtown Issaquah, then park in the lot 2.9 miles from the exit. For more information, visit the Washington Trails Association at www.wta.org.

>> Not only is Tiger Mountain great for hiking, it's a favorite launch point for local paragliders. Check out Parafly Paragliding at paraflyparagliding.com or Seattle Paragliding at www.seattle paragliding.com if you want to take a solo or tandem flight.

SWIM IN LAKE SAMMAMISH

2000 NW Sammamish Road, Issaquah

Walk through this 512-acre day-use park to get to Sunset Beach on Lake Washington. Compared to Seattle's scene, this sandy beach is tidy, with lots of amenities to make everyone feel comfortable, including a playground, zip line, and new bathrooms. Meaning: There will be families. Tibett's Beach, southwest of Sunset Beach, is smaller, and during the summer you can rent a kayak, SUP, or pedal boat there from Issaquah Paddle Sports (425-891-5039; www .issaquahpaddlesports.com). Discovery Pass required.

PET A WALLABY AT THE FALL CITY WALLABY RANCH

35303 SE Fish Hatchery Road, Fall City • wallabyranch.org • 206-354-8624

Located in Fall City, about halfway between Issaquah and Snoqualmie, baby kangaroos and wallabies are born, rescued, and put up for adoption. Yes, this is a real thing. Come take a group tour, in which you will learn all about macropods, then meet them face to face. You might even get to see a little joey popping out of her mama's pouch or hold a tiny roo. Group tour: $75 for 5 people.

ABOVE & BEYOND

Dogs | **Issaquah Highland Bark Park** (2203 NE Natalie Way, Issaquah) is a fenced-in grassy area—one section is mowed, the other is not, great for dogs who like to wander through long grass—located in a quiet suburban park that features a playground and on-leash walking trails.

Luther Burbank Dog Park (2040 84th Avenue SE, Mercer Island) has water access and is therefore a favorite for hot dogs and pups who enjoy a good session of water fetch. (If you have an escape artist, you'll have to keep an eye out because there are ways to leave the dog park via the water.) The park has two fenced-in areas: one for nervous and/or small dogs, and a bigger, sandy area for bigger and/or more confident dogs.

Skates | **Issaquah Skate Park** (965 12th Avenue NW, Issaquah) is a 10,500-square-foot park renovated in 2017, with a large bowl, a long run, and a variety of elements.

Mercer Island Skate Park (7706 SE 34th Street, Mercer Island) is a mostly flat surface with a few fun features. Best for beginners or old-timers hoping to practice more mellow tricks. For photos and more information, go to www.northwestskater.com.

Books | **Half Price Books** (15600 NE Street, Bellevue; www.hpb.com; 425-747-6616; open Monday–Saturday 9 a.m.–9 p.m., Sunday 9 a.m.–8 p.m.) is a chain with more than 120 stores in the United States, founded in 1972 and featuring new and used books for every taste.

Island Books on Mercer Island (3014 78th Avenue SE, Mercer Island; www.mercerisland books.com; 206-232-6920; open Monday–Friday 9 a.m.–7 p.m., Saturday 9 a.m.–6 p.m., Sunday 10 a.m.–5 p.m.) is a much-loved independent bookstore with a wide variety of new fiction, nonfiction, and children's books, a great staff, and a big selection of magazines.

CARNATION

FROM SEATTLE: 45 MINUTES · DAYS HERE: 0.5 TO 1

EAT	DRINK	DO	BUY
berries	hot cider	get sexy in a heart-shaped lake	*Bors Hede Boke of Cookry*

≡ *Getting There*

BY CAR | From Seattle, drive on WA-520 E or I-90 E for approximately 27 miles, then get on WA-202 or WA-203 E and continue for approximately 11 miles.

≡ *Plan Around*

FALL HARVEST CELEBRATION

September and October
Local farms host pumpkin-related fun.

>> Through November up until the big day, you can **cut down your own Christmas tree** at Carnation Tree Farm (31523 NE 40th Street; 425-333-4510), a 100-year-old family farm.

// Tomatoes from Carnation Farms, Carnation

TIMBER! OUTDOOR MUSIC FESTIVAL

July • Tolt-MacDonald Park, NE 40th Street • www.timbermusicfest.com

For one weekend, see some stellar live music and do a bunch of other fun activities, such as outdoor yoga, various water sports and playtime on the Tolt and Snoqualmie rivers. Screen movies, toast s'mores, climb a tree, and stargaze with professional stargazers from the Seattle Astronomical Society. Camp at first-come-first-served campsites for $40, glamp with pre-set-up tent sites for $400, park your RV for $500, or rent a six-person yurt, with additional space for two tents, for $1,000. No doggies. Tickets: $45–110.

>> There's also a **Timbrrr! Winter Music Festival in Leavenworth** (page 267).

≡ *Eat & Drink*

Get Caffeinated

SANDY'S ESPRESSO

4650 Tolt Avenue, Carnation • 425-549-0062 • Open Monday–Friday 5:30 a.m.–5 p.m., Saturday 6:30 a.m.–5 p.m., Sunday 7:30 a.m.–4 p.m.

Cute country café with good coffee, big breakfast sandwich bagels, baked goods, and paninis and salads for lunch.

Farm Fresh

CARNATION FARMERS' MARKET

Tolt Avenue and Bird Street • carnationfarmersmarket.org • Open May–November, Tuesday 3–7 p.m.

CARNATION FARMS

28901 NE Carnation Farms Road, Carnation • carnationfarms.org • 425-844-3100 • Open Thursday–Saturday 10 a.m.–dusk

On special designated Farm Days, visitors can tour the farm, do a tasting, and meet the cows. Otherwise, stop by the farm stand for fresh organic veggies and eggs, fresh honey, dried beans, and more.

// Carnation Farms, Carnation

REMLINGER FARMS RESTAURANT

32610 NE 32nd Street, Carnation • remlingerfarms.com • 425-333-4135

Pick some berries, pet a goat, then eat a farm-fresh salad made with produce sourced from approximately 100 yards away. Sandwiches with in-house slow-roasted meat are big and soups are satisfying. Take a U-bake pie to go—each berry pie contains 2 pounds of fresh berries. There will be kids.

FIRST LIGHT FARM

27307 NE 100th Street, Carnation • www.upickseattle.com • 206-719-8602

A farm stand, a picnic area, and an opportunity to get dirt under your nails while picking giant pumpkins and other vegetables.

Dining

IXTAPA CARNATION

4522 Tolt Avenue, Carnation • ixtapa-carnation.business.site • 425-333-6788 • Open daily 11 a.m.–9 p.m.

Quite amply portioned Mexican cuisine, great service, fun decor, nummy bottomless chunky salsa, and hot homemade tortilla chips. Get one margarita per person, then split an enormous burrito and the chicken tortilla soup.

CARNATION CAFÉ

4760 Tolt Avenue, Carnation • 425-333-4304 • Open Tuesday–Thursday 11:15 a.m.–8 p.m., Friday 8:30 a.m.–8:30 p.m., Saturday 8 a.m.–8 p.m.

Casual country look, solid Northwesty cuisine. They're known for their breakfasts, and the eggs Benedict are worth a weekend stopover. They're also known for lunchtime stacked sandwiches, burgers, and whipped cream–topped desserts.

SAM'S NOODLE TOWN

Tolt Town Center, 31722 W Eugene Street, Suite 7, Carnation • samsnoodletown.com • 425-333-6288 • Open Monday 11 a.m.–9 p.m., Wednesday–Saturday 11 a.m.–9 p.m., Sunday 11 a.m.–8 p.m.

Noted as "the best pho on the Eastside" by some, this small, family-owned restaurant serves fresh Asian fusion. The veggies are freshy fresh. Get a bubble tea and a bahn mi to go, or stay for some hot noodle soup.

PETE'S CLUB GRILL

4640 Tolt Avenue, Carnation • www.petesclubgrill.com • 425-333-4300 • Open Monday–Friday
11 a.m.–12 a.m., Saturday and Sunday 8 a.m.–2 a.m.

A 100-plus-year-old venue with lots of outdoor seating space and indoor games, good pub
grub plus salads, with 13 beers on tap and a full bar. It's a motorcycle bar/sports bar, so be prepared for some loud *vroom vroom* and sports-related cheering coming from the back room,
Hawks Nest. Get the basket o' fries. Check out their events calendar online for trivia night,
karaoke night, Texas Hold 'Em tournaments, and live music.

Booze and Beyond

MAC AND JACK'S BREWING COMPANY

17825 NE 65th Street, Redmond • www.macandjacks.com • 425-558-9697 • Beer Garden open
Thursday–Sunday 2–8 p.m.; free tours on Saturday and Sunday at 2 p.m.

The nearest brewery is in Redmond, about 13 miles west of Carnation toward Seattle. It's a
good one and worth stopping in for a free brewery tour and tasting.

Stay Over

LAKE JOY BEACH HOUSE

10908 W Lake Joy Drive NE, Carnation • lakejoybeachhouse.com • 425-788-6669

Pretend like you're a resident by renting a room at Lake Joy Beach House. Wake up to stunning views of the water and the Cascade Mountains, then walk out the front door and down
to the lake. The quaint little B&B serves a continental breakfast and has a variety of boats you
can take out on the water.

TOLT-MACDONALD PARK—TENT, RV, YURT CAMPING

31020 Northeast 40th Street, Carnation • 206-205-5434

To get the best darn sleep of your life, hunker down in a room without corners. Tolt-
MacDonald Park is a 574-acre park on the confluence of the Tolt and Snoqualmie rivers, and
it has six furnished yurts available to rent—each yurt can sleep up to seven people—plus 16 RV
campsites and 22 individual tent sites. The yurts and many of the campsites are walk-in only.
For more information, go to carnationwa.gov or kingcounty.gov. To make reservations, call the
number above or 206-477-6149.

≡ *While You're Here*

SWIM AND FISH IN LAKE JOY IN CARNATION

10911 E Lake Joy Road NE, 3.5 miles NE of Carnation

Think public property should be accessible only to rich people? If the answer is no, then head over to Lake Joy, the darn tootinest cutest heart-shaped lake in King County. Public access is basically a tiny slice of underdeveloped shoreline, and you're not going to find much information about it online. Still, no matter how difficult "they" make it to find, it exists on the east shoreline, just north of where E Lake Joy Drive NE and NE Moss Lake Road intersect. The rest of the shoreline is taken up by houses. The lake is small and so feels refreshingly bathwater-y come June, and it's an easy swim out to the dock that sits in the middle of the lake. There's a high dive on it if you're feeling brave. Bring a boat small enough to carry in, plus a fishing pole if that's your thing—rumor has it there's lots of bass.

VISIT CAMLANN MEDIEVAL VILLAGE

10320 Kelly Road NE, Carnation • camlann.org • 425-788-8624 • Village demonstrations May–September, daily noon–5 p.m.; dinner at Ye Bors Hede Inn Wednesday–Sunday 5–8 p.m.

Learn about the Middle Ages at this 14th-century village, where volunteers play lutes and do handcraft demonstrations and, obviously, joust. Check online for their schedule, including festivals held throughout the year and featuring medieval art, music, and food. While you're here, stop by Ye Scribes Shoppe to peruse the book selection—be sure to pick up your copy of *Bors Hede Boke of Cookry*—and the Clothier Shoppe to get your noble knight or fine lady outfit.

FLOAT THE SNOQUALMIE RIVER IN FALL CITY

4101 Fall City Carnation Road, Fall City • www.fallcityfloating.com • 1-844-831-0448

Take a 4-mile float from just below Snoqualmie Falls to the Fall City Bridge. Renting a tube, a life jacket, paddles, and a storage locker, and reserving a spot on the shuttle to the launch point costs $30 on weekends and $20 on weekdays. (A cooler plus tube costs $15, ice and beverages not included.) Book in advance. To save money, bring your own tube—the shuttle costs only $5. FYI: The water's not warm, so choose a sunny day and bring a ton of sunscreen.

Dogs welcome in shuttle and on river—don't forget the doggy life vest.

BIKE THE SNOQUALMIE VALLEY TRAIL

Bring your own bike or rent one from Valley Vignettes Tours (425-941-4459; valley vignettesbiketours.com) in Carnation, which happens to sit in the middle of the trail. You can bike north to Duvall or southeast to North Bend and beyond. The whole shebang is approximately 20 miles. See VVT's website for information on shuttles, route ideas, and other cool places to visit on bike, and/or check out savorsnoqualmie.com.

U-PICK BERRIES

If you hate children, then this is probably not the activity for you. If you love children, or at least feel neutral about them, then stop by these farms to pick your own produce.

HARVOLD BERRY FARM (STRAWBERRIES AND RASPBERRIES)

(32325 NE 55th Street, Carnation; 425-333-4185). Call ahead to make sure fields are open and the fruit is ripe.

GAME HAVEN GREENERY (PUMPKINS) (7110 310th Avenue NE, Carnation; 425-

333-4313). You can pick the perfect pumpkin for your jack-o'-lantern, plus other gourds. Family owned for more than 65 years. Open daily in October 9:30 a.m.–dusk.

BLUE DOG FARM (BLUEBERRIES) (7125 W Snoqualmie Valley Road NE, Carnation;

www.bluedogfarm.com). This farm is a membership u-pick farm, meaning you have to pay the $30 fee ($25 if you pay before July 1) and then you can come back again and again until your teeth are stained purple forever.

PET AN ALPACA AT CASCADE ROSE ALPACAS

1826 324th Avenue NE, Carnation • www.cascaderosealpacas.com • 425-224-7224

Because they're cute. This farm cares for more than 60 huacaya alpacas, and not only can you watch them do weird alpaca business, you can also purchase alpaca-made goods (not made by them, made *with* them).

ABOVE & BEYOND

Dogs | **Carnation Off-Leash Dog Park** (4300 Larson Avenue, Carnation) has 8 acres of grassy fields perfect for your pup to romp in. Great for those long-distance fetchers and dogs (and their humans) who like a little extra space.

Skate | **Carnation Skate Park** (3810 Tolt Avenue, Carnation) has a huge bowl, with clamshells, hips, and other spaces for catching some wind and doing some grinding. For more information and photos, go to northwestskater.com.

SNOQUALMIE & NORTH BEND

FROM SEATTLE: 45 MINUTES · DAYS HERE: 0.5 TO 2

EAT	DRINK	DO	BUY
honey from Heaven	whiskey at The Iron Duck Public House	a *Twin Peaks* Tour	a growler at Snoqualmie Brewery and Taproom

Getting There

BY CAR | Drive on I-90 E for 27 miles.

BY BUS | Take Sound Transit #554 to Issaquah, then transfer to the #208. Travel time: approximately 1 hour 45 minutes.

Eat & Drink

Get Caffeinated

COFFEE EXPRESS-O

7936 Railroad Avenue, Snoqualmie • 425-831-5226 • Open Monday–Friday 5:30 a.m.–7 p.m., Saturday 6 a.m.–7 p.m., Sunday 6 a.m.–6 p.m.

A wee roadside coffee hut with a drive-thru for you busy people on the go. Try the vanilla chai latte, but skip the baked goods.

CAFÉ MINEE

8150 Railroad Avenue, Suite B, Snoqualmie • www.cafeminee.com • 425-223-9889 • Open daily 8 a.m.–5 p.m.

If you like Caffe D'arte coffee, then Café Minee's got you covered. Delightful baked goods made on-site—get the rice crispy treats, or a slice of triple-layer cake, or a cinnamon roll, or a grilled panini, or a macaron . . .

GEORGIA'S BAKERY

127 W North Bend Way, North Bend • georgiasbakerycafe.com • 425-888-0632 • Open Tuesday–
Sunday 7 a.m.–5 p.m.

Satisfy your sweet tooth at this 90-year-old bakery, home of the giant doughnuts featured
on—you guessed it—*Twin Peaks*. The recipes are old but the pastries are fresh.

Farm Fresh

NORTH BEND FARMERS' MARKET

Si View Park, 400 SE Orchard Drive, North Bend • www.siviewpark.org/farmers-market.phtml •
425-831-1900 • Open June–September, Thursday 4–8 p.m.

Dining

AAHAAR INDIAN EATERY

7726 Center Boulevard SE #135, Snoqualmie • www.aahaaronline.com • 425-888-5500 • Open
Tuesday–Thursday 11 a.m.–2 p.m., 5–9 p.m.; Saturday and Sunday 11 a.m.–3 p.m., 5:30–9:30 p.m.

Multiregional Indian food with a focus on South Indian cuisine, specifically from Tamil Nadu
and Kerala. Local favorite and a destination restaurant for Seattle Indian food fans.

CAADXI OAXACA

8030 Railroad Avenue SE, Snoqualmie • facebook.com/caadxioaxaca • 425-434-9587

Drink yourself an Oaxaca martini, then order something that has molé on it followed by
Plátano Macho Frito for dessert. The food is from-scratch and authentic southern Mexican,
but the owners are nice enough to put a V for vegetarian and even a GF for gluten-free on the
menu. Amazing tamales.

Booze and Beyond

SNOQUALMIE BREWERY AND TAPROOM

8032 Falls Avenue SE, Snoqualmie • fallsbrew.com • 425-831-2357 • Summer and school vacation
hours: Wednesday–Saturday 11 a.m.–10 p.m., Sunday–Tuesday 11 a.m.–9 p.m.; winter hours: Monday–
Saturday 11 a.m.–10 p.m., Sunday 11 a.m.–9 p.m.

This brewery makes year-round and seasonal beer, plus small-batch special releases. Try them
all plus apps, sandwiches, wraps, soups and salads, and pizzas in the restaurant and taproom.
Don't forget to grab a growler or keg to go.

THE IRON DUCK PUBLIC HOUSE

101 W North Bend Way, North Bend • theironduckpublichouse.com • 425-292-9196

A whiskey library with 350 entries. That should say it all, but if not, then just know that there's a great happy hour with a side-by-side menu in which whiskeys are paired with draft beers. The tap features rotating local brews, and the menu has decent pub fare plus unique offerings such as Duck Drummies and Black Duck Pizza.

Stay Over

THE ROADHOUSE RESTAURANT & INN

4200 Preston–Fall City Road SE, Fall City • fcroadhouse.com/the-inn • 425-222-4800

Built in 1916, The Roadhouse Inn was originally a one-story tavern and lodge. Later a second story was added to house school teachers new to the area, so if you feel the presence of a marmish ghost, don't be alarmed. Now it's a charming inn near Snoqualmie and all the fun to-do's to do, with a restaurant featuring a classic pub fare/fancified Northwest cuisine hybrid, such as the Original Ugly Breakfast, a grilled steelhead salad, and six kinds of mac and cheese.

While You're Here

GAMBLE AT THE SNOQUALMIE CASINO

37500 SE North Bend Way, Snoqualmie • www.snocasino.com • 425-888-1234

It's a casino where you can do all the things you do at a casino. Once you've won the jackpot on the slots or at the blackjack table, check out the—*ahem*—eclectic entertainment.

DRIVE AT DIRTFISH

7001 396th Drive SE Snoqualmie • dirtfish.com • 1-866-285-1332 • Open daily 8 a.m.–5 p.m.

Live out your rallycross fantasies at Dirtfish, where you can drop in for a car-control fundamentals course. There are longer, more advanced courses, too, if you want to learn how to really *vroom* in a high-performance rally car on loose surfaces.

ABOVE & BEYOND

Dogs | **Three Forks Off-Leash Dog Park** (39903 SE Park Street, Snoqualmie) is a wide-open grass field with plenty of space for your pup, and a track and views of Mount Si for you.

Skates | **Snoqualmie Skate Park** (Snoqualmie Community Park, 35016 SE Ridge Street, Snoqualmie) offers a clover bowl, a hubba, a ledge, a flat rail, and other fun elements. You can also check out **North Bend Skate Park** (712 E North Bend Way, North Bend), though it did not get a stellar review by Skater Dan of northwestskater.com. For more information and photos, go to northwestskater.com.

Books | Apparently, Snoqualmie Valley's only bookstore is the **Depot Bookstore**, located at the Northwest Railway Museum (38625 SE King Street, Snoqualmie; www.trainmuseum.org; 425-888-3030). Not a ferroequinologist? On your way east, be sure to stop by **Island Books on Mercer Island** (3014 78th Avenue SE, Mercer Island; www.mercerislandbooks.com).

Bikes | Snoqualmie is a big biking, hiking, and skiing town. Stop by the following stores to get a tune-up, a new ride, and/or the outdoorsy gear necessary to get you up and down the mountain: **Northwest Bicycle** (7811 Center Boulevard SE, Snoqualmie; northwestbicycle.com; 425-363-2100); **Single Track Cycles** (119 W North Bend Way, North Bend; www.stcycles.com; 425-888-0101); and **Pro Ski and Mountain Service** (108 W North Bend Way, North Bend, www.proskiservice.com; 425-888-6397 ext 1).

Not Ready to Go Home | Get a glimpse of the real Laura Palmer house (708 33rd Street, Everett), about 30 miles north of Seattle.

Good to Know |
· The Snoqualmie tribe lived in the Snoqualmie Valley for thousands of years. Tolt, the original name of the town, came from the Tolt River or *Tolthue*, a Snoqualmie word that means "river of swift waters."
· Carnation/Tolt has been indecisive about its name. Non-natives started homesteading the area known as Tolt in the 1850s, and the area was eventually renamed Carnation after the famous dairy operation moved there in 1910. Then they changed it back in 1928. It's been Carnation since 1951, though there are some people who still call it Tolt.
· Another Tolt/Carnation nickname is "Home for Contented Cows." Apparently a cow by the name of Possum Sweetheart won a world record by producing 37,000 pounds of milk in a single year. That's a lot of nipple juice!

Been There, Done That | For wine, head north to Woodinville (page 15).

TAKE A *TWIN PEAKS* TOUR

You can find many itineraries online, but the one at savorsnoqualmievalley.org is comprehensive, easy to use, and includes a map. Or book a guided tour at www.twinpeakstour.com.

WALK THE SNOQUALMIE TUNNEL

150 Eastern State Park Road, North Bend • Open May–October

Once part of an active railroad path, this abandoned tunnel is about as pitch black as they come. Take the 2.3-mile trek, most of which will be in utter darkness—flashlight or headlamps are recommended for when things get weird down there in the dark. You will be walking into the mountainside, and the farther in you go, the colder and darker it gets. Discovery Pass recommended.

SKI THE SUMMIT AT SNOQUALMIE

1001 WA-906 Snoqualmie Pass • www.summitatsnoqualmie.com

Drive 23 miles east to get to The Summit, which has four base areas with a total 2,000 vertical feet for all your downhill adventures. Summit West is for the kiddos and the newbies; Summit Central and Summit East, with their Black Diamond and beginner runs, claim all-levels; and the Alpental Back Bowls are for backcountry experts. The Nordic Region has more than 50 kilometers of groomed trails for snowshoers and cross-country skiers. Then there's the tubing lanes. There are coffee, food, and booze establishments located throughout The Summit, and lodging at the Summit Inn (603 State Route 906, Snoqualmie Pass; 425-434-6300) and LOGE Camps (www.logecamps.com). For more information on LOGE Camps, see pages 266–267.

>> Looking for a **backcountry ski guide**? Get away from the crowds and explore the snow-covered ridges, peaks, mountains, and buttes of the area with someone who knows where the most fun—and safe—runs are. Contact Gray Bird Guiding (www.graybirdguiding.com).

// Ski Snoqualmi

7

Small-Town Vibes in Bainbridge Island

FROM SEATTLE: 0.5 HOUR · DAYS HERE: 0.5 TO 2

DO	EAT	DRINK	BUY
sail	Sunday roast at Harbour Public House	coffee at Storyville	a shirt at Bay Hay & Feed

Bainbridge Island sits smack dab in the Kitsap Peninsula, which is named for the Squamish Tribe's Chief Kitsap. Kitsap County was also home to a guy you might've heard of by the name of Chief Seattle. His gravesite is on Bainbridge Island, as are the graves of the diverse settlers who lived and died there. (The 10-mile-by-5-mile island has a total of five cemeteries.) As logging and shipbuilding became a thing in the mid- to late 1800s, the island became a mill town, with many Japanese, Filipino, and European immigrants working in Port Blakely Mill, once known as the largest and highest-producing sawmill in the world.

After the bombing of Pearl Harbor, the United States forced many of its citizens into concentration camps, including the Japanese Americans living on Bainbridge Island. Unlike many communities, who were all too willing to seize the property of their Nikkei neighbors, the community of Bainbridge worked to preserve their fellow Islanders' farms while they were imprisoned, and 150 of the 272 exiled Islanders were able to return to the area. (For more information, see Bainbridge Island Japanese American Community [BIJAC] at www.bijac.org and biajema.org.)

Bainbridge Island has a rich history and a thriving foodie/boozie and outdoor enthusiast scene. Tour the cemeteries, then go sailing, or wine tasting, or strolling the promenade in Winslow. If you don't have a car or are just plain sick of driving, you're in luck: You don't need one to make the half-hour voyage to Bainbridge Island and enjoy all the island has to offer.

═ Getting There

BY FERRY | From the Seattle Ferry Terminal at Pier 52, take the Seattle–Bainbridge Ferry across Elliot Bay. Travel time: approximately 35 minutes.

BY BIKE | Bring your bike on the ferry or rent one at Classic Cycle (206-842-9191; classic cycleus.com) or Bike Barn Rentals (206-842-3434; www.bikebarnrentals.com).

BY CAR | Go the long way around by driving approximately 32 miles south on I-5 S to WA-16 W in Tacoma, then take the Narrows Bridge to the Kitsap Peninsula and drive north for approximately 21 miles to WA-3 N. Drive approximately 18 miles on WA-3 N to WA-305 toward Poulsbo/Bainbridge Island. Drive 15 miles. Travel time: approximately 1 hour 45 minutes.

BY BUS | Walk onto the ferry and, at the Bainbridge Island Ferry Terminal, catch the BI Ride for transit around Bainbridge Island (www.kitsaptransit.com).

// Bloedel Reserve, Bainbridge Island

☰ *Highlight Reel*

PACWESTY

pacwesty.com • 1-888-212-3546 • #vanlife

The nice people at PacWesty can pick you up at the ferry in a meticulously maintained, 100 percent ready-to-go vanagon. This vehicle truly has all you need for the #vanlife: sleeping space and linens for up to four people, plenty of room to store your gear, all the equipment needed for that beach campfire dinner or camping in the woods. Truly, all you have to do is show up. Then you can take the vanagon wherever want: around Bainbridge Island or into the wilds of the Olympic Peninsula and beyond. PacWesty offers more than an amazing ride; it is an adventure travel company, and the PacWesty folks are happy to help you plan your trip—which hikes to do, which beaches to visit, which campgrounds to overnight park in or which lodges to stay in— or you can go full-on spontaneous and just drive and see where the road leads. There's nothing more romantic than a long day of adventure followed by a night under the moon. $1,795-plus.

SET SAIL WITH SAIL BAINBRIDGE

233 Parfitt Way SW, Bainbridge Island • sailbainbridge.com • 206-788-6512

From the Harbour Marina, set sail for an excursion into Puget Bay in a renovated classic boat, built in the 1960s and designed by famous naval architect John Alden. You can have two glorious hours with the wind in your hair and cell phone reception a distant memory—the sunset

// Sail Bainbridge, Bainbridge Island

sail is popular for heightening the romance—or take a five-hour day trip to Blake Island, a state park only accessible by watercraft, for remote beach time and hiking. You can also sign on for longer trips, such as the multiday Port Townsend or Gig Harbor sails, in which you arrive by boat, wander the town at your leisure, and then come back to spend the night on the docked boat, which comfortably sleeps up to six people. For those who are really trying to get away from it all, the nice sailor will drop anchor in the Bainbridge Island's Eagle Harbor and then paddle his little rowboat home so you can have the open water and big starry night all to yourself. $395-plus.

☰ *Plan Around*

JAPANESE AMERICAN MOCHI TSUKI FESTIVAL

January • IslandWood, 4450 Blakely Avenue NE, Bainbridge Island • www.bijac.org

In honor of the Japanese New Year and sponsored by the Bainbridge Island Japanese American Community, come warm your hands over an open fire and make (and eat) sweet rice mochi, watch taiko performances, and learn how to fold origami. This is a popular event, so registration is required.

TASTE OF LYNWOOD

September • Lynwood Center, Point White Drive NE and Pleasant Beach Drive NE, Bainbridge Island • tasteoflynwood.org

Like a big block party, with good bands, good foods, and arts and crafts vendors.

CELLULOID BAINBRIDGE FILM FESTIVAL

November • www.celluloidbainbridge.com

From 1999 to 2016, the Celluloid Bainbridge Film Festival showcased films by filmmakers from Bainbridge Island only. Then it was opened to filmmakers from the greater Pacific Northwest, and today submissions are welcome from everyone. Because everyone is great and love is the answer. There are, however, special screen times for hyperlocal and local films.

WINE ON THE ROCK

Seasonal • www.bainbridgewineries.com

Four times per year, the wineries of the Bainbridge Winery Alliance host an event in which you can do tastings at all seven Bainbridge wineries in the course of two days. For each event, wines are paired with a local food—for example, it's chocolate for the Valentine's Day–adjacent February event. Registration required.

☰ *Eat & Drink*

Get Caffeinated

STORYVILLE

9459 Coppertop Loop NE, Bainbridge Island • www.storyville.com • 206-780-5777 • Open Monday–
Friday 6:59 a.m.–4 p.m., Saturday and Sunday 7:59 a.m.–4 p.m.

The coffee shop is located in the loft of the Roasting Studio, a big open space with high ceilings, a copper roof, and a cozy feel. This is where the roasting magic happens, and on any given
day you might just get to test certain trial recipes before Storyville rolls them out at the other
locations. The baristas know just about everything, but if you want a special tour, call ahead
and they'll try to arrange it.

>> The Storyville love affair doesn't have to end once you leave Bainbridge Island. Check out the
Seattle locations in the Queen Anne neighborhood, Pike Place Market, and downtown.

PEGASUS COFFEE HOUSE

131 Parfitt Way SW, Bainbridge Island • 206-842-6725

A long list of teas, lots of space, comfy couches to sit on, and an outdoor patio for summertime
sipping. It's a locals' spot, so if they're on island time, just be chill, OK? If you want a waterfront
view, get your scone and chai to go and walk a little ways down to the public picnic patio.

SWEET DAHLIA BAKING

9720 Coppertop Loop, Ste 103, Bainbridge Island • sweetdahliabaking.com • 206-201-3297 • Open
Tuesday–Thursday 7 a.m.–5 p.m., Saturday 8 a.m.–6:30 p.m., Sunday 8 a.m.–3 p.m.

Self-proclaimed "sweetest thing on Bainbridge Island" and deservedly so. The scones—both
the sweet ones and the savory—might make you cry tears of joy. They offer lunch, too, on
their own fresh-baked bread. Whether you love gluten or not, try the casually wheat-free
peanut butter cookie.

Farm Fresh

BAINBRIDGE ISLAND FARMERS' MARKET

280 Madison Avenue N, Bainbridge Island • www.bainbridgeislandfarmersmarket.com • Open April–
mid-December, Saturday 9 a.m.–1 p.m.

BAY HAY & FEED

10355 NE Valley Road, Bainbridge Island • bayhayandfeed.com • 206-842-2813 • Open Monday–
Saturday 9 a.m.–5:30 p.m., Sunday 10 a.m.–4 p.m.

The building is more than 100 years old and the product line includes hog feed and horse pellets, so it's no wonder that Bay Hay & Feed considers itself an old-fashioned farm store. But
not all old-fashioned farm stores get featured in *Vanity Fair*. Yes, *that Vanity Fair*. Beyond the
grain, hay, tools, and farm supplies, the store has a post office just as it always has, plus a grocery and pet supplies store, plant nursery, gift shop, and the work/living clothing store. The
store as a whole is on trend with the green and locally sourced movement, and its claim to the
fashion hall of fame is its many variations of the multianimal T-shirts and hoodies of *Vanity Fair*
renown. Choose from row upon row of duckies, horsies, chickies, oinkers, goats, or other various farm animals and wear it with pride.

Dining

SUBI

403 Madison Avenue N #150, Bainbridge Island • www.sushibi.com • 206-855-7882 • Open lunch
Tuesday–Saturday 11:30 a.m.–1:45 p.m., dinner Monday–Saturday 5–8 p.m.

Get off the ferry and get into some sushi at this warm, intimate little restaurant. The sushi is
fresh and beautifully crafted, the noodle soup is scrumptious, the vegetarian options are bountiful, and the atmosphere is perfect for date night.

ROLLING BAY CAFÉ

10355 NE Valley Road, Bainbridge Island • www.rollingbaycafe.com • 206-780-6788 • Open
Monday–Saturday 7 a.m.–5 p.m., Sunday 8 a.m.–4 p.m.

After stocking up on hog feed and horse pellets at Bay Hay & Feed, step over to the Rolling
Bay Café for some simple farm fare, including granola from Poulsbo's Farm Kitchen, locally
baked muffins, and homemade soups and salads. The garden seating is great for sipping that
Italian soda under the shade of the trees.

THE MARKETPLACE AT PLEASANT BEACH

4738 Lynwood Center Road NE, Bainbridge Island • www.marketplaceatpleasantbeach.com •
206-866-6122 • Open daily 7 a.m.–4 p.m.

It's a coffeehouse, bakery, deli, and taproom all rolled into one. Get one of their super scrumptious sandwiches and then a brownie.

TREEHOUSE CAFÉ

4569 Lynwood Center Road NE, Bainbridge Island • treehousebainbridge.com • 206-842-2814 •
Open Monday–Saturday 11 a.m.–11 p.m., Sunday 11 a.m.–10 p.m.

The pizza is the main attraction, though, like any good American restaurant, the menu
includes tacos. Sit down for a bottle of beer or a glass of wine, and be sure to catch a show—
the lineup is surprisingly good for such a small and out-of-the-way venue.

HARBOUR PUBLIC HOUSE

231 Parfitt Way SW, Bainbridge Island • harbourpub.com • 206-842-0969 • Open Monday–Saturday
11 a.m.–12 a.m., Sunday 10 a.m.–10 p.m.

Originally the home of the Grow family, who settled in Eagle Harbor in 1881, the house was
refurbished and converted to the Harbour Public House in 1991. If you're there on a Sunday,
stop in for the Sunday Roast in the British style, with meat and potatoes and veg with gravy;
on Fridays during the oyster season of October through April, you can get fresh-shucked oysters from local Port Madison Shellfish. Daily you'll find burgers, bar food, locally sourced seafood, and a whole collection of local beers, ciders, and wines.

HITCHCOCK RESTAURANT

133 Winslow Way E #100, Bainbridge Island • www.hitchcockrestaurant.com • 206-201-3789 • Open
Tuesday–Sunday 5–10 p.m.

Everything in this acclaimed restaurant is real pretty. Much of the produce is sourced from Chef
Brendan McGill's own Shady Acres working farm and is served in a Northwest, seasonally inspired
style. The menu changes daily, but you're guaranteed fresh-caught, locally sourced, and delicious.

>> If you liked Hitchcock, then try Bruciato, a pizzeria dedicated to wood-fired Neapolitan
   pizza and seafood and the chef's latest project (236 Winslow Way E, Bainbridge Island; www
   .pizzeriabruciato.com; 206-201-3462).

// Hitchcock Restaurant, Bainbridge Island

Booze and Beyond

BAINBRIDGE VINEYARDS

8989 NE Day Road, Bainbridge Island • www.bainbridgevineyards.com • 206-842-9463 • Open Thursday–Monday noon–5 p.m.

In 1977, each vine was selected for its ability to thrive in the Puget Sound American Viti-cultural Area, the only AVA west of the Cascades, from varietals that were successful in the similar climes of France, Germany, and Austria. Certified organic in 2014, the wine is made exclusively from island-grown grapes and fruits. You can find bottles on the island and throughout the region or stop by for a tasting.

ROLLING BAY WINERY

11272 Sunrise Drive NE, Bainbridge Island • www.rollingbaywinery.com • 206-419-3355 • Open Friday 3–7 p.m., Saturday and Sunday noon–5 p.m.

What started as a hobby in the 1980s officially went pro in 2007. Try the award-winning artis-anal wines in one of Seattle Met's "Top 22 Tasting Rooms in Washington."

BAINBRIDGE ORGANIC DISTILLERY

9727 Coppertop Loop NE Suite 101, Bainbridge Island • www.bainbridgedistillers.com • 206-842-3184 • Open May–September, daily 11 a.m.–5 p.m.; October–April, Monday–Saturday 11 a.m.–5 p.m.

As Washington's first USDA-certified organic producers of gin, whiskey, and vodka, Bain-bridge Organic Distillery is real hands-on when it comes to their spirits. From choosing grains to distillation, every step of the process is done on-site, and the grains themselves come from nearby Skagit County, Snohomish County, and, farther afield but still local, Walla Walla. Come for a tour of the facilities and a tasting of the award-winning spirits.

>> You could spend an entire day at **Coppertop Park**, a business park 2.5 miles north of the ferry terminal. Fuel up with coffee at Storyville Coffee and a scone at Sweet Dahlia Baking, then head over to Island Rock Gym (9437 Coppertop Loop NE, Bainbridge Island; www .islandrockgym.com; 206-451-4020) and climb the wall (refill at Storyville as needed). Once you've murdered your fingers, stop in at Fletcher Bay Winery for wine tasting, followed by a beer at Bainbridge Brewing's brewery and taproom (9415 Coppertop Loop NE; bainbridge-beer.com/brewery-taproom; 206-451-4646), then a spirit at Bainbridge Organic Distillery. Order of drinking is open, just be sure to do it *after* the climbing.

FLETCHER BAY WINERY

9415 Coppertop Loop NE, Suite 102, Bainbridge Island • www.fletcherbaywinery.com •
206-780-9463 • Open Monday and Tuesday 1–7 p.m., Wednesday 2–8 p.m., Thursday and Friday
1–7 p.m., Saturday and Sunday noon–7 p.m.

Using grapes from three vineyards in the Yakima Valley and Walla Walla, FBW has managed to
win a whole lot of awards. In 2018 alone, the cabernet sauvignons won SavorNW gold, Cascadia International gold, and *San Francisco Chronicle* International bronze. Come on Wednesday
for Wine Down, featuring live music, food from the Grub Hut food truck, and half-priced
glasses of wine.

Stay Over

Inn It to Win It

INN AT PLEASANT BEACH

4633 Woodson Lane NE, Suite 349, Bainbridge Island • www.pleasantbeachvillage.com/inn •
206-842-7800

Located right on the edge of Lynwood Center, this beachy inn has 12 cozy rooms, each with
a gas fireplace. Many of the rooms have views of Rich Passage, and all rooms have access to
the outdoor pool and hot tub at Pleasant Beach. Reserve Suite 3 for the reading nook (rule of
thumb: *always* go for the reading nook). Pet-friendly rooms available for an additional $50 fee.
$150–400.

EAGLE HARBOR INN

291 Madison Avenue S, Bainbridge Island • www.theeagleharborinn.com • 206-207-6796

An easy walk from the ferry terminal and to the restaurants and shops of Winslow, the Eagle
Harbor Inn is ideally situated for those who like their fine dining close and their marina closer.
Get the Harbor Suite to watch the ships' pokey masts bobbing about in Eagle Harbor. The inn
rents out two lovely townhomes, if you're coming down with friends/polyamorous sex partners. $180–600.

>> Bainbridge Island is bursting at the seams with **Airbnbs**. You can find mother-in-laws, backyard
   yurts, cute cottages, and more.

#farmlife

HEYDAY FARM

4370 Old Mill Road NE, Bainbridge Island • heydayfarm.com • 206-201-1770

Spend the night at a 25-acre sustainable and historic farm, in a house built in the 1890s. The farm kitchen is right downstairs, and there you'll eat your farm-fresh breakfast once the rooster crows (or whenever you feel like it). Tuesdays are community dinner days at the farm kitchen, no reservation required, and there are ongoing cooking classes and dinners prepped with seasonal vegetables straight out of the garden and humanely harvested meat, dairy, and eggs.

// Heyday Farm, Bainbridge Island

TEPEE AT SWEET LIFE FARM

9631 Summer Hill Lane NE, Bainbridge Island • sweetlifefarm.com • 206-842-6577

The owners of Sweet Life Farm are living the retirement dream: gardening, cooking, and making things. One of those things that they've made is a tepee, available May through September. Inside is a queen bed, some rocking chairs, reading lamps, and even an outlet for all your various devices. Step outside and into the open-air bath hut with composting toilet and on-demand water, or to explore the miles of hiking trails just beyond the 10-acre property. In the evening, sit by the fire pit and think deep thoughts before heading off to bed. If you've never had sex in a round, semipermeable room, then get ready for a treat. $175 per night.

Camping

FAY BAINBRIDGE PARK & CAMPGROUND

15446 Sunrise Drive, Bainbridge Island • biparks.org/fay-bainbridge-park-campground • 206-842-2306, ext. 118

Sleep near the sound at Fay Bainbridge Park, a 17-acre marine camping park with more than 1,400 feet of shoreline. Just a 10-minute drive from Bainbridge Island's wee downtown, it's well maintained and quietly popular. There are 14 tent sites, 26 RV sites, and two cabins, all with access to central water and a portable toilet. If you want a sure spot, make a reservation more than 10 days in advance per park policy. Pet friendly. $20 per night.

☰ *While You're Here*

VISIT BLOEDEL RESERVE

7571 NE Dolphin Drive, Bainbridge Island • bloedelreserve.org • 206-842-7631 • Summer hours: end of May–beginning of September, Tuesday and Wednesday 10 a.m.–4 p.m., Thursday–Sunday 10 a.m.–6 p.m.; winter hours: beginning of September–end of May, Tuesday and Wednesday 10 a.m.–4 p.m.

Built by a lumber company owner's son gone green, this renowned 150-acre public garden and forest preserve has 12 gardens, plus the founders' massive 1920s-era mansion and a Japanese guest house. Interesting tidbit: Mr. Bloedel was colorblind, so though you will find some pretty pinks, purples, and yellows, especially when the rhododendrons bloom in the glen come spring, the focus is on textures and shades. A big favorite is the moss garden, which has 40 species of moss and is basically a forest with floor-to-ceiling live green carpet. It smells nice. The Japanese garden has all kinds of trees, including a 150-year-old lace maple and a

// Bloedel Reserve, Bainbridge Island

katsura tree, which give off a sweet smell that some claim reminds them of cotton candy. Bloedel Reserve hosts only two weddings a year—if they catch you wearing wedding-like attire, they will ask you to leave—but there's plenty nonmatrimonial romance to be had walking hand in hand with your honey on the roughly 2 miles of trails throughout the grounds, or taking in the views of Puget Sound, or simply sitting and staring into one another's lovelorn eyes as birds sing around you. This is like a living outdoor museum, so leave your dog, ham sandwich, and drone at home. $17.

>> Up the romance by coming in February for the annual **Cupid's Walk**, in which you'll tour the grounds and learn about the true love story that is at the foundation of Bloedel Reserve. Or come for the Winter Solstice Walk, poetry in the garden in April, music with a view all summer long, and/or the plays of Shakespeare in July.

SEE A MOVIE AT LYNWOOD THEATRE

4569 Lynwood Center Road NE, Bainbridge Island • farawayentertainment.com/location/lynwood-theatre • 206-842-3080

Opened in 1936, the Tudor-style house-turned-talking-picture-theater opened its curtains to *Times Square Playboy* and *She Couldn't Take It*. (No, these were not talking-picture porns, despite their obviously pornographic titles.) Since then, the theater has made the necessary improvements, including—and most importantly—getting a bigger popcorn machine. Tickets: only $11.50!

>> Take a photo with Frog Rock (14607 Phelps Road NE, Bainbridge Island), a funny-shaped granite bolder painted in 1971 to resemble a frog.

PAY RESPECTS AT A CEMETERY

SUQUAMISH TRIBAL CEMETERY

Suquamish Museum, 6861 NE South Street, Suquamish • suquamishmuseum.org Visit the grave of Chief Seattle, the legendary leader of the Suquamish Tribe and namesake of our great city, in Suquamish Village on the Port Madison Indian Reservation. An interpretive kiosk at the cemetery entrance and a new monument at the gravesite honor the chief and the impact he had on the region. Once you've paid your respects, go into the museum proper to learn about the tribe, take a turn at the Clearwater Casino Resort, or walk down to the Suquamish Dock and onto the waterfront.

PORT BLAKELY CEMETERY

4375 Old Mill Road NE Bainbridge Island; portblakelycemetery.org • 206-717-4900 • Open daily; summer hours: 9 a.m.–7 p.m.; winter hours: 9 a.m.–4 p.m. Every cemetery is a history lesson. The first section of Port Blakely Cemetery was opened in 1880, and many of Bainbridge Island's prominent residents, the ones who have streets named after them, are buried there, along with farmers and the millworkers of Port Blakely Sawmill from days gone by. You can find

1 Chief Sealth Gravesite, Bainbridge Island
2 Port Blakely Cemetery, Bainbridge Island
3 Bloedel Reserve, Bainbridge Island

many monuments there, too: to the victims of the 1906 SS *Dix*'s sinking, members of the Woodmen of the World fraternal organization, and to the graduating class of 1961, installed by Secretary of State Ralph Monroe. It's also an American melting pot of sorts, with the graves of Jews, Japanese, and non-Jewish European immigrants intermingling. It's quiet, too.

ABOVE & BEYOND

Dogs | Located within a circle of trees, the 2-acre **Strawberry Hill Dog Park** (7666 NE High School Road, Bainbridge Island) features lots of shade, a mini-park for the mini and/ or nervous, and a dog wash station. Near the skate park. For **Eagledale Park** (5050 Rose Avenue NE, Bainbridge Island), follow the signs from the parking lot up to the off-leash area. Even though it's at the top of the hill, it can stay soggy for a while post-rain. More mud for your doggie to roll in!

Skate | **Bainbridge Island Skatepark** (7760 NE High School Road, Bainbridge Island) is made up entirely of a big fun bowl. For photos and more information, go to www. northwestskater.com.

Books | **Eagle Harbor Books** (157 Winslow Way E, Bainbridge Island; www.eagleharbor books.com; 206-842-5332; open Monday–Friday 10 a.m.–7 p.m., Saturday and Sunday 10 a.m.–6 p.m.) is a proudly independent bookstore that supports the 70-plus local public book groups, including the speculative fiction book group, the mystery book group, and the Eagle Harbor Readers' Circle, and frequently hosts Washington State authors. Great used and new books, too.

At **The Traveler** (256 Winslow Way E, Bainbridge Island; www.thetraveler.com; 206-842-4578; open Monday–Saturday 9:30 a.m.–7 p.m., Sunday 10:30 a.m.–6 p.m.), you can buy guidebooks, travel lit, and maps, plus luggage, clothing, and other accessory essentials for the travel enthusiast.

For military and aviation books, including rare finds and first editions, visit **Barbarossa Books** (5660 NE Tolo Road, Bainbridge; www.barbarossabooks.com; 206-780-8452).

TAKE A TOUR

www.tourbainbridge.com; 206-359-2201

Meet your Tour Bainbridge tour guide at the ferry terminal, then go on a three- or four-hour tour. You can focus on the historical in the Chief Seattle Adventure Tour or History and Hiking Tour, or go the libation sensation route on the Bainbridge Winery Tour or the Craft Beer and Spirits Tour. $79-plus.

Disclaimer: **Backstreet Beat** (265 Winslow Way E #102, Bainbridge Island; 206-780-6721) is not directly related to the Backstreet Boys. This hole-in-the-wall book and music shop does, however, have other good music—though not Brian Littrell inspired—in the form of a wide selection of vinyl records, plus used books.

Not Ready to Go Home | Drive north on WA-305 to Poulsbo for some more small-town vibes. Known as "Little Norway on the Fjord" because of the Scandinavian roots of its early white settlers, the town hosts Viking Fest (www.vikingfest.org) every summer, featuring a lutefisk-eating contest, a strongman competition, and a Viking parade.

Good to Know | Snow Falling on Cedars, set in the Pacific Northwest, was written by Bainbridge High School teacher David Gutterson.

Been There, Done That

- Take WA-305 W to get to Port Townsend (page 91) and the Olympic Peninsula (page 175).
- Whidbey Island (page 249) is nearby as the crow flies, but you have to go the long way around to get there.
- Take WA-3 S to get to the Hood Canal (page 44).

8

Pure Hedonism in Portland

FROM SEATTLE: 175 MILES, 2.5 TO 4.5 HOURS · DAYS HERE: 1 TO 3

DO	EAT	DRINK	BUY
dress up like a mermaid	food cart food	a flight from Distillery Row	a lap dance and a rose tattoo

Portland is the epicenter of all things hip. Like Seattle, it's a city with everything: amazing food, easy access to the great outdoors, a culture of acceptance and celebration of diversity. But it is smaller than its neighbor to the north (though it's still the second-biggest city in the Pacific Northwest), and it's managed to maintain a sliver of the small-town feel that Seattle used to have, before the latest tech boom. There are some key differences, however, when it comes to culture that makes it ideal for a romantic weekend. First, you can eat your fill without draining your bank account or spending a thousand hours in traffic, thanks to the collection of food carts scattered throughout the city. Second, the terrain is flatter, making it much easier to get around via bike (the public transit system is good, too). Third, the attitudes around sex are a little looser, at least as far as sanctioned and safe strip clubs and respect of those who work in them. You don't have to venture into some sleazy underbelly to enjoy the jiggle and wiggle of the human body, nor do you have to feel like you're preying on the vulnerable. Granted, most of the strip clubs only feature entertainers of the female variety, but there are a few with people on the male side of the spectrum. More importantly, misogyny and other forms of violence are not tolerated, and regardless of your gender identity or sexual proclivity; you will be welcome as long as you treat the performers with kindness—and tip well. This is the city to visit when you want to get out of the city and go to a different city, when you want to live the hedonist dream.

≡ Getting There

BY CAR | Drive south on I-5 for approximately 174 miles. Travel time: 2.5 hours.

BY BUS | From 5th Avenue S at S Dearborn Street, catch the Bolt to Portland, NW Everett at NW 8th Avenue. It's a nonstop, approximately four-hour trip. Ticket: $17–25. 1-877-BOLTBUS; www.boltbus.com.

BY TRAIN | Take the Amtrak Coast Starlight or the Cascades lines to Portland's Union Station. Travel time: 3.5–4.5 hours, $26–64.

BY BIKE | Take your bike on the train for easy cruising once you've reached your final destination. In July, you can join the **Seattle-to-Portland Ride**, a one- or two-day affair in which you and your fellow cyclists cruise the 200-mile route to Portland. The starting line is the University of Washington E-1 parking lot, with the midpoint at Centralia College and the finish line at Holladay Park. There are rest stops with free food and rest stops with food to buy along the way. You can use the 30 acres of camping space on the Centralia College campus as a rest stop or overnighter. They'll have 200-plus showers, food vendors, a beer garden, TV with the Tour de France playing, and on-site massage therapists to help you relax and refuel after the long day. For more information, go to www.cascades.org.

// Jupiter Hotel, Portland

☰ *Highlight Reel*

THE JUPITER: JUPITER HOTEL AND JUPITER NEXT

900 E Burnside Street, Portland • jupiterhotel.com • 503-230-9200

Spruce up a motor lodge built in the 1960s, add an art gallery and a world-renowned music venue, throw in some eco-friendly bath supplies, and what do you get? Jupiter Hotel, vintage flavored, that's what. The 81 rooms have chalk doors on which to write jaunty messages, and the two sides of the building are split for those who want a more chill experience versus a party time. (It is just a hop, skip, and stumble from Distillery Row, after all.) In lieu of a mint on the pillow, guests can look forward to a Jupiter-branded condom on the nightstand. Let John Lennon or Marilyn Monroe gaze down upon you in one of the modern-style beds, or rent the Dream Suite so you can gaze upon yourselves via the floor-to-ceiling mirrors. Across the street, Jupiter NEXT, at an epic six-floor height, features ginormous windows in each room so that guests can overlook the city. NEXT leans sleek over vintage, with X, XX, and XL rooms and in-room digital concierge Roxy available to satisfy your every whim. Both NEXT and Jupiter Hotel have easy access to the Doug Fir Bar and Lounge, open from dawn until way past dusk and serving breakfast, lunch, dinner, and many booze-related drinks. $100–800.

>>   Book the Ink 'n Drink package (discounted tats and a bucket of brews) or the 420 package (paraphernalia, munchie kit, latest issue of *Oregon Leaf*—everything but the weed). Or, to up the sexy ante, ask for the off-the-menu **Fantasy Kit**, which is not explicitly listed on the website.

// Jupiter Hotel, Portland

ACE HOTEL

1022 SW Stark Street, Portland • www.acehotel.com/portland • 503-228-2277

If you're there to get it on with your bae, then rent one of the rooms that has a queen-size bed and private bath. If you're going with friends, want to save a few bucks, or prefer an audience, then reserve a shared room with multiple twin beds. The lobby has a big, comfy sectional, Stumptown coffee, lots of succulents, walls decorated with locally made artwork, plus a functioning record player and a refurbished vintage photo booth for all of your analog black-and-white photo needs. For room service, order some European-style peasant food from Clyde Common (www.clydecommon.com). $100-plus. Pet-friendly accommodations available.

THE SOCIETY HOTEL

203 NW 3rd Avenue, Portland • thesocietyhotel.com • 503-445-0444

Even the bunk beds are seriously cute. Located inside the bunk room, which sleeps up to 24 people, these are great for resting your weary head among your fellow travelers. For medium privacy, reserve the private rooms with shared bathrooms, and for max privacy, get a suite, where you won't have to talk to a single damn person if you don't want to for the duration of your stay. Tall windows let in the gray morning light, and the rooftop gives you a panoramic view of the city. Downstairs in the lobby is a lounge, café, and bar, with fresh food and coffee, and Northwest wines and beers on tap. $45-plus.

HOTEL VINTAGE

422 SW Broadway, Portland • www.hotelvintage-portland.com • 503-228-1212

Hotel Vintage is obsessed with wine. In tribute to Oregon's Willamette Valley, each floor is dedicated to different viticultural areas of the region, and each room to one of its wineries. The rooms go for quirk, with ornate headboards and cork-built artwork. And, of course, you'll receive a bottle of wine with your room's namesake. Splurge for an urban soak room and its outdoor hot tub, or the sky loft room with its huge solarium windows. The Bacchus Bar downstairs has live music and frequent wine tastings, and the bring-your-drink-into-the-game lounge for some pool or shuffleboard. In-room yoga mat (and yoga channel) and spa and dining services mean you never have to leave the room.

Pet-friendly accommodations available. $100–900.

SEX, DRUGS, AND FOOD CARTS: TAKE A TOUR

THE POTLANDIA EXPERIENCE

1821 NE 91st Avenue, Portland • potlandiaexperience.com • 503-409-3975

All aboard the "consumption bus" for a 420-friendly sight-seeing tour to dispensaries, microbreweries, food carts, and more. Yes, you can smoke weed on the bus. P.S. The bus is purple.

HIGH 5 TOURS

www.high5tours.com • 503-303-2275

High 5 offers two kinds of tours: cannabis or strip club. Tour local grower Green Choice Farms, marijuana dispensaries, breweries or coffee shops, with a farm-made lunch or final munchie stop at Cartlandia. Book a private tour or purchase a self-guided tour of the Green Mile, a.k.a. Sandy Boulevard in the Hollywood District, which houses six dispensaries. Rent the bus for a private strip club adventure for $699. P.S. The bus is yellow.

BREWVANA (www.brewvana.com; 503-729-6804) Drinking and driving is dumb. So let someone else shuttle you hither and yon as you geek out on brewing systems and best practices, learn how to scale-up small operations and how to ferment, get your bias for Pacific Northwest beer confirmed (West Coast is the best coast), and drink. Tours last between four and six hours, during which you might reach "brewvana"—the euphoric state of awareness, appreciation, and LOVE for Portland's finest craft beers, as defined by the ones who made up the term. Every tour includes beer sampling, lunch or dinner, transportation, a journal, and, most importantly, a pretzel necklace. $69–109.

PORTLAND SHORT BUS (portlandshortbus.com; 971-209-2895) Lucille is just a tiny yellow school bus trying to make a name for herself. She's a feisty cute one who wants to take you on a four- or five-hour guided urban wine tour to local wineries around PDX. Lucille would like to remind you to talk to your fellow riders even if you don't know them, and to not forget to shower your driver with monetary affection. $85–135.

PDX PEDICAB BOOBS AND BREW TOUR (pdxpedicab.com; 503-828-9888) PDX Pedicab offers all kinds of great alcohol-related tours. This particular three- or four-hour one, in which you will visit two breweries and two strip clubs, has the fun addition of boobs. The pedicab drivers are not only very knowledgeable about Portland itself, they have the insider scoop on strip club etiquette (tip $1 per song no matter what, no touching), and they'll make sure you don't get arrested. The tour always includes a stop at Sassy's Bar and Lucky Devil Lounge, but you can tailor the brewery part of the tour to your liking, or simply hand over the reins to the experts. Cost of the tour covers one beer and one shot per strip club, plus a tasting flight at each brewery. It doesn't cover tipping of strippers or tipping of the pedicab drivers—make sure you bring cash. $85 per person.

FOOD CARTS PORTLAND (www.foodcartsportland.com) Curious as to why Portland is so obsessed with food carts? Me too. For answers, book a food cart tour, a 60- to 90-minute extravaganza of all things food cart, including eating at them. Monday–Friday by appointment only. $60.

>>   Want a different sort of tour? Then check out the **free Secrets of Portlandia tour** to get the real intel from Rose City natives. The two-hour tour is offered daily starting at 11 a.m., and features fun factoids about the city's weird past and trendsetting residents, as well as restaurant and other tourist-related recommendations. There is no fee, but tips are happily accepted (secretsofportlandia.com).

WORLD NAKED BIKE RIDE

June • Cathedral Park, 6905 N Portland Avenue, Portland • pdxwnbr.org

Imagine a world in which we are free of oil dependence and carbon emissions. Take off your clothes and bike on down to the World Naked Bike Ride. On second thought, ride down to the starting point first, then take off your clothes. Portland's WNBR is one of nearly 100 naked bike rides across the world. This is not about sex, it's about saving the planet, so don't come expecting an orgy. Meet at 8 p.m.

PORTLANDIA MERMAID PARADE

July • Waterfront Promenade • www.portlandiamermaidparade.com

A family-friendly, gender-neutral, body-positive celebration of mermaids featuring an opening ceremony, a parade along the waterfront of the Willamette River, and a beach party stuffed to the gills with photo ops.

 *Plan Around*

PORTLAND INTERNATIONAL BEERFEST

June • North Park Blocks, 235 NW Park Avenue, Portland • www.portland-beerfest.com • 503-902-4666

Come for the 200-plus world-class beers and ciders from all over the planet, stay for the pie jousting. You can get in for free, which is great if you want to watch other people get sloshed and have fun. But you're no teetotaling wallflower, so buy their ticket deals, which include a beerfest glass and beer tix, which you'll use to pay for your beer in lieu of cash. Once you're good and sloshed, head over to the beer joust pop-up bar, where you can ride one of the official bikes and try to hit your adversary in the face with pie, then drink some more as you drink from the sidelines. Viking hats optional. It's a three-day event, so don't forget your wristband for free re-entrance for hair of the dog.

PORTLAND ROSE FESTIVAL

June • www.rosefestival.org

There's a reason they call Portland "Rose City." For over a hundred summers, out-of-towners have flocked to town to . . . stop and smell the roses at the annual Rose Festival. There are three parades, urban street fairs, and concerts at the waterfront Rozone.

>> Have you always dreamed of being a clown? Apply way in advance and go through their rigorous process to join the other doctors, financial planners, and writers who've exchanged business casual for red noses, bright wigs, and the ability to strike terror in the hearts of children. www.rosefestival.org/programs/clown-prince-clowns

PICKATHON

August • Pendarvis Farm, 16581 SE Hagen Road, Happy Valley • pickathon.com

A four-day event featuring amazing bands and Laugh, Spoken, and Imagine Storytelling line-ups on three stages that are also art installations. Bring extra cups and/or cutlery and dishware, because it's eco strict and you won't find extras lying around. Tent camping in the woods is included in weekend admission tickets. Single day tickets $125–150, plus $30 for parking; weekend tickets $320, parking included.

>>   Spend all day on **Sandy Blvd NE**, eating until you can't eat no mo. From the central east side to Portland International Airport, the boulevard features a cornucopia of restaurants, from cheap eats to fine dining.

≡ *Eat & Drink*

Get Caffeinated

As is the case in Seattle, there are too many coffee shops in Portland to describe them all. Suffice it to say that, on the whole, they serve good, fair-trade coffee in a hip atmosphere and everyone is super cool.

BARISTA

www.baristapdx.com

Pearl: 539 NW 13th Avenue, Portland • Open Monday–Friday 6 a.m.–6 p.m., Saturday and Sunday 7 a.m.–6 p.m.

Alberta: 1725 NE Alberta Street, Portland • Monday–Friday 6 a.m.–6 p.m., Saturday and Sunday 7 a.m.–6 p.m.

Downtown: 529 SW 3rd Avenue, Unit 110, Portland • Open Monday–Friday 6 a.m.–6 p.m., Saturday and Sunday 8 a.m.–5 p.m.

Nob Hill: 823 NW 23rd Avenue, Portland • Open Monday–Friday 6 a.m.–7 p.m., Saturday and Sunday 7 a.m.–7 p.m.

Brass Bar: 126 SW 2nd Avenue, Portland • Open daily 8 a.m.–6 p.m.

Coffee, house-made sandwiches, wine.

COAVA COFFEE ROASTERS

coavacoffee.com; 503-894-8134

Coava on Grand, 1300 SE Grand Avenue (A), Portland • Open Monday–Friday 6 a.m.–6 p.m., Saturday and Sunday 7 a.m.–6 p.m.

Coava on Hawthorne, 2631 SE Hawthorne Boulevard, Portland • Open Monday–Friday 6 a.m.–6 p.m., Saturday and Sunday 7 a.m.–6 p.m.

Coava on Jefferson, 1171 SW Jefferson Street, Portland • Open Monday–Friday 6 a.m.–6 p.m., Saturday and Sunday 7 a.m.–6 p.m.

The Public Brew Bar & Roastery, 1015 SE Main Street, Portland • Open Monday–Saturday 8 a.m.–2 p.m., public cuppings 1 p.m.

Through long-term partnerships with coffee growers—you can look at and learn about the farms in Nicaragua, Kenya, Honduras, Columbia, Brazil, Guatemala, and Ethiopia on the website—Coava brings in stellar green coffee to be processed and roasted with hardcore meticulousness. Watch the roastery in motion at the Public Brew Bar & Roastery, where you can do a free public cupping at 1 p.m., Monday through Saturday.

TEA CHAI TÉ

www.teachaite.com

Tea Chai Té on Burnside, 616 E Burnside, Portland • 503-447-6544 • Open daily 9 a.m.–9 p.m.

NW 23rd Ave Tea Shop, 734 NW 23rd Avenue, Portland • 503-228-0900 • Open daily 9 a.m.–10 p.m.

Sellwood Caboose Tea Shop, 7983 SE 13th Avenue, Portland • 505-432-8747 • Open daily 9 a.m.–9 p.m.

With over 100 handcrafted and award-winning teas, including herbal medicinals and chai blends, bubble tea, house-made kombucha, and all kinds of fancy teaware, Tea Chai Té is a teaphile's dream.

>> Are you a **Stumptown** fan? The roaster is originally from Portland, and the city has six locations. Come in for a tasting at the Portland headquarters (100 SE Salmon Street, Portland) on Friday at 2 p.m.

VOODOO DOUGHNUT

Portland Downtown: 22 SW 3rd Avenue, Portland • 503-241-4704

East Side: 1501 NE Davis Street, Portland • 503-235-2666

Cartlandia: 8145 SE 82nd Avenue, Portland

Good things come in pink boxes, like the classic yeast-raised doughnut with glaze or the powdered sugar cake doughnut. But wait, there's more! Put favorites in your face like the Old Dirty Bastard, the Grape Ape, and the Bacon Maple Bar, then get the Maple Blazer Blunt, a blunt-shaped delight with red sprinkle embers, or the Voodoo Doll, a voodoo doll-shaped doughnut with filling that squirts out when you take a bite. The Cock-n-Balls tastes like heaven.

PIP'S ORIGINAL DOUGHNUTS

4759 NE Fremont Street, Suite C, Portland (or hire their custom hand-painted and -lettered classic Chevy P-10 van to come to you); www.pipsmobile.com; 503-206-8692 • Open daily 8 a.m.–4 p.m.

Pip's Original Doughnuts is less about creative and penis-shaped doughnuts like Voodoo's and more about bringing back simplicity in the form of mom-and-pop-style, fried-to-order dough-nuts, though they do go seasonal and fancy, too. The handcrafted chai is their special hook, with five or so delectable varieties. Order the chai flight to try them all.

>>   "Chai" means tea in a bunch of languages. So when you say "chai tea," you are saying "tea tea" (or "chai chai" for those who aren't Anglo-centric). Once is plenty!

MAURICE BAKERY

921 SW Oak Street, Portland • www.mauricepdx.com • 503-224-9921 • Open Tuesday–Sunday 10 a.m.–4 p.m.

Named one of *Bon Appétit*'s Top 10 Best New Restaurants in America in 2014, Maurice Bak-ery calls itself a "pastry luncheonette." Its menu changes daily and satisfies those with a sweet tooth, with its delicate French pastries, cakes, and other scrumptious desserts. For those who prefer savory, the luncheonette part of the menu offers an ever-changing range of items, from *poulet au pain* ("chicken bun") to seasonal salads to *fromage plat* ("cheese plate").

Food Carts

Seattle loves its food trucks, actual trucks that drive around the city, distributing their fares to those who can afford a $10 grilled cheese. But, day and night, Portland has more than 500 food *carts* open. These stay in one place, and you can find them solo or in "pods." In the neigh-borhoods, they tend to gather in groups of 8 to 10, while in the city center they can gather in as many as 60.

We've surveyed locals on their favorites, but these food cart aficionados demurred because a) "that's like asking a child which single Lego is their favorite," as food cart expert Brett Bur-meister says, and b) the world of food carts is constantly shifting, with today's sweetheart shuttering its lid tomorrow and a new batch rolling on in the day after that. Many up-and-comers start in the food cart biz and then move on to restaurants once they've earned the funds and the reputation for making such a move viable. Or they shut it down, because such a business (as any business in the food industry) is subject to the whims of Lady Luck—a single robbery or equipment malfunction can signal a food cart's doom. Therefore, we can't name any must-eat-ats, so go down there with an open mouth and an open mind, ready to eat to your heart's content while meditating on the nature of impermanence.

The following four pods are, at the time of this writing, the biggest in the city. That is, of course, subject to change, and there are a ton of other great food carts and food cart pods worth exploring. For more information, go to www.portlandneighborhood.com/portland-food -carts.html.

CARTLANDIA

8145 SE 82nd Avenue, Portland • www.cartlandia.com • 503-358-7873 • Open daily 7 a.m.–9 p.m.

Like a food court but a thousand times cooler. Self-proclaimed bike-centric food cart super pod Cartlandia hosts 30-plus food carts, a beer garden, and everything your little foodie heart could desire. Dog and horse friendly.

CARTOPIA

1207 SE Hawthorne Boulevard, Portland • Open Wednesday–Sunday 11:30 a.m.–12 a.m., Friday and Saturday 11:30 a.m.–3 a.m.

With a covered, heated seating area and long hours, Cartopia is popular with the cool weather, late-night type of crowd.

PORTLAND STATE UNIVERSITY

www.pdx.edu/foodcarts/home; 503-725-2394

Millar Library Food Carts, SW Park Avenue and SW Harrison Street

UCB Food Carts, SW 5th Avenue and SW Harrison Street

Site A, at the PSU library, is near a pedestrian corridor and two big residence halls, so prepare to see students. The second site is by a bus stop, perfect for getting your grub to go.

THIRD AVENUE FOOD CART

SW Third Avenue and Washington Street, Portland

Pick up your food and walk down to nearby Waterfront Park.

>> Want someone to do the work for you? Go to page 144 for info on food cart tours. Also, for the latest news and reviews, check out the blog on www.foodcartsportland.com.

Farmers' Markets

It should be no surprise that, in such a foodie town, there are farmers' markets every day of the week.

SATURDAY

HOLLYWOOD FARMERS' MARKET NE Hancock between 44th Avenue and 45th Avenue • hollywoodfarmersmarket.org • open 8 a.m.–1 p.m.

PORTLAND FARMERS' MARKET at Portland State University (South Park blocks between SW Hall Street and Montgomery Street) • portlandfarmersmarket.org/our-markets/psu • open April–October 8:30 a.m.–2 p.m., November–March, 9 a.m.–2 p.m.

ST. JOHN'S FARMERS' MARKET St. John's Plaza N, between Lombard Street and Philadelphia Avenue • open May–October 9 a.m.–2 p.m.

WOODLAWN NEIGHBORHOOD FARMERS' MARKET NE Dekum Street and Durham Avenue • open May–October 10 a.m.–2 p.m.

SUNDAY

HILLSDALE FARMERS' MARKET SW Capitol Highway and Sunset Boulevard • www.hillsdalefarmersmarket.com • open April–November 9 a.m.–1 p.m.

KING PORTLAND FARMERS' MARKET NE 7th Avenue and Wygant Street • www.portlandfarmersmarket.org/our-markets/king • open May–November 10 a.m.–2 p.m.

LENTS INTERNATIONAL FARMERS' MARKET SE 92nd Avenue and Reedway, between Foster and Harold • www.portlandfarmersmarket.org/our-markets/lents-international • open June–November 9 a.m.–2 p.m.

MONTAVILLA FARMERS' MARKET 7600 Block of SE Stark Street • www.montavilla-market.org • open May–October 10 a.m.–2 p.m.

WOODSTOCK FARMERS' MARKET SE 46th Avenue and Woodstock Boulevard • woodstockmarketpdx.com • open June–October 10 a.m.–2 p.m.

MONDAY

PORTLAND FARMERS' MARKET AT THE SQUARE Pioneer Courthouse Square, SW 6th Street and SW Yamhill • portlandfarmersmarket.org/our-markets/pioneer-courthouse-square • open June–August 10 a.m.–2 p.m.

TUESDAY

LLOYD FARMERS' MARKET NE Holladay Street between 7th Avenue and 9th Avenue • lloydfarmersmkt.net • open year-round 10 a.m.–2 p.m.

OHSU FARMERS' MARKET OHSU Auditorium Courtyard near the fountain, 3181 SW Sam Jackson Park Road • www.ohsu.edu/farmersmarket • open June–September 10 a.m.–2 p.m.

WEDNESDAY

KENTON PORTLAND FARMERS' MARKET N McClellan Street and Denver Avenue • www.portlandfarmersmarket.org/our-markets/kenton • open June–September 3–7 p.m.

MORELAND FARMERS' MARKET SE Bybee Boulevard and SE 14th Avenue • www .morelandfarmersmarket.org • open May–October 2–7 p.m.

PEOPLE'S FARMERS' MARKET 3029 SE 21st Avenue • www.peoples.coop/farmers-market • open year-round 2–6 p.m.

PORTLAND FARMERS' MARKET AT SHEMANSKI PARK Shemanski Park, SW Park and Salmon • www.portlandfarmersmarket.org/our-markets/shemanski-park • open May–October 10 a.m.–2 p.m.

THURSDAY

CULLY PORTLAND FARMERS' MARKET NE 42nd Avenue, between Alberta and Sumner • www.cullyfarmersmarket.com • open June–August 4 p.m.–8 p.m., September 4–7 p.m.

SOUTH WATERFRONT FARMERS' MARKET Elizabeth Caruthers Park, 3508 SW Moody Avenue • www.southwaterfront.com/farmers-market • open June–October 2–7 p.m.

NEW COLUMBIA FARMERS' MARKET 4632 N Trenton Street • villagegardens.org/ farmers-market • open June–August 4–7 p.m.

Brick and Mortar

SHUT UP AND EAT

3848 SE Gladstone Street, Portland • www.shutupandeatpdx.com • 503-719-6449 • Open daily 10 a.m.–9 p.m.

A former food cart, Shut Up and Eat is famous for its "big fat" Italian-inspired sandwiches. They offer breakfast all day, lunch starts at 10 a.m., and you can order beer or wine whenever you damn well please. All the bread, which is strong enough to support such fat fixings, is freshly made from Pearl Bakery (pearlbakery.com). Get the chicken or eggplant parm, a seasonal salad, and the shoestring fries.

TEOTE HOUSE CAFÉ AND MEZCALERIA

www.teotepdx.com • Open Sunday–Thursday 11 a.m.–10 p.m., Friday and Saturday 11 a.m.–11 p.m.

South: 1615 SE 12th Avenue, Portland • 971-888-5281

North: 2700 NE Alberta Street, Portland • 971-288-5688

Start with an arepas, a Venezuelan deep-fried corn cake, and add your choice of smoky meat or black beans, topped with something green (cilantro, cabbage salad, mixed greens, verde sauce, depending) and varying quesos, sauces, or plantains. You can order shareable or family-style meals—we suggest the Masa Nosh, because when a Yiddish word shows up on a Latin American restaurant's menu, you know world peace is possible. The house café has a full bar and upstairs patio, and the mezcaleria has a very long list of mezcal. Bet you can't try just one.

PÉPÉ LE MOKO

407 SW 10th Avenue, Portland • pepelemokopdx.com/ • 503-546-8537 • Open daily 4 p.m.–2 a.m.

Spanish-ish restaurant serving oysters, stylish bar snacks such as quicos and Matiz Gallego sardines, and bocadillos, plus classic cocktails and house cocktails. If you like uppers with your downers, try the espresso martini, featuring Stumptown coffee extract.

CHICKEN AND GUNS

1207 SE Hawthorne Boulevard, Portland • www.chickenandguns.com • 503-234-7236

By "guns," Chicken and Guns means crispy potatoes, and by "chickens" they mean a quarter, half, or whole bird that's been oak- and mesquite-smoked to pure deliciousness. Get the Peruvian Aji sauce. Actually, get the chimichurri. Actually, just do yourself a favor and pay the 50 cents for both.

Booze and Beyond

DISTILLERY ROW

www.distilleryrowpdx.com

The Portland Distillery Passport features those on Distillery Road and three in the Northwest Distiller's District. Consider hiring a PDX pedicab (pdxpedicab.com; 503-828-9888) to take you on a Distillery Row tour.

STONE BARN BRANDYWORKS

3315 SE 19th, Suite B, Portland • www.stonebarnbrandyworks.com • 503-341-2227 • Open for tastings Friday–Monday noon–6 p.m., or by appointment

Regional fruit brandies during harvest season and rye whiskey when not. The offerings are constantly changing: get the grappa or cranberry liqueur if you can.

WILD ROOTS VODKA

135 NE 6th Avenue, Portland • wildrootsvodka.com • 971-254-4617 • Open Thursday–Sunday noon–6 p.m.

Vodka flavored with Pacific Northwest's favorite crop: the berry. Marionberry, red raspberry, cranberry, and dark sweet cherry. While you're at it, don't forget the pear and Washington apple.

VINN DISTILLERY

222 SE 8th Avenue, Portland • www.vinndistillery.com • 503-807-3826 • Open Thursday and Friday 1–4 p.m., Saturday noon–5 p.m., Sunday 1–5 p.m.

Rice-based spirits from recipes passed down for seven generations and counting. Includes baijiu, a drink that's been popular in China for thousands of years. Bonus: All spirits are gluten-free.

ROLLING RIVER DISTILLERY

1215 SE 8th Street, Suite H, Portland • 503-236-3912 • Tasting room open Friday–Sunday noon–5 p.m.; weekdays by appointment)

Vodka, gin, and aquavit handcrafted using fresh organic ingredients.

NEW DEAL DISTILLERY

900 SE Salmon Street, Portland • newdealdistillery.com • 503-234-2513 • Tasting and tours daily noon-6 p.m.

Small batch, including the more familiar rums, gins, and whiskeys alongside moonshines and white dog whiskey, an unaged and fiery spirit. You can also get an "island getaway flight," which includes three tropical-inspired cocktails.

HOUSE SPIRITS DISTILLERY

65 SE Washington Street, Portland • www.housespirits.com • 503-235-3174 • Tasting room open daily noon–7 p.m.

Limited-edition small-batch spirits, such as Swedish-style aquavit and Volstead vodka. Weekday tours run start at the top of the hour between 1 and 5 p.m. Saturday tours are at 1 p.m. and 3 p.m., and Sundays at 3 p.m. $20 includes tour and full tasting.

EASTSIDE DISTILLING

Southeast Distillery Row Tasting Room: 1512 SE 7th Avenue, Portland • ww.eastsidedistilling.com • 971-703-4712 • Open Sunday–Thursday noon–8 p.m., Friday and Saturday noon–10 p.m.

Award-winning small-batch bourbons, American whiskeys, potato vodka, naturally flavored rums, and seasonal liqueurs.

APEX: A BEER BAR

1216 SE Division Street, Portland • apexbar.com • 503-APEX-BAR • Open daily 11:30 a.m.–2:30 a.m.

Known for their swag—one recent long-sleeve favorite proclaimed "Drink beer, ride bikes, go fuck yourself"—and outdoor beer garden. Oh, and the 50 beers on tap. They serve no food on-site, so bring some along if you need some grease to soak up the alcohol. Cash only, no dogs or kids, lots of bike parking.

STORMBREAKER BREWING AND JOHNS

www.stormbreakerbrewing.com • Open Sunday and Monday 11 a.m.–10 p.m., Tuesday–Thursday 11 a.m.–11 p.m., Friday and Saturday 11 a.m.–12 a.m.

832 N Beech Street, Portland • 971-703-4516

8409 N Lombard Street, Portland • 971-255-1481

They love beer a lot, and you can tell. Beers are handcrafted, with some regulars and some seasonals on tap. If the timing works out, get the Triple Double IPA, which has an ABV of 8.5% and a basketball theme, or order off the whiskey and beer pairing menu. Decent bar food; dog and kid friendly.

ECLIPTIC BREWING

825 N Cook Street, Portland • eclipticbrewing.com • 503-265-8002 • Open Sunday–Thursday 11 a.m.–10 p.m., Friday and Saturday 11 a.m.–11 p.m.

Great bar with good bar food and beyond. If you're feeling the citrus, try the Espacio Mexican-style lager with lime zest, limed so you don't have to, or the Moonbase Blood Orange Saison. Or, for the sweet-toothed, order a porter float, which features the daily house-made ice cream and Capella Porter. Tours run at noon on Monday, Tuesday, and Friday. Monday is also all-day happy hour.

BASE CAMP BREWING

930 SE Oak Street, Portland • basecampbrewingco.com • 503-477-7479 • Open Sunday–Thursday noon–10 p.m., Friday and Saturday 11 a.m.–12 a.m.

Good beer made by Pacific Northwest outdoor enthusiasts—when they're not brewing, they're climbing/swimming/camping/fishing. The taproom partners with a rotation of food carts for the best of Portland eating. Come on Monday for all-day happy hour. Dog friendly.

 *Stay Over*

For hotels, see page 142.

Hostels

NORTHWEST PORTLAND HOSTEL & GUESTHOUSE

479 NW 18th Avenue, Portland • www.nwportlandhostel.com • 503-241-2783

From a single 36-room building to a five-building citadel, the Northwest Portland Hostel & Guesthouse has all the amenities without arm-and-a-leg costs. Remember, this is a hostel, so you have to ask for towels and most rooms share a bathroom. On the plus side, the front desk is staffed 24 hours a day! Choose from one of the 160 beds in the eight- or four-bed dorm rooms, or one of the 32 private rooms with either a queen, a double, a single, or some combination of the three. All rooms share a garden and courtyard, and everyone gets a complimentary bagel breakfast. Dorm beds: $27–49; private rooms: $67–159 (prices before lodging tax).

HI PORTLAND HAWTHORNE HOSTEL

3031 SE Hawthorne Boulevard, Portland • www.portlandhostel.org • 503-236-3380

Located in southeast Portland's bohemian Hawthorne district, this homey house was built in 1909 and converted into a nonprofit hostel 75 years later. It includes a total of 34 beds, with two private rooms, two co-ed dorms, and two segregated dorms (based on a binary definition of gender, one would presume). They're classified as a Designated Sustainable Living Center, and you can get an eco-tour to see the eco-roof, vegetable garden, rainwater collection system, permeable wall, and other various green features. If you biked all the way there—bringing your bike on train, bus, or car is considered cheating—then you get a $5 discount. Dorm beds: $27–45; private rooms: $68–80.

While You're Here

STOP BY THE ZYMOGLYPHIC MUSEUM

6225 SE Alder Street, Portland • www.zymoglyphic.org

Willamette Weekly calls it "a self-contained world of rogue taxidermy and steampunk." The curator, a former software engineer, takes found objects, photographs, and exoskeletons, and makes oddities and artifacts, dioramas, sketches, and entire imagined worlds and made-up

// The Zymoglyphic Museum, Portland

eras. This is some weird-ass and brilliant shit. Visit this garage-size curiosity cabinet (it's above a detached garage) at the curator's home on the second and fourth Sunday of the month, 11 a.m.–4 p.m. Free.

Visit a Strip Club

Portland has the most strip clubs per capita of any city in the United States. Part of the reason is that people in Portland skew sex-positive, and stripping is considered a viable profession. This means that most of the clubs have a noticeably unseedy feel, and they offer a wide range of actually good food and drinks, including a plethora of local beers and/or vegan fare. Most of them are open all day, seven days a week.

MARY'S CLUB

129 SW Broadway, Portland • www.marysclub.com • 503-227-3023 • Open Monday–Saturday 11 a.m.–2:30 a.m., Sunday 11:30 a.m.–2:30 a.m.

Mary's Club's claim to fame is that it's Portland's first topless club, offering "entertainment of the girlie variety" since 1965.

DEVILS POINT

5303 SE Foster Road, Portland • www.devilspointbar.com • 503-744-4513 • Open daily 11 a.m.–2:30 a.m.

Voted #3 Best Karaoke Bar in America by *Maxim*, Devils Point is home to the groundbreaking and world-famous **Stripparaoke** since 2005. Starting at 9 p.m. on Sunday, you can get up and belt out whatever song moves you while a dancer makes her moves. Don't forget to tip the dancer for making your terrible singing look good.

ABOVE & BEYOND

Dogs | There are **33 public off-leash dog parks** in Portland. Check out the Portland Parks & Recreation website (www.portlandoregon.gov) for information on each park, organized by district, and *Willamette Week* (www.wweek.com) for ranking.

Skate | Some of the key parks to check out include: **Burnside Skate Park** (SE 2nd Avenue, Portland); **Ed Benedict Skatepark** (10125 SE Powell Boulevard, Portland); **Alberta Skate Spot** (NE Alberta Street and 52nd Street, Portland,); **Pier Park** (9001 N Bruce Avenue, Portland); **Glenhaven Park** (7900 NE Siskiyou Street, Portland); **Holly Farm Park** (10819 SW Capitol Highway, Portland); **Gabriel Skatepark** (SW 45th Avenue and SW Nevada Street, Portland); **Gateway Discovery Park Skate Dot** (NE 106th Avenue and Halsey Street, Portland 97220).

Also check out these great indoor skate parks: **Commonwealth Skateboarding** (1425 SE 20th Street, Portland, www.cwskate.com) and **Skatechurch** (8815 NE Glisan Street, Portland, skatechurch.net).

Bikes | Bikes are another alternative form of transportation that's celebrated in Portland. There is a ton of places to rent bikes, and you can find more information on the city website (www.portlandoregon.gov). For bike share, including maps, go to **BIKETOWN** (www.biketownpdx.com) and download the app.

Books | **Powell's Books** (www.powells.com; 503-228-4651) is a Portland institution. It is the world's largest indie bookstore—the flagship location, **Powell's City of Books** (1005 W Burnside Street), has over a million books. There are four additional locations around Portland: **Powell's Books on Hawthorne** (3723 SE Hawthorne Boulevard), **Powell's Books for Home and Garden** (3747 SE Hawthorne Boulevard), **Powell's Books at PDX** (7000 NE Airport Way, Suite 2250), and **Powell's Books at Cedar Crossing** (3415 SW Cedar Hills Boulevard). There is also a location in nearby Beaverton.

At **Wallace Books** (7241 SE Milwaukie Avenue, Portland; wallacebookspdx.blogspot.com; 503-235-7350; open Monday–Saturday 10 a.m.–7 p.m., Sunday 10 a.m.–6 p.m.), the shelves are warped by the weight of great new and used books.

Longfellow Books (1401 SE Division Street, Portland; www.longfellowspdx.com; 503-239-5222; open Monday–Saturday 2 p.m.–5 p.m.) specializes in fine used, rare, and antiquarian books, with a price range from $10 to $5,000. They like to pick up entire estates' worth of books as well as vintage photos, posters, and paper ephemera.

Not Ready to Go Home | Stop by **The Brautigan Library** (1511 Main Street, Vancouver; www.thebrautiganlibrary.org), located in the Clark County Historical Museum, to see over 300 unpublished manuscripts, classified in accordance to the Mayonnaise System. Each manuscript has its own story to tell (as all manuscripts do).

Good to Know |
· Portland is the city with the most dogs per capita in the country and is ranked the #1 friendliest dog city by dogtime.com. Seattle is ranked #2—we have more dogs in the city than kids.

· The naming of Portland came down to a coin toss between the two biggest landowners in the area, one of whom was from Boston, Massachusetts, the other from Portland, Maine. You can probably guess who one. The reason why they didn't at least try to be a little creative is lost to history.

· Stumptown Coffee borrowed Portland's nickname. Stumptown was one of its oldest nicknames and is based on rapid urban growth and logging of the area during the 1840s.

Been There, Done That | Stop by Olympia in South Puget Sound (page 33) or Whidbey Island (page 249) on the way home.

LUCKY DEVIL LOUNGE

633 SE Powell Boulevard, Portland • www.luckydevillounge.com • 503-206-7350 • Open daily 11 a.m.–2:30 a.m.

Red velvet walls, puma-print carpet, custom-built steel cage with monkey bars. Sunday is ladies' night.

SASSY'S BAR

927 SE Morrison Street, Portland • www.sassysbar.com • 503-231-1606 • Open daily 10:30 a.m.–2:30 a.m.

Three stages with women at three stages of undress, and 24 micro- and craft beers on tap.

CASA DIABLO AND DUSK 'TIL DAWN CASA DIABLO 2

2839 NW St Helens Road, Portland • 503-222-6600

8445 SE McLoughlin Boulevard, Portland • www.casadiablo.com • 503-222-6610 • Casa Diablo and Dusk 'Til Dawn Casa Diablo 2: daily 2 p.m.–2:30 a.m.

Self-proclaimed "vegan house of sin," Casa Diablo is a more advanced strip club—you'll see some things here—with a vegan menu. As one reviewer wrote, "I can get down with seitan and Satan at the same time."

SILVERADO

318 SW 3rd Avenue, Portland • www.silveradopdx.com • 503-224-4493 • Open daily 9 a.m.–2:30 p.m.

The premier gay men's nightclub, with a lounge for quiet drinking and a night club for dancing and male exotic entertainment after 10 p.m. Monday night is amateur night.

>> Need more weird back in Seattle? Go to **Ye Olde Curiosity Shop** (yeoldecuriosityshop.com).

9

Fantasy in Forks

FROM SEATTLE: 4 HOURS · DAYS HERE: 1-PLUS

DO	EAT	BUY
take a *Twilight* tour	Bella's Mushroom Ravioli at Bella Italia	plaid Bite Me pants from Native to Twilight #twication

If you don't like paternalistic sparkly vampires and hunky werewolves, then a) skip to the next section, and b) why the heck not? Since Stephenie Meyer's best-selling 2005 debut, *Twilight*, members of both Team Edward and Team Jacob have flocked to Forks and La Push, Washington, to see the misty land that inspired this fantasy yarn. Because vampires don't like too much sun, see, and the Olympic Peninsula has low lighting.

The first drafts of Meyer's first book were titled *Forks*, which, admittedly, doesn't have the same ring to it as *Twilight*. Since made famous, this teeny town, population a few thousand, has been hosting *Twilight*-related tours and *Twilight*-related events, and you can download a *Twilight* map at the Forks Chamber of Commerce website (forkswa.com). Those who had formative crush experiences and learned fantasy-style romance from *Twilight*, you are now all grown up, hopefully with money in your pocket, sexual experience, and a more pragmatic view of the logistics of modern romance—but without it dampening your nostalgia for romance stories of days gone by. At the very least, stop by on your way from the Hoh Rain Forest to the Pacific Coast of the Olympic Peninsula (page 175).

☰ *Getting There*

BY CAR AND FERRY | Take the Seattle–Bainbridge Ferry to Bainbridge, then get on WA-3 N to Poulsbo. Drive 13 miles to WA-104 W to Highway 101, then drive for 115 miles.

☰ *Highlight Reel*

FOREVER TWILIGHT IN FORKS FESTIVAL

September • forkswa.com/ftffestival

For a few days in September, you can travel back to a simpler time, when *Twilight* was fresh on the scene and we didn't yet know the glory of Michelle Obama. For one nice price of $250 to $275, you'll receive special meals with the Olympic Coven at Bella Italia, the location of Bella and Edward's first date; an autograph/photograph event; access to many dance parties, including ones that involve dancing; a Forever Twilight in Forks Festival goodie bag; and more.

TAKE A TOUR WITH TWILIGHT TOURS IN FORKS

130 Spartan Avenue, Forks • 360-374-5634

But of course. Ride a bus around the town where Bella and Edward fell in love and Jacob felt unrequited—and also a bunch of other crazy stuff happened. There are three types of bus tours to choose from, all of which make eight stops around the city where Bella's dad, Bella, Edward, and Dr. Carlyle lived, worked, and went to school, and other interesting spots you'll recognize from the movies. There's a special stop, too, in a top-secret locale to see a top-secret prop. Along the way, you'll be able to take photos with any of the tour guide's life-size cardboard cutouts. The guide, whose family has lived in the area for generations, will talk about both *Twilight* and the history of Forks. Reservations encouraged.

THE BELLA TOUR | The eight-stop OG tour. Lasts 1.5 to 2 hours, depending who's on it. $30.

THE JACOB TOUR | The Bella Tour plus a trip to La Push to see Jacob's motorcycle and Jacob's beach (a.k.a. First Beach). Lasts three hours. $45.

THE SUNSET TOUR

The third and final tour must be made by special appointment. It's for those who want to take the *Twilight*-themed romance to the next level. Includes the eight stops, the trip to La Push and Jacob's beach, and an additional stop at Rialto Beach, where the guide will roast hot dogs and smores over an open fire as you and your boo-boo watch the sun setting over the water. Lasts five or six hours. $65.

>> Watch the documentary, *Twilight in Forks: The Saga of a Real Town*, to get an inside look at this teeny town made unexpectedly popular.

MILLER TREE INN

654 E Division Street, Forks • millertreeinn.com • 360-374-6806

It has been decided that the Miller Tree Inn is the Cullen house, as described in the book. Go to the website to read the breakdown of why this quaint inn deserves this honor and how the owners have, since 2005, revamped the place to make the resemblance even clearer. Beyond *Twilight*, the inn is quiet and cute, with a well-stocked library, private baths, pasture views, a breakfast served hot each morning, and a tabby cat to scratch under the chin. From October through April, you can get a pre-dawn breakfast and a thermos of coffee before you head down to the river for some fishing.

>> Established almost 10 years before Edward and Bella's first date, **Bella Italia** (118 E 1st Street, Port Angeles; bellaitaliapa.com; 360-457-5442; open daily at 5 p.m.), located in Port Angeles on the northern shore of the Olympic Peninsula, sources locally as much as possible, bringing in halibut caught in Neah Bay, Quillette king salmon, and shellfish from the Hood Canal, plus mushrooms from the Olympic National Forest and produce from farms in Sequim and nearby. Obviously get Bella's Mushroom Ravioli.

☰ *Plan Around*

DRAG RACING

One weekend a month, May through September • Forks Municipal Airport, S Forks Avenue, Forks • www.westendthunder.com

Get your motor running at West End Thunder Drag Races. Features 1/8-mile drags, a classic car show, and a Show 'n Shine. Vroom vroom! $10.

☰ *Eat & Drink*

Despite being a tourist trap, this is still a very small town with limited food options.

PACIFIC PIZZA

870 S Forks Avenue, Forks • 360-374-2626 • Open Sunday–Thursday 11 a.m.–9 p.m., Friday and Saturday 11 a.m.–10 p.m.

A more casual pizza joint that, besides the many kinds of pizza, also serves fresh salads, paninis, back east grinders, pastas and larger entrées, hot baked potatoes, nachos, wings, and craft beers on tap.

FORKS OUTFITTERS

950 S Forks Avenue, Forks • forksoutfitters.com • 360-374-6161 • Deli/bakery hours: daily 8 a.m.– 8 p.m.; espresso hours: Monday–Friday 5 a.m.–7 p.m., Saturday and Sunday 6 a.m.–7 p.m.

A sporting goods/grocery store, with espresso and smoothies, deli sandwiches, baked goods, and booze.

GOLDEN GATE RESTAURANT

11 S Forks Avenue, Forks • 360-374-5528

Decent Chinese food for a small town, with the fun addition of more *Twilight* cutouts.

PLAZA JALISCO

90 N Forks Avenue, Forks • 360-374-3108 • Open Sunday–Thursday 11 a.m.–9 p.m., Friday and Saturday 11 a.m.–10 p.m.

Authentic Mexican, with huge portions and icy margaritas. Split the fiesta platter.

☰ *Stay Over*

Small-town vibes, with many cabins, tents, rooms, and a yurt or two available on Airbnb and VRBO.

B&Bs

KALALOCH LODGE

157151 Highway 101, Forks • www.thekalalochlodge.com • 1-866-662-9928

The main lodge has been offering travelers wireless refuge for nearly a century. The Bluff Cabins provide privacy, and the sound of the Pacific waves roiling nearby will wash out the howls of your lovemaking. Every room in the Seacrest House faces the ocean, and the group campsite, a quarter-mile from the main lodge, is perfect for those on a budget and a propensity for sea-salted air and the freedom of the outdoors. Everyone gets access to fire circles, gazebos, and a daily bundle of firewood. Please note that there's no WiFi, and intentionally so. The outdoors is calling. Pet-friendly cabins available.

MANITOU LODGE B&B

813 Kilmer Road, Forks • manitoulodge.com • 360-374-6295

The Manitou Lodge B&B has options: rooms in the main lodge, rooms in the two detached cottages, two "outback" camping cabins, and three ready tents (no pitching required). Inside the proper buildings is lots of wood for that cabin feel. The lodge offers a hiker's portable breakfast basket for those itching to get out for some *Twilight* touring or to go down to the beach. Pet-friendly accommodations available.

Motels

PACIFIC INN MOTEL

352 S Forks Avenue, Forks • pacificinnmotel.com • 360-374-9400

Although this average motel does offer regular rooms, the kind with white walls and patterned carpet, why not get a *Twilight*-themed room? There, you can let your vampire fantasies be inspired by the black-and-red bedding, curtains, and walls, as well as the framed posters of Edward and Bella looking moody over the bed. All rooms have flat-screen TVs.

DEW DROP INN

100 Fern Hill Road, Forks • www.dewdropinnmotel.com • 360-374-4055

Small, family-owned inn in downtown Forks. Has cable and one *Twilight*-themed room. Pet-friendly accommodations available for a $15 fee.

Camping and Cabins

BOGACHIEL STATE PARK

185983 Highway 101, Forks • 360-374-6356

According to Hipcamp, Bogachiel campground is shaped like "an infinity symbol of awesome." In a more technical sense, it's a 127-acre camping park along the Bogachiel River, between the Hoh Rain Forest to the east and Ruby Beach and Rialta Beach to the west. Bring a tube for some nearby river floating. Includes 35 campsites, two restrooms, showers, three picnic tables, and a kitchen shelter with electricity. First come, first served year-round, with option of reservations at 1-888-CAMPOUT or washington.goingtocamp.com.

BOGIE BUNGALOW

101 Hollow Road, Forks • www.bogiebungalow.com

Sick of *Twilight*? Then rent this secluded cabin in the woods, with easy access to hiking trails, the beach, and the river. In fact, you're only 55 feet from the Bogachiel River, and in season you can step out the door with your raft or tube and get in the water. There's a fully equipped kitchen, a riverbank fire pit, and an almost guarantee of elk sighting. On a clear night you can see the stars.

≡ *While You're Here*

GO FISH

Year-round, Forks is a fishing destination. Chinook and coho salmon and steelhead trout make their migratory runs through the waters of the Sol Duc, Bogachiel, Calawah, Hoh, and Quillayute rivers. If pulling these fish out of the water and then eating them (after taking a pic to post) is your thing, then Forks is the right place to throw out your line. There are a few fishing

If you're looking for a five-star situation, go elsewhere. If, however, you're on a tight budget and open to a "unique" experience in a Bernie Sanders time machine, come to **Rainforest Hostel** (169312 Highway 101, Forks; www.rainforesthostel.com; 360-374-2270). The owner, who lives there, is less about dusting or decluttering and more about socialism. As a result, the cost of stay is sliding scale and all guests are encouraged to do 15 minutes of chores per day. There are two rooms: one room has three double bunks, and the other has one full-size and a double bunk. Families and couples can make special arrangements. Think of payment as you would universal healthcare: If you have more to give, then you can help to cover those who have little or nothing.

guide services to choose from, each offering some variation on drift boat fishing, fly-fishing, specialized raft fishing, jet sled fishing, and more.

ANGLER'S GUIDE SERVICE (www.anglersguideservice.com; 360-374-3148) Drift boat or specialized raft $350.

WESTSIDE GUIDE SERVICE (westsideguide.com; 360-640-0546) $225-plus.

MIKE Z'S GUIDE SERVICE (mikezsguideservice.com; 360-640-8109)

PISCATORIAL PURSUITS (www.piscatorialpursuits.com; 1-866-FISH2DAY) $250-plus.

DON KINSEY FISHING (www.pacificnwguide.com; 253-670-8923) $200-plus.

SHOP AT NATIVE TO TWILIGHT

Highway 101/Main Street, on the west corner of the only stoplight in town • www.nativetotwilight.com • 360-374-2111

For all the must-have *Twilight*-themed gear, stop by Native to Twilight. The souvenir/clothing shop also sells handmade and local items made by First Nation artists, such as traditional grass and cedar baskets, woven and beaded barrettes, bentwood cedar boxes, and more.

ABOVE & BEYOND

Dogs | There are no off-leash dog parks in the city of Forks, but you can walk your dog on-leash on the Spruce Railroad Trail, Peabody Creek Trail, the Kalaloch Beaches, and Rialto Beach. For more, check out olympicpeninsula.org/stories/pet-friendly-travel.

Skate | The skate park in Tillicum Park (437 Tillicum Lane, Forks) is well appointed, with a big bowl, half pipe, and some other unique elements worth putting your wheels on. For more information and photos, go to northwestskater.com.

Good to Know
· Members of the Quileute Tribe probably don't shape shift into werewolves.
· Although it continues to be a logging town, Fork's timber industry has been in decline since the 1980s due to new rules regarding the protection of old-growth forests.

Been There, Done That | For more on La Push, the Hoh Rain Forest, and the Olympic Peninsula, go to page 175.

JOHN'S BEACHCOMBING MUSEUM

143 Andersonville Avenue, Forks • 360-640-0320

An incredible and random collection of found objects discovered on local beaches and curated by the founder since the 1970s. See the totem pole made of buoys, the Raggedy Ann dolls, and the letters written by Japanese children, washed ashore following the tsunami in 2011.

// Beach at Forks

10

Soak in Soap Lake

FROM SEATTLE: 2.5 TO 4 HOURS · DAYS HERE: 2

DO	EAT	DRINK
smear mud on yourself	Russian-style smoked fish from Mama's	lots of (fresh) water

There are a few agreed-upon stories about Soap Lake. The main one goes like this: For a few thousand years, the indigenous people believed that the Smokiam carried healing powers, and the sick and injured would come from far and wide to rest and rejuvenate. What's not totally clear is what *Smokiam* actually means—is it "healing waters," as the city's website's reproduction of a Wikipedia page suggests? Or is that a misinterpretation? Well, genocide, cultural genocide, and the shunting of indigenous people onto the nearby Colville Reservation has made it hard to track down this information. But whatever you want to call it, the tradition of visiting this mineral-heavy lake for its restorative properties has continued, first in the form of a sanatorium in the 1900s and now as a destination for sunbathing, spreading black mud over skin, and float-ing in water with a uniquely high mineral content, particularly high levels of sulfate, carbonate, bicarbonate, sodium, and chloride. Like the reputed health benefits of the mud and waters of the Dead Sea, this area attracts a wide range of health seekers, and a large Russian population has settled in for the long haul. Today, with a population of just over 1,500, Soap Lake feels small town because it is. The whole natural spa vibe is quite relaxing, and all that skin softening and sunshine—the area gets kissed by the sun 300 days per year—is sure to put anyone in the mood.

☰ *Getting There*

BY CAR | Get on I-90 and drive east for about 150 miles to Exit 151. Follow WA-283 N for approximately 26 miles.

☰ *Highlight Reel*

SOAP LAKE RESORT

236 Main Avenue E, Soap Lake • soaplakeresort.com • 509-246-0462

The Soap Lake Spa and Resort side of the business includes inn and cottage rooms, which are like standard, homey hotel rooms, with a bed, a TV, and air conditioning. Some have a two-person Jacuzzi tub, some have a private patio. Now, the Notaras Lodge part of the business features 15 "luxury in log" rooms, each of which has a different theme—e.g., "memories," "honeymoon"—plus a kitchenette, cable TV, and WiFi. Seven of the rooms have their own two-person Jacuzzi tubs, some have giant bath tubs, all have Soap Lake mineral water.

Pet friendly, $25 fee.

SMOKIAM RESORT

22818 WA-17 N, Soap Lake • smokiamrvresort.com • 509-246-0413

The Smokiam Resort is located on the north side of Soap Lake and includes RV sites, campsites, tepees, and cabins available to rent. Some of the tepees are right next to the water, with a swimming dock nearby, and a sports court and playground between them and the cabins and tent and RV sites. These are "dry" tepees, meaning they have no electricity or running water, though lanterns and linens are provided. Tepees include futon beds or sleeping cots, a fire pit and grill, and a stunning view of the lake and basalt cliffs beyond. Other tepees are farther back, with the resort's sauna, putt-putt golf course, swimming pool (for when your skin needs a break from all those

// Smokiam Resort, Soap Lake

minerals), clubhouse, fire pit, two hot tubs (one is adults-only), and a café between them and the sandy beach that leads into the water. Water is available in the shared restrooms and showers. The 51 campsites are spread out across the property, some closer to the water, some in a large grassy area nicely shaded by trees. The cabins are fully appointed and family-size, with bedding, a kitchen, a TV, and various combinations of beds. There's a range of prices, depending on where you're staying and the season, from $40 per night to $260 per night.

MOM'S EUROPEAN FOOD & DELI

331 Main Avenue E, Soap Lake • 509-246-1121

Known locally as Mama's, this Russian grocery store-slash-deli has a good selection of Eastern European snacks and deli delicacies such as borscht, sour cream–topped piroshki, pelmeni, cheeses and sausages, and the (in)famous smoked fish, which you can purchase whole, eyeballs and all. Get a big loaf of dark rye bread to go with it and you have yourself a delightful fishy snack.

LASER LIGHT SHOW AT GRAND COULEE DAM

May–September • Grand Coulee Dam Visitor Center, WA-155, Coulee Dam • www.usbr.gov/pn/grandcoulee/visit/laser.html • 509-633-9265

At 550 feet high and nearly a mile long, Grand Coulee is one of the largest structures built by human hands. It serves to distribute power to a big chunk of the United States and covers 75 percent of the power needs of the Pacific Northwest. The power production facilities are awe inspiring, and you can take a guided tour April through October. During the summer, however, things get special. Smoke a blunt, sit back and relax, and let the One River, Many Voices laser show take you to another plane.

 **Plan Around**

SOAP LAKE HYDRO REGATTA

June

For two days, a mini-Seafair lands on Soap Lake. During that time, instead of soaking, you can watch the speed demons of the Seattle Drag and Ski Club race hydroplane boats.

CANNABIS KICKBALL CUP

August

For one day toward the end of August, watch stoners play kickball. There's also a parade. For more information, visit www.thecannabisalliance.us.

RUN TO DESERT BIKE RALLY

September • 3953 Airway Drive NE, Moses

Every year near Moses Lake, motorcyclists and friends gather for a bike show, swap meet, music, fireworks, and more. It gets loud, and many of the attendees camp in Soap Lake, where they don't get any quieter. If motorbiking is your thing, then mark your calendar. If motorbiking is not your thing, also mark your calendar.

≡ Eat & Drink

Soap Lake is a very small town, meaning, food-wise, there's not a ton of choices. Please don't expect deep-urban quality. People looking for haute cuisine, an epicurean adventure, a divinely orchestrated culinary experience, ingredient-inspired/wild-crafted/high-vibration/bold-flavored anything, or food-adjacent things deconstructed or made out of foam, this is not the town for you. Enjoy!

JOHN'S FOODS

115 Daisy Street, Soap Lake • 509-246-1332

Perhaps the only place in town where you can buy fresh produce, John's Foods has the basics for a price *because it is not a corporate chain.* When you go there, please don't complain about the fact that it's not Whole Foods and that the employees live on a small-town schedule. The doughnuts are made fresh daily, the produce is seasonal and locally sourced, and the people are generally chill.

LAKESIDE BISTRO

14 Canna Street N, Soap Lake • soaplakeresort.com/lakesidebistro • 509-246-1217 • Open Monday–Saturday 4–10 p.m., Sunday 8:30 a.m.–12 p.m.

For 50-plus years, this little spot was known as Don's Restaurant, but recently it got a rebranding and a revamped menu to appeal to people like you. They've kept some Don's favorites, such as a 12-ounce steak and a prime rib special every Friday and Saturday. Lakeside Bistro features what you'd expect in a small town catering to a tourist audience—seafood, burgers, and broiler entrées—with the happy addition of small plates and veggie creations. There's ample outdoor seating (with umbrellas over every table to protect diners from that bright Eastern Washington sun). Try the walnut and smoked salmon salad, any of the burgers, and the bourbon brown betty.

SOAP LAKE FARMERS' MARKET

Soap Lake Park East Beach, Daisy Street N and Main Avenue E, Soap Lake • 509-312-9826 • Open June–October, Sunday 10 a.m.–2 p.m.

DEL RED PUB

311 Main Avenue E, Soap Lake • 206-246-1867

This is a small-town, dive-adjacent sort of restaurant, so don't go in expecting fancy. Do expect good karaoke, good beers, and decent bar food. No kids allowed after 8 p.m.

 # Stay Over

MASTERS INN

404 4th Avenue NE, Soap Lake • www.mastersinnsoaplake.com • 509-246-1831

Masters Inn is a quaint, a.k.a. not fancy, motel that's kept its classic '60s-era charm (read: wood paneling). It's clean, quiet, and, more importantly, affordable. There's even a meditation and yoga room for when you're done doing it and need a moment to regroup. You get breakfast every morning and many trees to sit under and watch the sun go down. Pet-friendly rooms available.

Camping

SMOKIAM CAMPGROUND

www.cityofsoaplake.org/smokiam-campground-rates

On the southeast shore of the lake, the Smokiam Campground is open year-round, with eight tent sites and 28 RV sites, plus shower and restroom accommodations.

$15 per tent, $3 per car. Pet friendly.

While You're Here

GOLF AT LAKEVIEW GOLF AND COUNTRY CLUB

19547 Golf Club Road, Soap Lake • lvgcc.com • 509-246-0336

Remember that teacher freshman year who wouldn't sign off on your application to get into sophomore honors English? Visit Lakeview Golf and Country Club's driving range and imagine his smug face while smacking some golf balls into the wide blue sky.

SEE THE LENORE LAKE CAVES AND THE BLUE LAKE RHINOCEROS CAVE

Lenore Lake Road, Coulee City • 1.5 miles round-trip • Elevation gain: 1,300 feet • Trailhead: 47.5174, -119.4938 • www.wta.org/go-hiking/hikes/lenore-lake-caves

A cave that was once a Diceratherium, ancestor of the modern rhinoceros—true story! In the mid-1930s, some hikers stumbled upon a cave in the shape of an upside-down rhinoceros. Eventually a geologist examined the cave and the bones resting nearby and decided that it had in fact been a rhinoceros who'd met its doom in a basaltic magma flow approximately 15 million years earlier. The trailhead is located near the north end of Lake Lenore. Beware of rattlesnakes. Discover Pass required.

ABOVE & BEYOND

Not Ready to Go Home | A 7,124-acre park at Wanapum Recreation area, with 3 miles of hiking trails, 27,000 feet of freshwater shoreline, swimming and boating in Wanapum Reservoir, and camping, the **Gingko Petrified Forest** (4511 Huntzinger Road, Vantage; parks.state.wa.us) is worth a stop. The pièce de résistance: a huge fossil forest, discovered in the 1920s. The Trees of Stones trail runs along 20 untampered-with petrified logs and the interpretive center displays one of the most petrified wood collections in North America. It's located at the junction of WA-28 and I-90.

Good to Know |
- People claim that the waters of Soap Lake provide relief from everything, from rheumatoid arthritis to neuropathy, Buerger's disease to psoriasis.
- Soap Lake is on the Coulee Corridor Scenic Byway, which runs approximately 150 miles along I-155, I-17, and US-2. It includes many attractions, like Steamboat Rock State Park, Columbia National Wildlife Refuge, and Dry Falls Visitor Center, plus the cities of Othello, Moses Lake, Ephrata, Coulee City, Electric City, Grand Coulee, Omak, and Okanogan.
- The Cariboo Cattle Trail, used by Natives for hundreds of years, follows the Okanogan River from the Columbia River to Lake Osoyoos in British Columbia, with a healing pit stop in Soap Lake.

Been There, Done That | Leavenworth lies to the west, along US-2.

Part Three

The Great Outdoors

11

Rain Forest and Coast of the Olympic Peninsula

FROM SEATTLE: 2 TO 4 HOURS · DAYS HERE: 2-PLUS

DO	EAT	DRINK	BUY
hike	a burger at the Hard Rain Cafe	rain falling from the sky	an Olympic National Park Pass and a Wilderness Camping Permit

Based on findings at more than 650 archaeological sites, it's estimated that people have lived in and around the Olympic Peninsula for more than 12,000 years. The names of the rivers, regions, and forests come from the names of those who have lived and continue to live here: the Hoh, Ozette, Makah, Quinault, Quileute, Queets, Lower Elwha Klallam, and Jamestown S'Klallam.

On the peninsula there's just about every kind of Pacific Northwest ecosystem you can imagine. Looking for a stormy coastline? It's got 70 miles of it, from Ozette in the north near Neah Bay to Queets Valley in the south. What about old-growth rain forest, with dripping moss and towering cedars? It's got that, too. Then there's the mountains, like Mount Olympus, and the hot springs in Sul Duc, and the spits on the shores of the Strait of Juan de Fuca . . .

Much of the Olympic Peninsula, a.k.a. "Little Alaska," consists of the approximately 1 million acres of the Olympic National Park. The park itself got its first designation in the late

1890s, and then President Franklin Roosevelt made it official in 1938. (The Pacific Coast part of the park was designated 15 years later.) Olympic National Park is widespread and diverse, with little to no development within its interior. Check out the **Highlight Reel** for the top outdoor activities and locales, but be aware that there are over 100 trailheads in the region and about a million outdoor activities that, once you become addicted to the Olympic Peninsula, you'll want to learn more about through Olympic Peninsula–specific guidebooks. The closest towns and cities are along the northern and western coast, all of which are within driving distance from many great outdoor destinations. (Much of the credit for this delineation of the northern shore of the Olympic Peninsula goes to the good people at the Peninsula Trails Coalition, who've spent more than 30 years working their buns off to get the Olympic Discovery Trail up and running. For an itinerary based on this gorgeous 130-mile biking trail, see page 285.) Imagine an inverted L, branching from Port Townsend though not including it (see page 91 for information on Port Townsend), to Cape Alava, the westernmost tip of the peninsula and the contiguous 48, then heading south past La Push of *Twilight* fame to Ocean Shores and the North Bay. The main stopping points along the way are **Sequim**, **Port Angeles** (including **Lake Crescent**), and **La Push**. (See page 160 for information on the city of Forks and page 44 for the Hood Canal.)

☰ Getting There

BY CAR | Drive south on I-5 to Tacoma, then keep going on WA-16. Approximately 160 miles.

BY FERRY | Take the Seattle–Bainbridge Ferry to Bainbridge Island, then get on WA-3 N in Poulsbo. Drive west for 14 miles, then drive on WA-104 W and Highway 101 N. Or take the Edmonds–Kingston Ferry to Kingston and get on WA-104. Approximately 101 miles.

BY BUS | Catch the Dungeness Line from one of the Seattle or Edmonds bus stops and take it to Port Angeles, Sequim, Discovery Bay, or Port Townsend. www.olympicbuslines.com.

☰ Highlight Reel

OLYMPIC DISCOVERY TRAIL

The 130-mile Olympic Discovery Trail runs from Port Townsend along the northeast edge of the Olympic Peninsula to La Push on the Pacific Coast (or vice versa). It's a work in progress, with constant updating over the last 30 years, since the trains officially gave up the ghost and the Peninsula Trails Coalition started vying to turn the rail lines into a community trails system. In partnership with the Clallam Tribe, this trail has been painstakingly reclaimed and reworked for ease of use. Today, more than half of the route is motorized vehicle–free.

// Olympic Peninsula

Riding the Olympic Discovery Trail can be a four-day trip, with overnights at each quarter of the ODT (for an itinerary, go to page 285). Or it can take less time, depending on how far you want to go each day and how many stops you want to make. Every 5 to 10 miles there's a kiosk with maps and info, and there's a bathroom every 2 to 3 miles. Between the four main stops, there's little by way of restaurants, It's recommended that you pick up a sandwich and a drink to take with you, then stop by whatever pretty point along the trail strikes your fancy for a picnic. Check out the interactive map and get more information at olympicdiscoverytrail.org.

>>   For bike shops along the way, visit the **Olympic Peninsula Bicycle Alliance** at olympicpeninsula cycling.com.

HOH RAIN FOREST

At more than four hours' distance from Seattle, the **Hoh Rain Forest**, on the northwest side of the Olympic National Park, is one of the farthest escapes in the book. But it's definitely worth the drive. Each year, the area receives 12 to 14 *feet* of rain, making it the moistest, mossiest fairyland in the region (and, perhaps, the world). There, you'll find all-encompassing moss and ferns, nurse logs nursing the next generation, herds of wild Roosevelt elk herd wandering, eagles soaring, fish swimming. There are

// Hoh Lake, Olympic Peninsula

over 800 miles of trails to explore within this magical forest, under trees as old as 500 years and as large as 250 tall and 30 to 60 feet in circumference. This is a hiker's paradise, with so much canopy to keep you cool.

>> **Wilderness Camping Permits are required** for all overnight hikes. Obtain your permit at the Wilderness Information Center (WIC) in Port Angeles. Contact the WIC for more information (360-565-3100).

EAT AND STAY AT HARD RAIN CAFE

5763 Upper Hoh Road, Forks • hohrainforest.wixsite.com/hardrain • 360-374-9288

One of the only blips of civilization out among the trees and the forest creatures, this little off-the-beaten-path café has been feeding hungry hikers for more than 35 years. There's a seasonal campground, too, for when you've been lost for a while and are finally feeling found, or if you just want to take a much-needed shower.

HALL OF MOSSES

0.8 mile round-trip • Elevation gain: 100 feet • Trailhead: Hoh Rain Forest Visitor Center, 18113 Upper Hoh Road, Forks

Take this easy loop to get a sense of the magic of moss. This is more of a meander than a hike, and you'll be sharing the trail with kids, old people, and everyone in between. Great if you've got a bum knee. If you see a banana slug, lick it. (Legend has it that it'll give you magical powers. Or make your tongue slightly numb for a minute. Either way, what do you have to lose?) Requires National Park Pass. Nearest campground: Hoh Campground; nearest town: Forks.

SPRUCE NATURE TRAIL

1.2 miles round-trip • Elevation gain: Less than 100 feet • Trailhead: Hoh Rain Forest Visitor Center, 18113 Upper Hoh Road, Forks

Another easy loop like the Hall of Mosses, with flat grounds and many a moss curtain. It goes down to the Hoh River and then back around to the visitor center. Requires National Park Pass. Nearest campground: Hoh Campground; nearest town: Forks.

BOGACHIEL RIVER TRAIL

12 miles round-trip • Elevation gain: 5,879 feet • Bogachiel Rain Forest River Trailhead: 47.8822 N, -124.2750 W

With many miles and a solid climb, this trail is for the experienced hiker (or horseback rider). Though, of course, you can just turn around when you feel like you've hit your edge. Like all trails, and rain forest trails especially, the Bogachiel River Trail is vulnerable to erosion caused by rain. You will likely run into very few people, if any. The trailhead is located on Undi Road, 5 miles south of Fork on Highway 101 and across the highway from Bogachiel State Park.

All-wheel or four-wheel drive is recommended. Requires National Park Pass—for more information, go to www.nps.gov/planyourvisit/passes.htm. Nearest campground: Hoh Oxbow Campground; nearest town: Forks.

HOH RIVER TRAIL TO GLACIER MEADOWS

34.8 miles round-trip • Elevation gain: 3,700 feet • Trailhead: Hoh Rain Forest Visitor Center, 18113 Upper Hoh Road, Forks

This trail is considered moderate because it's mostly flat for the first 13 miles. There are many spots along the way where you can turn around without feeling like a failure—Mount Tom Creek at the 3-mile point and the campsites at Five Mile Island. Depart from the Spruce Nature Trail, get on at mile 3 or so you'll cross a bridge over the river, another river crossing near the 8-mile point, and some streams beyond that. After those first 13 miles, the trail

CAMPING

HOH CAMPGROUND Upper Hoh Road, Forks

At the terminus of Upper Hoh Road, Hoh Campground is near many natural trails through old-growth forest and includes 78 total sites, including some near the Hoh River, each with a picnic table and fire grate, plus access to potable water and a restroom. It's a popular campground and fills up fast, so come during the fall or spring (if you can handle the moisture) to avoid the crowds. This campground can be a little damp. Such is life in a rain forest. Dogs must be on-leash, but are not allowed on trails in national parks. First come, first served.

HOH OXBOW CAMPGROUND 17602 Highway 101, Forks

Located between Hoh Rain Forest Visitor Center and Ruby Beach, this campground has only eight sites and is therefore nice and quiet, near an oxbow-shaped bend in the Hoh River. Each site has a picnic table and fire pit, and everyone shares an outhouse. Discover Pass required.

HOH RIVER TRAIL Trailhead: Hoh Rain Forest Visitor Center, 18113 Upper Hoh Road, Forks
Five Mile Island: 5 miles
Happy Four: 5.5 miles, primitive wooden shelter
Olympus Guard Station: 9.1 miles
Lewis Meadow: 10.5 miles
Blue Glacier Overlook: 19.5 miles

There are five campsites along the Hoh River Trail. Some, like Five Mile Island, are easy to get to and perfect for an afternoon rest or an overnight. The others are for the legit backpacker and are worth planning an entire weekend around.

ramps up as you head to Glacier Meadow. Requires National Park Pass. Nearest campground: Hoh River Trail; nearest town: Forks.

>> The quietest spot on earth, according to Emmy Award–winning acoustic ecologist, is the **One Square Inch of Silence**, located 3 miles up the Ho River Trail and marked by a small red pebble on top of moss on top of a log. This is one of 12 "quiet zones" in the United States.

The Pacific Coast

HOLE-IN-THE-WALL ON RIALTO BEACH

4 miles round-trip • Elevation gain: 0 feet • Parking area: the end of Mora Road, Forks

Near where the Quillayute River meets the Pacific Ocean, just north of La Push, this beach is pure Pacific Northwest, with lots of rocks, scraggy driftwood, cool breezes, and nearly perpetual cloud cover. Looking south, you can spot James Island and Little James Island sitting pretty; heading north, you'll pass the sea stacks pointing toward the sky. Along the way, you can spot sea lions and otters nearby, eagles above, whales out yonder. When the tide's out, explore the tide pools teeming with bright green sea anemones and little barnacles sticking out their cirri and thick-limbed starfish plotting their next very slow move. The Hole-in-the-Wall is a giant rock formation carved into an arch by the sea, under which you can stand and gape. If you happen to be there when the fog disperses just in time for a crimson and gold sunset, consider yourself one of the lucky ones. Olympic National Park wilderness permit required. Pets on leash permitted during daylight hours. Nearest campground: Mora Campground; nearest town: La Push.

OLYMPIC SOUTH COAST WILDERNESS TRAIL

17 miles one-way • Elevation gain: 250 feet • Third Beach Trailhead: 47.8906, -124.5990 • Oil City Trailhead: 47.7493, -124.4085

Walk along the coast from the Third Beach Trailhead in La Push to the Oil City Trailhead, or vice versa. You'll traverse fords and be at the whim of the tides in terms of dry passage along the beaches. There's little elevation to deal with, but the trail is undeveloped and moderately difficult. Check out the tide pools at Strawberry Point and Toleak Point, and the "Giants Graveyard," a collection of a dozen or so sea stacks. This is for people who know what they're doing (or are open to a learning curve). Make this a multiday backpacking trip, or go as far as you want and then turn back. Call ahead (All Points Charters & Tours, 360-460-7131) to reserve shuttle service from either of the trailheads. Wilderness Camping Permit and National Park Pass required, no pets. Nearest town: La Push.

KALALOCH

From Kalaloch Lodge, at low tide you can walk north along rugged coastline for miles and miles: approximately 3 miles to Kalaloch Beach 4, with Beaches 1, 2, and 3 along the way, as well as Browns Point, a little dollop of land sticking out from the coast at the 2-mile point, or head approximately 3 miles south to South Beach. For longer hikes or a drive, head up to Ruby Beach, one of the area's most popular destinations, approximately 8 miles from Kalaloch.

LAKE OZETTE

Trailhead: Ozette Ranger Station, Hoko-Ozette Road, Clallam Bay

At 7,700 square acres, Lake Ozette is the third-largest natural lake in Washington, yet it's relatively unknown because it's hard to get to. Which means there's lots of space to be alone on the trails around its perimeter. (There are three main hiking options from the lake to the coast: Cape Alava, a 3.1-mile hike, Sanpoint, a 2.8-mile hike, or the Ozette Loop, a 9-mile hike. Or just hang out and get in the water, which is as cold as a frozen hell, so make sure you allow yourself time post-swim to dry off and warm up before dusk falls. Wilderness Camping Permit and National Park Pass required, no pets. Nearest campground: The Lost Resort at Lake Ozette, Ozette Campground.

CAMPING

MORA CAMPGROUND Mora Road, Forks
Camp in coastal forest 2 miles from Rialto Beach. Ninety-four first-come-first-served sites, fire rings, flush toilets, and potable water. Open year-round. $20 per night.

KALALOCH CAMPGROUND Kalaloch Campground F Road, Forks
Camp on a bluff overlooking the Pacific Ocean, with the mossy forest at your back and tide-pool-speckled shoreline down below. You can reserve one of the 170 sites online during the summer, and all campsites are first-come-first-served during the other times of the year. Includes flush toilets, potable water, picnic tables, and campfire rings.

OZETTE CAMPGROUND 21083 Hoko Ozette Road, Clallam Bay
Stay by the lake in one of 15 first-come-first-served sites. Pit toilets, potable water. $20 per night.

SOUTH BEACH CAMPGROUND Highway 101, Forks • Open May–September
Camp above the beach, on the bluff south of Kalaloch Campground. Fifty-five first-come-first-served sites, flush toilets, no potable water. $15 per night.

// Lake Ozette, Olympic Peninsula

THE LOST RESORT AT LAKE OZETTE

20860 Hoko-Ozette Road, Clallam Bay • www.lostresort.net • 360-963-2899

Stay at the westernmost outpost in mainland US. Featuring 30 tent sites spread out from shore to forest, three rustic cabins, and lots of space to roam. There's a cute little store/deli serving breakfast and lunch daily during the summer. $25–90. No pets.

Lake Crescent

LAKE CRESCENT

The water of Lake Crescent is incredibly clear and surprisingly blue, the kind of stunning blue you'd generally see in a tropical locale. This subalpine lake is low in nitrogen, so there are fewer green things, a.k.a. phytoplankton, that usually occupy the Pacific Northwest's water space. That's why people don't just swim, canoe, kayak, SUP, and fish for Beardslee and Crescenti trout (two kinds of trout that thrive only in Lake Crescent), but also scuba and snorkel. At around 60 feet, the visibility is remarkable for this part of the world. It's cold as hell, however, so if you're going to spend some time in it, you better have the right gear. There are many spots to get in—just circle the perimeter and get in where you can. Turn off Highway 101 at the west beach area on Camp David Jr. Road, then drive approximately 1.5 miles to the North Shore Day-Use Area. There's camping down there, along with picnic tables, a grill, and a dock with a panoramic view of the lake and the Olympic Mountains.

>> Rent snowboards, surfboards, and wetsuits at North By Northwest Surf Co (902 S Lincoln Street, Port Angeles; nxnwsurf.com; 360-452-5144). During the summer, they also have a popup store in Hobuck Beach Resort in Neah Bay.

LAKE CRESCENT LODGE

416 Lake Crescent Road, Port Angeles • www.olympicnationalparks.com/lodging/lake-crescent-lodge • 1-888-896-3818

Built in 1915, this historical lodge sits on the south shore of Lake Crescent, next to the easy Moments in Time trail. There are cabins, rooms, and cottages on the property, no TVs, and internet access only in the lobby, so get outside already. Bring a book, too, and enjoy a cup of tea and some reading time in the idyllic sunroom. Rent boats and paddleboards at the dock. You can eat at the certified green restaurant, open for all three meals April through January. Pet-friendly accommodations available for a $25 fee.

LOG CABIN RESORT

3183 E Beach Road, Port Angeles • www.olympicnationalparks.com/lodging/log-cabin-resort • 1-888-896-3818 • Open end of May–September

From the more chi-chi two-bedroom kitchenette cabins and lakeside chalet to the plumbing-free camper cabins, Log Cabin Resort offers a range of accommodations. Some are next to Lake Crescent, some are a little bit farther away, all are close. These are great for group rentals. Pet-friendly accommodations are available.

FAIRHOLME CAMPGROUND

Olympic National Park Visitor Center • 360-564-3130

There are 88 first-come-first-served lakeside campsites on the western tip of Lake Crescent, with access to Fairholme Beach. It's a popular campground, so come early to get your spot. Includes potable water, restrooms, and a picnic table and fire pit at each site. National Parking Pass required, $20 per night.

Hot Springs

OLYMPIC HOT SPRINGS

4.8 miles round-trip • Elevation gain: 600 feet • Appleton Pass Trailhead: 47.9775, -123.6925

An easy hike on a paved path, across a log bridge over Crystal Creek and then another bridge over Boulder Creek. Once you cross that bridge, there are 21 hot spring pools along the trail to try out. They tend to be shallow at 1-foot depth. The biggest one is about 100 yards up the hill from the trail's end. Bathing suit optional. National Park Pass required. Check Washington Trails Association (www.wta.org) for road alerts. Nearest town: Port Angeles.

// Sol Duc Falls, Olympic Peninsula

SOL DUC HOT SPRINGS

12076 Sol Duc Hot Springs Road • www.olympicnationalparks.com • 360-327-3583

Soak in the three mineral pools, each with a different temperature, plus a freshwater pool. The last is generally between 50 and 85°F, while the other three are kept at different temperatures, the coldest being 99°F, the hottest at a toasty 104. Like all neato and easily accessible outdoor activities, there are times of great business, shoulder season, and the off-season, when there's a little more quiet to be found. Once you've reached max wrinkleyness, get out for lunch at the Poolside Deli. $15, or free if staying at the Sol Duc Hot Springs Resort.

STAY AT SOL DUC HOT SPRINGS RESORT 12076 Sol Duc Hot Springs Road • www.olympicnationalparks.com • 360-327-3583

Rent a cabin so you don't have to go too far from mineral springs to bed to the Springs Restaurant and around again.

SEQUIM

FROM SEATTLE: 2.25 HOURS · DAYS HERE: 1-PLUS

EAT	DRINK	DO	BUY
charcuterie	Italian wine	hike Dungeness Spit	anything with lavender

☰ *Getting There*

BY CAR | Drive south on I-5 S for 32 miles to Exit 133. Drive on WA-16 W and WA-3 N for approximately 54 miles, then drive on WA-104 W and Highway 101 N for another 36 miles. (Total miles: 122; approximate travel time 2.25 hours.)

BY FERRY | Take the Seattle–Bainbridge Ferry to Bainbridge, then drive on WA-3 N in Poulsbo for 14 miles to WA-104 W and Highway 101 N. Drive for another 42 miles or so. (Total miles: 66; approximate travel time 2.25 hours.)

BY BUS | From the Seattle Greyhound Bus Terminal, take the Dungeness Line to Sequim. Travel time: 3 hours. Cost: $83 round-trip (1-800-457-4492; www.olympicbuslines.com).

☰ *Plan Around*

SEQUIM LAVENDER FESTIVAL

July · www.lavenderfestival.com

A three-day celebration of the sensory experience of lavender. There are some great events the week before, such as Lavender Afternoon Tea and Brunch in the Blooms. Many of the local lavender farms will host beer and wine gardens and serve lavender-seasoned food, such as lavender tamales, lavender sausages, and, of course, lavender lemonade and cookies.

JAMESTOWN S'KLALLAM TOTEM TOUR

June or July · www.bensbikessequim.com/totem-tour-recumbent-rally

Visit more than 40 totem poles in a 30-mile ride along the Olympic Discovery Trail and local bike paths in Blyn and by 7 Cedars Resort.

TOUR DE LAVENDER

August • tourdelavender.com • 971-704-1156

Choose from the 35-mile "family fun" ride or the Metric Century, then bike your buns off to local lavender farms, along the Olympic Discovery Trail, and around the Sequim–Dungeness Valley. $60.

>> For a bike tune-up, a bike rental, or some detailed maps of bike routes in the area, stop by **Ben's Bikes** or call them up for a special bike delivery (1251 W Washington Street, Sequim; www.bensbikessequim.com; 360-683-2666).

>> Take the **Olympic Culinary Loop** (www.olympicculinaryloop.com), a food-centric self-guided tour of the Olympic Peninsula.

Eat & Drink

Get Caffeinated

ADAGIO BEAN & LEAF

881 E Washington Street, Sequim • m.adagiobeanandleaf.com • 360-582-0024 • Open daily 6 a.m.–7 p.m.

Handcrafted coffee and tea drinks, pastries and sandwiches, fresh salads, daily specials, and dog treats for Lucy. Sit in the main café, on the outdoor patio, or in the reading room, or drive up to the drive-thru window to get a sandwich or muffin to go. Bonus: bidet in the bathroom.

RAINSHADOW COFFEE ROASTING COMPANY

157 W Cedar Street, Sequim • www.rainshadowcoffee.com • 360-681-0650 • Open Monday–Saturday 8 a.m.–4 p.m.

Coffee roasted in small batches, using 100 percent Grade I, directly traded and handpicked Arabica beans. Come in for a cup of joe roasted on-site and some fresh-baked goodies, a bowl of homemade soup, or a breakfast burrito.

Farm Fresh

SEQUIM FARMERS' MARKET

Civic Center Plaza, N Sequim Avenue, Sequim • sequimmarket.com • 360-582-6218 • Open May–October, Saturday 9 a.m.–3 p.m.

Most of the 60 vendors are from Sequim proper, with the leftovers being slightly farther afield in the Olympic Peninsula. Lots of art, crafts, jewelry, and nontraditional leashes, cute collars, and harnesses from Canine Connected.

>> Stop by the **Olympic Peninsula Authors** booth at Sequim Farmers' Market to buy a book by a local writer.

DUNGENESS VALLEY CREAMERY

Farm store: 1915 Towne Road, Sequim • www.dungenessvalleycreamery.com • 360-683-0716 • Open Monday–Saturday 10 a.m.–5 p.m.

A family-owned and -operated dairy since 1971. Get certified raw milk and cream from their team of Jersey cows, which you can meet at the farm itself, right behind the store! Also pick up beef, eggs, and aged garden manure to take home.

PACIFIC PANTRY ARTISAN DELI

229 S Sequim Avenue, Sequim • 360-797-1221 • Open Monday–Saturday 11 a.m.–7 p.m.

A charcuterie and café where you can find brats and sausages made from Washington pasture-raised pork, as well as fresh sandwiches, salads, and craft beers. Stop by on your way out of town to get some house-cured meat and canned mustards.

Dining

DOCKSIDE GRILL

2577 W Sequim Bay Road, Sequim • www.docksidegrill-sequim.com • 360-683-7510 • Open Wednesday–Thursday lunch: 11:30 a.m.–3 p.m., apps only: 3–4 p.m., dinner: 4–8 p.m.

Enjoy epic views of Sequim Bay as you eat iterations of shellfish. Not into seafood? Get the chicken parm or some delightful pasta.

ALDER WOOD BISTRO

139 W Alder Street, Sequim • alderwoodbistro.com • 360-683-4321 • Open Wednesday–Sunday lunch: 11:30 a.m.–2:30 p.m., dinner: 4:30–8:30 p.m.

Walk the brick path through a lavender patch to get to the front door. Alder Wood Bistro uses local organic, sustainable ingredients, and they aren't shy about wood-firing their foods. Get the focaccia pizza of the day for lunch and, in the summer, eat in the garden courtyard.

NOURISH SEQUIM

101 Provence View Lane, Sequim • nourishsequim.com • 360-797-1480 • Open Wednesday–Saturday 11:30 a.m.–8:30 p.m., Sunday 11 a.m.–8:30 p.m.

A dedicated gluten-free zone, with veggies grown on-site at Bell House Farm, established in 1880, to supplement the organic produce, kindly raised meat, and sustainably harvested seafood that rotates on the seasonal menu. Tour the herb and vegetable gardens, then drink a Farm Margarita or Lavender Princess cocktail and eat a farm-fresh entrée at the homey restaurant, or call or email in advance to place an order with the Dine at Home program—get the same amazing food for a reasonable price, all boxed up and ready for you to enjoy at your campsite or B&B field picnic.

Booze and Beyond

WIND ROSE CELLARS

143 W Washington, Sequim • windrosecellars.com • 360-681-0690

If an Italian varietal is grown in Washington State, doesn't that make it Italian American? Taste Italian American wines crafted with food pairing in mind. Come on a Friday or Saturday night for live music. Hours and bistro menu change seasonally.

# *Stay Over*

GREENHOUSE INN BY THE BAY

630 Marine Drive, Sequim • greenhousebythebay.com • 360-504-2489

An inn with all the amenities, views of the mountains of Olympic National Park or Dungeness Bay, and friendly hosts. After a long day of hiking/biking/lavender farm sight-seeing, take a soak in the tub and/or order (in advance) an in-room massage.

CLARK'S CHAMBERS B&B

322 Clark Road, Sequim • clarkschambersbandb.com • 360-683-4431

Stay on the oldest continuously operated farm in Washington State. In the late 1990s, sisters Glenda Clark and Belinda Chambers turned the farmhouse into a bed & breakfast, maintaining the old-timey feel—much of the restored furniture is over 100 years old, and the wallpaper harkens to simpler times. $125.

DUNGENESS BARN HOUSE B&B AT TWO CROWS FARM

42 Marine Drive, Sequim • dungenessbarnhouse.com • 360-582-1663

The glorious views on the Olympic Mountains and Strait of Juan de Fuca just don't get old. The Dungeness Barn House B&B has its own private beach on Dungeness Bay, gorgeous flower and lavender gardens to stroll through, and the breakfasts are made from produce grown on-site and from other local farms. $140–230.

>> For more rental and B&B information, go to sequimrentals.com and olympicpeninsulabedand breakfast.com

Camping

DUNGENESS RECREATION AREA

554 Voice of America Road W, Sequim • www.clallam.net • 360-683-5847

Camp at one of the 66 first-come-first-served campsites available for year-round camping on a bluff above the Strait of Juan de Fuca in this 216-acre park. Includes two restrooms, potable water, and coin-operated showers.

SALT CREEK

3506 Camp Hayden Road, Port Angeles • www.clallam.net • 360-683-5847

West of the Dungeness Recreation Area, this is another first-come-first-served campground located on a bluff above the Strait of Juan de Fuca. The park itself is 196 acres and includes tide pools and sports courts and fields, along with two restrooms, potable water, and coin-operated showers.

 *While You're Here*

TRAVEL THE LAVENDER TRAIL

sequimlavender.org

The rain shadow of the Olympic Peninsula makes for an ideal lavender-growing climate (and wine grape–growing climate, and produce growing, etc.). Walk through waving fields of purple glory, your nose in ecstasy. Take the Sequim Lavender Trail to visit them all.

>> Most of the farms sell lovely lavender culinary and bath and body products. Eat lavender ice cream at Purple Haze Lavender Farm (180 Bell Bottom Road, Sequim; purplehazelavender .com; 360-683-1714) and purchase pet products at Victor's Lavender (3743 Old Olympic Highway, Port Angeles; victorslavender.com; 360-683-7830).

HIKE THE DUNGENESS SPIT

Dungeness National Wildlife Refuge, 554 Voice of America Road, Sequim • 11 miles round-trip •
Elevation gain: 130 feet • Open 7 a.m.–dusk

If you want to look at the longest natural sand spit in the United States, then hike down
from the wooded parking lot area to the beach and feast your eyes on this strange deposi-
tion bar, the Dungeness Lighthouse, and Dungeness Harbor, the small body of water the
spit mostly encloses. But why stop there? The walk to the lighthouse is flat, and you might
just spot some funky birds such as the red-necked grebe or black oyster catchers, amphib-
ians such as the rough-skinned newt, or other animal friends such as the harbor seal or
chickaree. Look but don't touch—this is a wildlife refuge, after all. Accessibility depends on

ABOVE & BEYOND

Dogs | **Sequim Dog Park** (202 N Blake Avenue, Sequim; www.sequimdogparks.org)
is a 1-acre dog park with separate fenced-in areas for small and large dogs, a bathroom,
benches, and doggie cleanup bags. Locals love it so much it even has its own website.

Skates | When it comes to **Sequim Skatepark** (E Cedar Street and N Blake Avenue,
Sequim), Skate Dan says, "If you think of it as a ditch, this place is pretty rad." It has a few
interesting transitions and a couple of flat rails.

Books | With puzzles and arts and crafts, along with twice-loved paperbacks, **Twice Loved
Books** (353 Bell Street, Sequim; 360-681-4937) is a cute cottage bookstore. It's open
Tuesday–Saturday 10 a.m.–4 p.m.

Good to Know |

· Sequim is home to the oldest remains of a mastodon in the Americas. It's called the
  Manis Mastodon site after local farmer Emanuel Manis, who found the tusks on his
  farm in 1977.

· Pilots call Sequim "the blue hole" because it is protected from extreme weather by the
  Olympic Mountains to the southwest.

Been There, Done That |

· For Forks, see page 160.

· For the Hood Canal on the east side of the Olympic Peninsula, see page 44.

· For Bainbridge Island, in the Kitsap Peninsula to the east of the Hood Canal, see
  page 125.

· For Whidbey Island and Camano Island, in the Kitsap Peninsula to the east of the
  Hood Canal, see page 249.

the tides, so check before you visit at the US Fish and Wildlife Service website at www.fws
.gov. $3 per group of up to four.

VISIT OLYMPIC GAME FARM

1423 Ward Road, Sequim • olygamefarm.com • 360-683-4295 • Open Sunday–Friday 9 a.m.–5 p.m.,
Saturday 9 a.m.–6 p.m.

Originally called Disney's Wild Animal Ranch, Olympic Game Farm was a "filming farm" for
Walt Disney Studios. Today, some of the animals are rescues, some are "overflow" from other
facilities, and some are gifts or donations—whatever that means. You can take a walking tour
or a driving tour. Be sure to bring some bread—wheat or whole grain—to feed the animals.
There are bison, elk, yaks, bobcats and lynx, Arctic foxes, coyotes, timberwolves, peacocks,
tigers and lions, oh my! When the bears are waving at you, that means they want bread. All
proceeds from ticket sales go to caring for the animals. $15.

GAMBLE AT 7 CEDARS CASINO

270756 Highway 101, Sequim • www.7cedarsresort.com • 360-683-7777

Tired of all that damn fresh air? Then head into 7 Cedars Casino, where you can lose all your
money and love every minute of it. Check the casino's events calendar for bingo games, blackjack and poker tournaments, comedy night, live music, and more. There are two casino restaurants, dining on the Dungeness Golf Course, and a market and deli.

PORT ANGELES

FROM SEATTLE: 2.75 HOURS · DAYS HERE: 1-PLUS

EAT	DRINK	DO	BUY
blackberry pie	fresh juice	swim in Lake Crescent	comic books

Getting There

BY CAR | Drive south on I-5 S for 32 miles to Exit 133. Drive on WA-16 W and WA-3 N for approximately 54 miles, then drive on WA-104 W and Highway 101 N for another 52 miles. (Total distance: 138 miles; approximate travel time 2.5 hours.)

BY FERRY | Take the Edmond–Kingston Ferry to Kingston, then drive on WA-104 W for approximately 9 miles. Continue on Highway 101 N for another 52 miles or so. (Total distance: 85 miles; approximate travel time 2.75 hours.)

BY BUS | From the Seattle Greyhound Bus Terminal, take the Dungeness Line to Port Angeles. Travel time: 3.25 hours. (1-800-457-4492; www.olympicbuslines.com; cost: $83 round-trip.)

Stay Over

B&Bs

DOMAINE MADELEINE BED & BREAKFAST

146 Wildflower Lane, Port Angeles • domainemadeleine.com • 360-457-4174

A luxury waterfront B&B with stellar sea views, natural murals above the comfy beds, jetted tubs and steam saunas, private gardens, personalized breakfasts and snacks to order, and bikes to rent. Make it romantic by getting an in-room couples massage or a four-course breakfast for two. $279–569.

GEORGE WASHINGTON INN & ESTATE

939 Finn Hall Road, Port Angeles • georgewashingtoninn.com • 360-452-5207

Get fancy at this sprawling B&B, located on 10 acres of oceanfront farmland including Washington Lavender Farm. The inn was built to resemble President Georgie W's Mount Vernon,

1 Domaine Madeleine, Port Angeles
2 The Nasty Habits, Port Angeles
3 Domaine Madeleine, Port Angeles

with rooms named in honor of the Father but with technology much more advanced than wooden teeth. You can book whale-watching and biking packages through the inn as well as get special lavender bath and body baskets and snack packs.

>>   Take the **Olympic Culinary Loop** (www.olympicculinaryloop.com), a food-centric self-guided tour of the Olympic Peninsula.

≡ *Plan Around*

DUNGENESS CRAB & SEAFOOD FESTIVAL

October • Port Angeles City Pier, 221 N Lincoln Street, Port Angeles • crabfestival.org • 360-452-6300

For one October weekend, "embrace your inner crab" at this acclaimed food festival located on the Port Angeles waterfront. The city is known for its whole Dungeness crab dinners, after all. Taste the crabtastic fares of local restaurants, watch cooking demos, participate in the chowder cook-off and Grab-a-Crab Derby, and experience the crafts and music of the community. Entrance is free, but for the low price of $30 you can get a ticket to the full crab dinner, where you will eat a whole, fresh Dungeness crab, some local corn on the cob, and organic coleslaw. Don't forget to buy a bib.

>>   **The Nasty Habits** is a local OP '80s and '90s cover band. To see if they're playing a show while you're in town (or if you want to plan your trip around their schedule), go to thenastyhabits.com.

≡ *Eat & Drink*

Get Caffeinated

BELLA ROSA COFFEE HOUSE

403 S Lincoln Street, Port Angeles • 360-417-5402 • Open Monday–Friday 6:30 a.m.–9 p.m., Saturday 7 a.m.–9 p.m., Sunday 7 a.m.–7 p.m.

Good coffee and excellent crêpes, both sweet and savory. The baked goods are fresh and the iced coffee and tea drinks are perfect for pre- or post-bike ride refreshment.

>>   Stop by **Celestial Espresso** coffee stand to grab a cup of drip and a muffin before getting on the ferry (111 Railroad Avenue, Port Angeles).

BADA NW COFFEE BAR

118 West 1st Street, Port Angeles • www.bada-nw.com • 360-797-1658 • Open Sunday–Wednesday 6:30 a.m.–8 p.m., Thursday–Saturday 6:30 a.m.–9 p.m.

Serving breakfasts and lunch seven days a week. Good biscuits, good burgers, good bar bites— bagel dog, chicken bacon pretzel melt—and good beer. Try the Bada NW Shake, a white coffee mixed with peanut butter, oats, chocolate protein, and banana, or get a coffee-infused cocktail to find the halfway point between upper and downer to drink on the outdoor patio.

THE BLACKBIRD COFFEEHOUSE

336 E 8th Street, Port Angeles • www.theblackbirdcoffeehouse.com • 360-452-3999 • Open Monday–Friday 6:30 a.m.–5 p.m., Saturday and Sunday 7:30 a.m.–5 p.m.

Been missing your Stumptown? Then come down to Blackbird to get your fix. As always with Stumptown Coffee Roasters, get the Hair Bender. All baked goods are made in-house, and there are plenty of gluten-free options for those in need. Good salads and smoothies using Pacific Northwest produce, too.

Farm Fresh

PORT ANGELES FARMERS' MARKET

133 E Front Street, Port Angeles • farmersmarketportangeles.com • 360-460-0361 • Open year-round, Saturday 10 a.m.–2 p.m.

Dining

BLACKBERRY CAFÉ

50530 WA-112, Port Angeles • 360-928-0141 • Open daily 7 a.m.–8 p.m.

A down-home roadside café, known for all things blackberry, in particular their fresh home-made blackberry pie. All-day breakfast, burgers, fries, and shakes are classic, without all the frills, and a reminder of simpler times.

COYOTE BBQ PUB

201 E Front Street, Port Angeles • coyotebbqpub.com • 360-477-4947 • Open Sunday–Thursday 11 a.m.–8 p.m., Friday–Saturday 11 a.m.– 9 p.m., or until they sell out

From two Texas transplants comes succulent West Texas BBQ. You don't have to choose between the 12-hour hickory- and oak-smoked prime brisket or the 14-hour pulled pork—just get the "Texas roundup" plate. Definitely order the chocolate peanut butter brownie with

// Coyote BBQ Pub, Port Angeles

house bacon crumbles. The vibe is steampunk adjacent, with pipe fixtures and tall ceilings and windows, plus five big-screen TVs on which you can watch your various sportsballs. Call 48 hours in advance to get whole smoked meats to go. Pets welcome on outdoor patio.

NEW DAY EATERY

102 W Front Street, Port Angeles • 360-504-2924 • Open Monday–Saturday 8 a.m.–4 p.m.

A fresh and clean breakfast and lunch joint with a commitment to organics and lots of options for the modern picky eater. Juices and smoothies are made fresh at the juice bar and named in the vein of '90s sitcom *Friends* (The Lemon Chia Seed One, The Very Green One), and meats are house-smoked and house-braised. For breakfast get the vegan pumpkin "Belgium" waffle or the gluten-free "Belgium" waffle, because when will you ever run into such foods again? For lunch, try any of their meaty or veggie burgers, all dressed to impress.

BELLA ITALIA

118 E 1st Street, Port Angeles • bellaitaliapa.com • 360-457-5442 • Open daily at 5 p.m.

Established almost 10 years before Edward and Bella's first date, this cozy Italian eatery sources locally as much as possible, bringing in halibut caught in Neah Bay, Quillette king salmon, and shellfish from the Hood Canal, plus mushrooms from the Olympic Forest and produce from farms in Sequim and nearby. Obviously get Bella's Mushroom Ravioli.

Booze and Beyond

OLYMPIC CELLARS WINERY

255410 Highway 101, Port Angeles • olympiccellars.com • 360-452-0160 • Open November–March, daily 11 a.m.–5 p.m.; April–October, daily 11 a.m.–6 p.m.

A boutique heritage winery in which the Washington-grown grapes are shoveled and then punched down by hand. You can try them year-round in the big barn and/or come to the summertime Saturday concerts; the proceeds of ticket sales are donated to local nonprofits.

CAMARADERIE CELLARS

334 Benson Road, Port Angeles • camaraderiecellars.com • 360-417-3564 • Open May–October, Friday–Sunday 11 a.m.–5 p.m.

For over 25 years, this boutique winery has used "oak to frame the picture," which means they use oak barrels but believe it's less about the barrel and more about the grape. Or something like that. Anyway, they love their Eastern Washington growers, cool fermentations, and the whole slow process that makes their wine perfect for pairing. To keep things fresh, they've made different kinds of wines, from riesling to classic bordeaux varieties to Italians and Spanish.

HARBINGER WINERY

2358 Highway 101 W, Port Angeles • www.harbingerwinery.com • 360-452-4262 • Tasting room hours: daily 11 a.m.–6 p.m.

A former logging truck stop, Harbinger Winery offers a whole bunch of classic and unique varietals. Try the award-winning syrah, bolero, and white table wine, plus the seasonal Bliss series, table wines comprising fresh Northwest raspberries, cranberries, and blackberries.

≡ *While You're Here*

SKI/SNOWBOARD/TUBE HURRICANE RIDGE

hurricaneridge.com • 848-667-7669 • Summit elevation: 5,240 feet

From Port Angeles, drive 17 miles south on Highway 101 into Olympic National Park and on to Hurricane Ridge Parkway. The area receives around 400 inches of snow per year, and the winter season is from mid-December through March, open on Saturdays and Sundays. Hurricane Ridge is much more chill than the more popular Whistler or Snoqualmie, with some mellow runs as well as bigger bowls and glades. There's no lodge, but you can get snacks in the Hurricane Ridge Visitor Center, which is worth the trip in and of itself because of the mile-

ABOVE & BEYOND

Dogs | The volunteers who fund and run **Lincoln Park** (1469-1737 W Lauridsen Boulevard; wa-portangeles.civicplus.com/Facilities/Facility/Details/Lincoln-Park-22; 360-417-4550;) are rightfully proud of it. It features picnic tables, small dog and large dog fenced-in areas, trees, and some walking trails.

Skate | **Port Angeles Skatepark** can be found between E 4th Street and S Race Street in Port Angeles.

Books | Boasting one of the largest magazine selections on the West Coast, **Port Book and News** (104 E 1st Street, Port Angeles; www.portbooknews.com; 360-452-6367) also has over 75,000 books, maps, and more. It's open Monday–Thursday 8 a.m.–7 p.m., Friday and Saturday 8 a.m.–8 p.m., and Sunday 9 a.m.–5 p.m.

There's a big selection of used and new books at **Odyssey Bookshop** (114 W Front Street, Port Angeles; 360-475-1045), plus games and other doodads. Puppets too. It's open Monday–Saturday 9 a.m.–7 p.m., Sunday 10 a.m.–5 p.m.

Anime, manga, games, and in-store events such as Pokémon League and Dungeons & Dragons make **Anime Kat** (114 W 1st Street, Port Angeles; www.animekat.com; 360-797-1313) special. They also buy and sell new and retro video games. They're open Monday, Wednesday, and Friday 11 a.m.–10 p.m.; and Tuesday, Thursday, and Saturday 11 a.m.–7 p.m.

Not Ready to Go Home | Take the Coho Black Ball Ferry from Port Angeles to Victoria, BC. It's a 90-minute, 22.6-nautical-mile trip through the Strait of Juan de Fuca. $18 one way (www.cohoferry.com).

Good to Know | Port Angeles includes 10 square miles of land and 53 square miles of water.

Been There, Done That |
· For Forks, see page 160.
· For the Hood Canal, on the east side of the Olympic Peninsula, see page 44.
· For Bainbridge Island, in the Kitsap Peninsula to the east of the Hood Canal, see page 125.
· For Whidbey Island and Camano Island, in the Kitsap Peninsula to the east of the Hood Canal, see page 249.

high viewpoint it gives you. Parking: $15 per car, or $30 for a yearly parking pass; $13–32 for day passes; $225 for a seasonal pass.

HIKE MARYMERE FALLS

1.8 miles round-trip • Elevation gain: 500 feet

Park at the large parking area with the sign for Marymere Falls and Lake Crescent, located on the south shore of the lake. At the Storm King Ranger Station to the east of the Lake Crescent Lodge and Beach, walk on the paved path through old-growth forest for 0.5 mile, then take a left to hike upstream, soon to turn right toward Marymere Falls. You can choose to either look up at the 90-foot-high waterfall from the lower platform, or walk up to the hillside to look down. Or do both. No park pass required.

>> To **encounter ghosts** of Port Angeles's past, take a tour with Port Angeles Underground Heritage Tours (121 E Railroad Avenue; www.portangelesheritagetours.com; 360-460-5748).

LA PUSH

FROM SEATTLE: 4 HOURS • DAYS HERE: 2-PLUS

EAT	DRINK	DO	BUY
salmon at River's Edge Restaurant	a glass of wine or whiskey while watching the storm	storm watch	firewood

The Quileute Tribe has lived in the La Push area for a thousand years, long before the world met Jacob Black and his pack of werewolves. The town is remote, 45 miles from Hoh Rain Forest and 12 miles from the city of Forks. The Pacific Ocean and the beaches of La Push are glorious year-round, with summertime being the best time for beach hikes, when the probability of your boots drying out is much higher. November through March is when storm watching is at its peak, and January is a popular month for daredevils, cold-loving surfers, and sea kayakers.

≡ *Getting There*

BY CAR | Take I-5 S for 32 miles, then continue on WA-16 W, WA-3 N, WA-104 W, and Highway 101 for 160 miles. Get on WA-110/La Push Road and drive for approximately 14 miles. Travel time: approximately four hours.

BY BIKE | Start the Olympic Discovery Trail in Port Angeles and ride for 130 miles.

≡ *Plan Around*

QUILEUTE DAYS

July

Come for the traditional fish bake, dancing, and stick games, watch the parade and outboard canoe races, eat good food, and buy some arts and crafts. There will be fireworks.

WHALE WATCHING

April–May

Simply stand on the beach and be patient, and you might just see orcas or humpbacks doing their thing. At Kalaloch Lodge, May is the unofficial Whale-Watching Month—gray whales do a drive-by as they migrate from Baja, California, to Alaska.

>> For more information on whale migration along the Pacific Coast, visit **The Whale Trail** at thewhaletrail.org.

STORM WATCHING

November–March

Rent a cabin, pour yourself a glass of something, and sit by the fireside to watch the waves pounding the shore. The violence of the ocean is all the more incredible when watched from a safe and warm distance.

Eat & Drink

RIVER'S EDGE RESTAURANT

41 Main Street, La Push • 360-374-5777 • Open daily 8 a.m.–9 p.m.

Known for their fresh seafood and incredible views of James Island and eagles and otters down in the marina. Get the salmon, either in entrée or salad or burger form, or really any of the other fish or shellfish options, and try the Indian fry bread for breakfast. This is the only restaurant in La Push, so enjoy!

Stay Over

QUILEUTE OCEANSIDE RESORT

330 Ocean Front Drive, La Push • quileuteoceanside.com • 1-800-487-1267

Equipped and appointed in Native American style, the 33 oceanfront cabins, two motel units, and 10 camper cabins of Quileute Oceanside Resort are right up from First Beach, as are the campground and two RV parks on-site. The cabins have fireplaces and incredible views, a great combo only improved by a bottle of wine. You'll be storm watching, not TV watching, so you won't miss the absence of televisions. WiFi available only in the main office. $69–299.

LONESOME CREEK STORE

490 Ocean Drive, La Push • 360-374-4338 • Open Monday–Thursday 6 a.m.–9 p.m., Friday and Saturday 6 a.m.–9:30 p.m., Sunday 7 a.m.–9 p.m.

Pick up ingredients for a beachside cookout or a wintertime in-cabin dinner at this little convenience store, which just so happens to be the only one around.

ABOVE & BEYOND

Good to Know |
- La Push has the westernmost ZIP code in the continental United States.
- There are no bike shops in La Push. For the closest bike shop, go the Olympic Peninsula Bicycle Alliance website (olympicpeninsulacycling.com).

Been There, Done That | Forks (page 160) is only 15 miles away, to the east.

≡ *While You're Here*

Take a Kayak Tour of the Quillayute Estuary

RAINFOREST PADDLERS

February–September • www.rainforestpaddlers.com • 360-374-9288

Take a three-hour tour of the route people have been kayaking for a thousand years. As you travel down the Quillayute River, you're bound to see a bald eagle or an otter, and if you're really lucky, an elk on shore or a whale way off near the La Push sea stacks. Tour conveniently ends near River's Edge Restaurant. $59–69.

>> Want more kayak tours? Rainforest Paddlers can take you on a rafting trip on the Elwha River, Sol Duc River, or the Hoh River. Or, for a self-guided tour, you can rent a kayak and gear for $11 per hour/$29 per day.

SURF

At the end of La Push Road/WA-110 and south of the mouth of the Quillayute River is a little cove, relatively sheltered from the rawer, more exposed parts of the coast in the area. Summertime is the best time for surfers of all levels, but if you're brave/experienced, come during January's Surf Frolic.

12

Waters of the San Juan Islands

In the 1790s, some white dude from Spain showed up and named an area that had already been populated for a couple thousand years after a viceroy back in España. More than 200 years later, in 2013, President Obama designated the more than a thousand acres of the San Juan Islands a national monument. Situated in the Salish Sea, with Seattle to the south, Bellingham to the east, Vancouver, British Columbia, to the north, and Victoria, British Columbia, to the west, San Juan County includes approximately 478 miles of shoreline, and the archipelago includes more than 400 islands, only 172 of which are officially named. Most of these islands are too small to set up the things most modern folks tend to expect—beds with clean sheets, farm-to-fork restaurants with well-curated wine lists, WiFi—but Orcas Island, San Juan Island, and Lopez Island have everything a city slicker craving outdoor adventure could want.

The area also has everything a whale could want. Some claim that San Juan County is the best place in the world to see orca, a.k.a. killer whales, all year-round. There are three pods, called the Southern Residents, who frolic spring through fall, while a group called the Transients come and go. The calm inland Salish Sea makes the area ideal for boaters who want to be near the whales and other animals that inhabit the area.

Orcas Island is the largest of the islands at 57 square miles. The main towns are Eastsound and Olga, and beyond that, it's a green rural landscape, including 5,252-acre Moran State Park.

San Juan Island is a close second in terms of size, with popular Roche Harbor. The county seat of Friday Harbor is the most populated town of the islands and hosts the Whale Museum (page 223), the first museum in the country dedicated to species living in the wild.

On **Lopez Island**, the Seattle Freeze will be but a distant memory. These mellow, friendly folk of Lopez are proud of their hometown's nickname, "Slowpez." They call themselves "Slowpezians," and they do this weird thing of smiling and waving to one another as they pass by. It's considered a **biking island** because its terrain is mostly level.

☰ *Getting Here*

BY SEAPLANE | From Seattle: Book a flight to San Juan Island, Orcas Island, or Lopez Island on Kenmore Air (1-866-435-9524; kenmoreair.com). You can catch the plane in one of four Seattle-area locations: Lake Union in the Westlake neighborhood, Lake Washington in Kenmore, Boeing Field, or Sea-Tac airport. Tickets are really not all that expensive, from $169 one-way.

From Anacortes or Bellingham: Take San Juan Airlines (1-800-874-4434; www.sanjuan airlines.com) to Orcas Island, Lopez Island, or Friday Harbor or Roche Harbor on San Juan Island. $65–89 one-way.

BY WASHINGTON STATE FERRY | From Anacortes, take the ferry to San Juan Island at Friday Harbor, Orcas Island, Lopez Island, or Shaw Island. Reservations recommended (www.wsdot.wa.gov). $13.50 for walk-on, add $4 for a bike. Motorcycle $18.90, vehicles $44.15–55.20.

// Orcas Island, the San Juan Islands

BY PERSONAL WATERCRAFT | Get in anywhere in the Puget Sound, Salish Sea, or the Pacific Ocean. You better know what you're doing. For information on the Cascadia Marine Trail, see below.

BY SHUTTLE | Catch a ride from Sea-Tac Airport or downtown Seattle with Island Airporter (360-378-7438; www.islandairporter.com; operates Monday–Friday; $50–67) or Bellair Shuttle (1-866-235-5247; www.airporter.com; operates daily, $33–82).

BETWEEN ISLANDS | For an interisland water taxi or charter, hire Outer Island Excursions (outerislandx.com). $150–400.

≡ *Highlight Reel*

CASCADIA MARINE TRAIL

For ten thousand years or so, people traveled the Salish Sea, Puget Sound, and Hood Canal. Get in your human- or wind-powered watercraft and carry on the tradition of exploring 150 miles of waterways, and stop by the 66 designated campsites and 160 day-use sites along the way. For information and maps, visit the Washington Water Trails Association at www.wwta.org.

EXPLORE THE ISLANDS ON BOAT

From wee 1-acre Posey Island and 3-acre Blind Island to 814-acre Sucia Island (360-376-2073), there are many islands of varying sizes on which you can pitch a tent. Most of the campsites are primitive, with no potable water or garbage service, and you can only get there by boat. For more information about these parks, visit parks.state.wa.us.

KAYAK ADVENTURES

It is mandatory that, while on in the San Juans, you take a kayak tour. There's a very high chance that you'll spot eagles, harbor seals and porpoises, ducks, and other marine animals, and if you're really lucky, you'll see an orca up close and personal. Through most of the kayak tours, you'll probably get to visit one of the many outer islands that are accessible only by boat. Some ask you to bring a lunch; others will cook up a beachside feast. Most tours, if not all, do not require prior experience. Bring phones at your own risk.

OUTER ISLAND EXCURSIONS KAYAKING

54 Hunt Road, Eastsound, Orcas Island • outerislandx.com • 360-376-3711

Offers kayak rentals and three-hour or all-day tours. The shorter tour leaves from Smuggler's Villa Resort and goes around St. Doughty State Park; the all-day tour includes a powerboat shuttle to Sucia Island, where you'll launch for a paddle around the island, eat lunch, and take a hike. $79–159.

// Kayaking in the Puget Sound

SHEARWATER KAYAK TOURS

138 North Beach Road, Eastsound, Orcas Island • shearwaterkayaks.com • 360-376-4699

Take a three-hour tour, an all-day tour, or design a custom one with this 35-plus-year-old kayak tour company. $85–120.

SPRING BAY ON ORCAS ISLAND KAYAK TOURS

464 Spring Bay Trail, Olga, Orcas Island • springbayonorcas.com • 360-376-5531

Two-hour tours launching directly from their private bay, morning and evening. You can also rent the private cabin, and so wake up and get in the kayak from there. $45.

OUTDOOR ADVENTURE CENTER

Lopez Island • www.outdooradventurecenter.com • 425-883-9039

Paddle at a leisurely pace for a three-hour sea tour of 2 or 3 miles of protected shoreline, with much opportunity for spotting bald eagles, porpoises, herons, and moon jellies.

>> Go on a three-day **Northwest Craft Beer Tasting and Kayaking Tour** or a three-day **Yoga and Kayaking Tour** with Outdoor Odysseys (www.outdoorodysseys.com).

WATCHING WHALES

It is mandatory that you watch some whales. See humpback whales, minke whales, gray whales, and resident and transient orcas, along with the other friends of mermaids—dolphins, porpoises, and seals. Bald eagles, too.

MAYA'S LEGACY

sanjuanislandwhalewatch.com • 360-378-7996

Snug Harbor Marina and Resort, 1997 Mitchell Bay Road, Friday Harbor, San Juan Island

Friday Harbor Marina, #14 Cannery Landing, Friday Harbor, San Juan Island

Step off the ferry on San Juan Island and onto the boat. Knowledgeable captain and marine naturalists will provide interesting factoids, and the hydrophones will allow you to hear the whales. Year-round, $119–129.

DEER HARBOR CHARTERS

deerharborcharters.com • 360-376-5989

A three- to four-hour tour, with seasonal and changing tours depending on the movement of these big wild animals. Naturalists, blankets and binoculars, and bathroom onboard. Sailing tours, wine-tasting sunset cruises, and private charters available. Year-round, $95.

OUTER ISLAND EXCURSIONS WHALE WATCHING

Lopez Islander Resort and Marina, 2864 Fisherman Bay Road, Lopez Island • outerislandx.com

This company offers a variety of tours launching from the San Juan Islands as well as the Bellingham area. Take the three-hour tour from Lopez Island, which has a 97 percent whale-sighting success rate. May–September, $109.

BIKE THE ISLANDS

See all three islands via bicycle. You can do this on your own—see the local bike shops listed in each individual island's section—or through the following organized trips and tours.

// Bike the San Juan Islands

WILDLIFE 100

350 N Beach Road, Eastsound • wildlifecycles.com/wildlife-100 • 360-376-4708

Join the unsupported bike ride, organized by Wildlife Cycles on Orcas Island, for an all-day coast around Orcas Island, Lopez Island, and San Juan Island, with ferry rides in between each route and food and refreshments in Friday Harbor at the end of the long day. Suggested $10 donation goes to the Orcas Island Recreation Program.

TERRA TREK

www.terratrek.com • 360-378-4223

Sign up for a bicycle tour that will take you through forests and along coasts, with optional hikes, whale watching, sea kayaking, wine tastings, and more. On the multiday trips—anywhere from two days/one night to six days/five nights—you'll explore one island, two islands, or all three, along with other non-bike outdoor adventures, fantastic meals, and either inn stays or camping, depending on the tour. Let them set the itinerary so you can focus on your burning thighs and the stunning views, or customize your own. $499–2,580.

SOUTH SOUND ADVENTURES

southsoundadventures.com • 360-970-9619

From Seattle or Olympia, take a customized, all-inclusive, guided two-day adventure of San Juan Island and Orcas Island. The rides can be long or short, the activities off-bike or on. Snacks, three meals per day, and ferry passes are included. $499.

ORCAS ISLAND

FROM SEATTLE: 3.5 HOURS • DAYS HERE: 2-PLUS

EAT	DRINK	DO
pizza at Hogstone	tasting flight at Island Hop Brewery	swim in Cascade Lake

☰ *Plan Around*

DOE BAY FESTIVAL

August

A four-day bluegrass ruckus, with festival tent camping, car camping, or boat camping. Wander Doe Bay's 30 acres of forest and beach bluff. Smoke pot and play the tuba (or watch someone do as much), relax into a sound meditation.

ORCAS ISLAND LIT FEST

April • oilf.org

Avoid the spring rain and come inside for Orcas Island Lit Fest. This celebration of all things writing—with readings; panel discussions; writers' workshops hosted by Pulitzer Prize–winning writers, critically acclaimed authors, and beloved regional and emerging writers; and a Lit Walk at venues around Eastsound.

☰ *Eat & Drink*

Get Caffeinated

KATHRYN TAYLOR CHOCOLATES

68 N Beach Road, Eastsound •www.kathryntaylorchocolates.com • 360-298-8093 • Open Monday–Saturday 9 a.m.–5 p.m.

Located in Eastsound Square, it's a cozy chocolatier featuring nummy bonbons, sipping chocolate, cakes and cookies, and Stumptown coffee. Design your own chocolate assortment to go.

BROWN BEAR BAKING

29 N Beach Road #1966, Eastsound • 360-855-7456 • Open Monday–Saturday 8 a.m.–4 p.m., Sunday 8 a.m.–5 p.m.

Wake up with a coffee, a sweet or savory croissant, and a scone. Breakfast deserves dessert, so get a lemon tart on your way out the door. You should probably come back for lunch—get any of the sandwiches and a salad. For lunch's dessert, get a chocolate muffin.

Farm Fresh

BUCK BAY SHELLFISH FARM

117 EJ Young Road, Olga • www.buckbayshellfishfarm.com • 360-376-5280 • Open Monday–Saturday 11 a.m.–6 p.m., Sunday 11 a.m.–5 p.m.

From Mountain Lake in Moran State Park runs Cascade Creek, which empties into Buck Bay, a little crevasse of the Salish Sea. There, at Buck Bay Shellfish Farm, you can eat fresh Buck Bay oysters, clams, Dungeness crab, prawns, shrimp, and fresh-caught fish separately, or throw everything in a bowl, call it ceviche, and then eat it.

》》   You can stay in the Buck Bay Getaway, just 100 feet from the shoreline. $90–135.

ORCAS ISLAND FARMERS' MARKET

Eastsound Village Green, N Beach Road, Eastsound • orcasislandfarmersmarket.org • 541-306-7084 • Open May–September, Saturday 10 a.m.–3 p.m.

In-Town Cuisine

HOGSTONE RESTAURANT

460 Main Street, Eastsound • www.hogstone.com • 360-376-4647 • Summer hours: Thursday–Monday 5 p.m.–close

Get your pizza, veggies, and seafood wood-fired by one of *Food & Wine* magazine's Top 10 New Chefs of 2017 while drinking earnestly curated wines. The produce comes from Orcas Island's own Maple Rock Farm and is, therefore, very fresh. Reservations recommended, or sign up for Aelder, a set tasting menu available four nights a week.

MIJITA'S

310 A Street, Eastsound • 360-376-6722 • Open Sunday–Tuesday 4–9 p.m., Wednesday–Saturday 11 a.m.–2:30 p.m.

The outdoor courtyard seating is open seasonally; the food is fresh and beautifully presented year-round. Get the homemade salsa and chips, the esquites, any and all tacos, and, of course, a margarita. Reservations recommended.

THE KITCHEN

249 Prune Alley, Eastsound • www.thekitchenorcas.com • 360-376-6958

Sticking to the philosophy of organic, locally produced, and fresh, The Kitchen is a small café that offers "fast Asian food," wraps and salads, and weekly specials. Build your own meal by choosing a rice or noodle, vegetables and/or protein, and a sauce or broth, or trust the staff picks. A glass of organic white wine pairs perfectly with the coconut rice pudding.

Booze and Beyond

ISLAND HOPPIN' BREWERY

33 Hope Lane, Eastsound • www.islandhoppinbrewery.com • 360-376-6079 • Tasting room open daily 11 a.m.–9 p.m.

Get a pint or tasting flight in the tasting room's outdoor patios or indoor seating. Sample the nice locally sourced and seasonal tasting menu, or bring your own picnic to go along with the brews. Casual tours available on demand.

DOE BAY WINE COMPANY

109 N Beach Road, Suite D1, Eastsound • www.doebaywinecompany.com • 360-376-7467 • Open daily 11 a.m.–6 p.m.

A bottle shop and tasting room with special events and tasting. During the summer, register for a "wine experience," a 12-person tasting centered around a nightly theme such as "Boutique Producers of the Northwest" or "Top Grapes of Southern Italy." $35.

ORCAS ISLAND WINERY

2371 Crow Valley Road, Eastsound • www.orcasislandwinery.com • 425-314-7509 • Open Friday noon–4 p.m., Saturday noon–6 p.m., Sunday noon–5 p.m.

Hike Turtleback Mountain, then drive 1 mile down the road to Orcas Island Winery, where you can see their 3 acres of grape vines on this 15-acre farm. Try the dry riesling or petit verdot, then get a bottle of cab sauvignon or the malbec to take home.

☰ *Stay Over*

KANGAROO HOUSE BED & BREAKFAST

1459 N Beach Road, Eastsound • www.kangaroohouse.com • 360-376-2175

The longest-running B&B on the islands, Kangaroo House provides organic, from-scratch break-fasts and garden and hot tub access. Each room is named after a bird that visits their backyard sanctuary, and each has a private bathroom. Walk to nearby North Beach to watch the sun set.

TURTLEBACK FARM INN

1981 Crow Valley Road, Eastsound • www.turtlebackinn.com • 360-376-4914

Built in the late 1800s and carefully restored, the farmhouse has seven bedrooms, each with a private bath. You can also get your pals together and rent the four-bedroom Orchard House for more privacy. Eat breakfast using fine bone china, and at the end of the day drink a glass of sherry by the roaring fire.

DOE BAY RESORT & RETREAT

107 Doe Bay Road, Olga • doebay.com • 360-376-2291

Car camp, set up a tent, or stay in a cabin, yurt, or geodesic dome at this famous Pacific Northwest resort. Whether it's beachside, forest enclosed, or on a bluff, you'll have easy access to the Salish Sea; the all-organic, farm-sourced Doe Bay Café; yoga classes; and clothing-optional soaking tubs. They offer massages and kayak tours, too. Pet-friendly accom-modations available for a $20 one-time fee. Two-night minimum.

// Doe Bay Resort and Retreat, Olga

#farmlife

PEBBLE COVE

3341 Deer Harbor Road, Eastsound • pebblecovefarm.com • 360-376-6161

This south-facing farm is right on the water, overlooking Massacre Bay. All accommodations have a 180-degree view of the water and access to an organic u-pick garden, rowboats, a hot tub, gas barbecues, kayak rentals, hammocks, an expansive lawn with farm animals, and the beach. Pet-friendly accommodations available, small dogs $15 per night, big dogs $25 per night. Three-night minimum, $150–200.

Camping and Glamping

MORAN STATE PARK

3572 Olga Road, Olga • 360-376-2326

Moran State Park has 124 standard campsites, six primitive campsites, and one 60-person group campsite. Five restrooms and 10 coin-operated showers. There's also one vacation house, which is available for overnights of up to eight guests; it has two bedrooms, a bathroom and shower, an equipped kitchen, and a TV. Bring towels and linens. Discover Pass required. For reservations, call 1-888-CAMPOUT or visit www.parks.state.wa.us. (For more information on Moran State Park, go to page 214.)

>>   Sleeping on the ground is optional. Reserve one of the five glamping sites in Moran State Park through LEANTO. Each site has one or two canvas tents with either a fully outfitted queen-size bed or two twins (www.stayleanto.com).

MOUNT BAKER FARM

706 Mount Baker Road, Eastsound • mountbakerfarm.com • 360-376-2425

Originally a dairy farm, this 80-acre campground has two train stations, 2 miles of train tracks, and a wittle functional train thanks to a former ferroequinologist owner. (It's no longer a working farm, which is why it's in the camping category.) It also has a ton of campsites both in open meadow and closer to treelines, hot showers, and camping gear available for rent if you didn't bring your own. A four-bedroom guest house is also available to rent. Pet friendly.

>>   **Good to Know:** An approximately 80-foot, three-masted barkentine vessel rests on private property off Mount Pickett Road, 6 miles from the ocean and 400 feet above sea level. It has never seen water.

// Wildflowers in the San Juan Islands

≡ *While You're Here*

MORAN STATE PARK

3572 Olga Road, Olga • moranstatepark.com • 360-376-2326

The more than 5,400-acre park includes 38 miles of hiking, biking, and equestrian trails; five freshwater lakes to swim or boat on; and three named, plus a few unnamed, waterfalls along Cascade Creek. Rent paddleboards, paddleboats, inflatable SUPs, kayaks, rowboats, and canoes at Orcas Adventures (www.orcasadventures.com; 360-376-4665; $18–75) on Cascade Lake and Mountain Lake. Discover Pass required.

TREE JUMP INTO CASCADE LAKE

Walk the 2.7-mile loop around the lake to find your best spot to throw down a towel and catch some sun. About 0.5 mile counterclockwise from the public beach, a full-scale bonsai-like tree juts out of a rock. Climb to the top and jump into the deep blue water, then swim back to shore and do it again. And again.

SWIM OUT TO AN ISLAND WITHIN AN ISLAND IN MOUNTAIN LAKE

In the middle of Mountain Lake sit two mini-islands, easily accessible by swim or paddle. The lake is higher up and a little more remote than Cascade Lake, so there's a chance that there won't be as many people. Pick a spot around the 3.9-mile circumference for a rest stop between swim sessions and a quiet afternoon.

HIKE MOUNT CONSTITUTION

At 2,409 feet above sea level, Mount Constitution is the biggest mountain in the San Juan Islands. Add to that the Civilian Conservation Corps tower, built during the Great Depression, and you've got the highest point in the islands, from which you can see all the way to the North Cascades, the Olympic Mountains, the other San Juan Islands, and several Gulf Islands across the Canadian border. Wake up before light and climb to the top to watch the sunrise.

Check out these two eateries located smack dab in Moran State Park.

SUGAR SHACK • The beach of Cascade Lake

SUGAR ON TOP • The top of Mount Constitution

Both locales serve Lopez Island Creamery ice cream, hot dogs, grilled cheese sandwiches and paninis, and other goodies, plus homemade strawberry lemonade, iced tea, and coffee drinks.

// Biking Friday Harbor

HIKE TURTLEBACK MOUNTAIN

3 miles round-trip • Elevation gain: 830 feet

A lesser-known hike, and a steep one, so you're more likely to have the trail to yourself. Come in the spring for the gorgeous wildflowers in full bloom. Climb to the top to watch the sunset.

BIKE THE SCENIC ROUTES

Bring your bike or rent a human-powered or electric bike for a day or two or more from **Wildlife Cycles** (350 N Beach Road, Eastsound; wildlifecycles.com; 360-376-4708). Stay off Horseshoe Highway, where you're sure to face vehicle traffic, and hit the winding scenic routes. Mount Constitution in Moran State Park is the pièce de résistance for cyclists with buns of steel, and the park as a whole has several decent mountain bike routes. Or head to Obstruction Pass or Deer Harbor. For maps and friendly advice, stop by Wildlife Cycles.

Take a Tour

SALISH SEA TOUR CO.

www.salishseatourco.net • 360-525-5014

Take the morning Art, History, & Local Legends tour for intel on how this tiny island ticks and has ticked for a long time. Come back in the afternoon for Fresh, Fermented, & Flying High, which starts after lunch and takes you on a tour of all the best foodie spots while educating on Orcas Island's farm-to-table situation.

ABOVE & BEYOND

Dogs | **The Orcas Off-Leash Area** (adjacent to Buck Park on Mount Baker Road, Eastsound) is tree-shaded, with separate sections for large and small dogs.

Skate | Funded by sports filmmaker Warren Miller and built by Seattle-based Grindline, **Orcas Island Skate Park** (Buck Park, 310-699 Mount Baker Road, Eastsound) is a must stop. The middle of the park is shaped like the island it sits on.

Books | With a wide selection of books, plus gifts, CDs, and coffee, **Darvill's Book Store** (296 Main Street, Eastsound; 360-376-2135) is a cozy bookstore with views of Fishing Bay and a penchant for nautical books. It's open Monday–Saturday 8 a.m.–5:30 p.m., and Sunday 8 a.m.–5 p.m.

SAN JUAN ISLAND

FROM SEATTLE: 3.5 HOURS · DAYS HERE: 2-PLUS

EAT	DRINK	DO	BUY
happy hour at Friday Harbor House	Westcott Bay Cider	zip line	whale adoption

☰ *Plan Around*

FRIDAY HARBOR FILM FESTIVAL

October • www.fhff.org • 360-298-1939

Each year since 2013, the Friday Harbor Film Festival invites filmmakers from far and wide to showcase their Pacific Rim–focused, positive-change-inspiring documentaries. The FHFF is on a mission to entertain, inspire, and enlighten all involved by creating awareness of and appreciation for our crazy little planet and its inhabitants.

LAVENDER FESTIVAL & ARTS FAIR

July • www.pelindabalavender.com

You can never have too much lavender. At the 25-acre Pelindaba Lavender Farm, more than 200 lavender-based botanicals, (non-pot-related) edibles, and bath and body care items are handcrafted on-site. Stroll through lavender fields, harvest your own lavender at the designated Cutting Field, and attend demonstrations about the history and uses of lavender and how to grow, harvest, cook, and distill it into essential oil. All day long you can get picnics to enjoy in the fields. Visit the craft tent to make wreathes and crowns, then eat lavender ice cream and cookies, and drink lavender lemonade, iced tea, and coffee.

☰ *Eat & Drink*

Get Caffeinated

LIME KILN CAFÉ

248 Reuben Memorial Drive, Friday Harbor • www.rocheharbor.com/dining • 360-378-9892 • Open daily 7 a.m.–3 p.m. and 5 p.m.–9 p.m.

Get the doughnuts, made fresh and in-house daily. The breakfasts are diner-style but with Northwest freshness, and the café offers salads, soups, sandwiches, and kiln-fired pizza starting at 11 a.m.

Farm Fresh

SAN JUAN ISLAND FARMERS' MARKET

Brickworks Building, 150 Nichols Street, Friday Harbor • www.sjifarmersmarket.com • Open April–October every Saturday, November–December and March first and third Saturdays, January–February first Saturday only, 9:30 a.m.–1 p.m.

WESTCOTT BAY SHELLFISH FARM

904 Westcott Drive, Friday Harbor • www.westcottbayshellfish.com • 360-378-2489

See how this family-owned farm operates, sit at the picnic tables overlooking the bay, and slurp some Pacific oysters, Mediterranean mussels, or Manila clams straight from the ocean.

>> While you're in the San Juan Islands, pick up **salt from the Salish Sea**, sun-dried and hand harvested by San Juan Sea Salt (www.sanjuanseasalt.com). You can also find this local delicacy in stores around Seattle and beyond.

Arrive sans car and rent an electric bike, moped, Scoot Coupe, or Chevy Tracker convertible from Susie's Mopeds (125 Nichols Street, Friday Harbor; www.susiesmopeds.com; 360-378-5244), just a five-minute walk from the ferry terminal. $30–70 per hour, $70–160 per day. Reservations highly recommended.

Dining

VAN GO'S PIZZA

180 Web Street, Friday Harbor • www.vangopizza.net • 360-378-0138 • Open Tuesday–Saturday
from 4 p.m. until they run out of dough

Named by the Dutch chef and owner after his favorite artist, this artisan pizza joint features
fresh-made dough, nummy pizzas, good salads, and ice cream. Come for the house-made
desserts—chef Daniel has a side hustle called Cake and Co (www.cakeandco.net) and therefore knows what he's doing when it comes to the sweets.

FRIDAY HARBOR HOUSE—THE RESTAURANT

130 West Street, Friday Harbor • fridayharborhouse.com/dining.php • 360-378-8455 • Brunch
Monday–Friday 7:30–11 a.m., Saturday 8 a.m.–noon, Sunday 8 a.m.–1 p.m.; dinner daily 5–9 p.m.

The chef has creds: He was once the sous chef at world-famous Willow Inn on Lummi Island.
Everything is so fresh it practically tastes green, and the seasonal cocktails—Smoking Jacket,
Chef's Garden, Ancient Fashioned—are truly creative. Fantastic views.

>> Come for the food and chichi cocktails, then spend the night at the Friday Harbor House Inn.
Whether you get a harbor view, a garden view, a partial view, or no view, all of the 24 rooms
have a two-person jetted tub. For reservations, call 1-866-722-7356 or go online.

Booze and Beyond

WESTCOTT BAY CIDER

12 Anderson Lane, Friday Harbor • www.westcottbaycider.com • 360-378-2606 • Tastings March–
December, Saturday and Sunday 1–4 p.m.; Memorial Day–Labor Day, Thursday–Sunday 1–4 p.m., or
by appointment

The cider makers of Westcott Bay mean business, growing traditional cider apples such as Yar-
lington Mill and Kingston Black in their very own orchard, which has been used to grow fruit
since the 1870s. Once harvested, their Sweet Coppins and Dabinetts are blended and fermented in the Normandy style to amber-gold perfection.

SAN JUAN ISLAND DISTILLERY

12 Anderson Lane, Friday Harbor • www.sanjuanislanddistillery.com • 360-472-1532 • Tastings
Saturday and Sunday 1–4 p.m., or by appointment

Along with the premium award-winning brandy from the same apple orchard at Westcott Bay
Cider, San Juan Island Distillery crafts liqueurs, flavored brandy, and, last but certainly not
least, 12 different gins.

// Wildflowers in the San Juan Islands

SAN JUAN ISLAND BREWING CO

410 A Street, Friday Harbor • www.sanjuanbrew.com • 360-378-2017 • Open Sunday–Thursday
11 a.m.–9 p.m., Friday and Saturday 11 a.m.–10 p.m.

Just get right to it by ordering the five-beer sampler, then, once you've taken your time with
your options, order off the seasonal drink menu. Get a wood-stone pizza, burger, or salad, too.

 *Stay Over*

Everything's Better on a Boat

THE WHARFSIDE BED AND BREAKFAST

204 Front Street, Friday Harbor • thewharfside.com

The 60-foot ketch *Slow Season* is the only floating B&B in the San Juans since 1986. It has
two spacious, private staterooms: The Forward Stateroom includes a bedroom, a sky-lit main
salon next to the main galley, and a full bath with shower; the Aft Stateroom is a low-beamed
captain's cabin with a fireplace and vintage movie player. $175–215.

Resorts

ROCHE HARBOR RESORT

248 Reuben Memorial Drive, Friday Harbor • www.rocheharbor.com • 360-378-2155

Established in 1886, this picturesque, full-service seaside resort includes historic and contemporary accommodations, gardens, restaurants, and stores, as well as a large marina and spa. Rent lodging on the waterfront, in historic cottages, and in hotel rooms with heated floors. You can rent a slip in the marina to park your yacht, too.

ISLAND INN AT 123 WEST

123 West Street (check in on Front Street), Friday Harbor • 123west.com • 360-378-4400

Originally a fuel and oil storage facility for the fishing fleet, ferry, and cannery, this place did a 180 by getting Silver LEED certified. Now you can rent cute contemporary rooms, some with a harbor view and some without, some with Euro-style washrooms and some with a wet bar. The penthouses are big and blingy. $200–280.

#farmlife

SWEET EARTH FARM

sweetearthfarm.com

This 20-acre organic working farm has a diverse fruit orchard, an herb and vegetable garden, and oodles of berries, as well as a pasture for chickens, ducks, turkeys and Kunekune pigs. Glamp near-ish these animal friends in comfy tents that come with new queen-size beds and linens, a covered outdoor kitchen, and rechargeable lantern. Two-night minimum, $120–140.

FREE HORSE FARM

215 Crow Valley Lane, Friday Harbor • www.freehorsefarm.com • 360-378-2968

Take a lesson or attend a workshop with Essential Horsemanship, then stay at the campsite, in the tepee, or inside the farmhouse on this 20-acre farm. Cook at the rustic outdoor kitchen or roll into town for some fine dining. You're welcome to care for the horses or do other farm chores. $40–115.

Camping and Glamping

LAKEDALE RESORT

4313 Roche Harbor Road, Friday Harbor • www.lakedale.com • 360-378-2350

The resort as a whole covers 82 acres, with numerous hiking trails and paths to go with the many, many accommodations. There's a main lodge, separate log cabins, a 10-person lake house, a yurt with a private hot tub, a fully renovated 1978 Excella Airstream, and many campsites to pitch your tent or rent one then pitch it. The canvas glamping tents and cottages come with a nightly "Toasty Toes" turndown service, which includes the delivery of two fleece-covered hot-water bottles "to keep your tootsies warm." Includes complimentary continental breakfast. Pet-friendly accommodations available for a one-time $35 fee. $50–645.

≡ *While You're Here*

VISIT SAN JUAN ISLAND NATIONAL HISTORICAL PARK

4668 Cattle Point Road, Friday Harbor • www.nps.gov/sajh/index.htm • 360-378-2240

In 1859, the United States and Great Britain nearly went to war over an American shooting a Hudson Bay Company pig. They'd long been squabbling over the region, and this peccary homicide added bacon fat to the fire. After much tedious posturing, they ended up working it out, and this park celebrates people acting like grown-ups. (Of course, we have to forget that whole messy business of Manifest Destiny, and how the Salish tribes had been living in the area for thousands of years and probably didn't relinquish the land because they were asked to oh-so nicely. Also, what about the pig?) Visit English Camp and American Camp, the two 1860s military barracks, if that's your thing. Or skip the glorification of imperialism and use the two camps as bases for hiking, tide pooling, picnicking, frolicking on the beach, bird-watching, and more.

WHALE WATCH AT LIME KILN POINT STATE PARK

1567 West Side Road, Friday Harbor

This 41-acre day-use park is considered one of the best spots to watch whales on earth. From May through September, climb up on the bluff and look for water spouting and fins slapping down below. You might also see advanced divers in the water below the 100-year-old lighthouse—the rocky cliff drops steeply to a depth of almost 120 feet.

// Lime Kiln Lighthouse, Friday Harbor

VISIT KRYSTAL ACRES ALPACA FARM
AND COUNTRY STORE

3501 W Valley Road, Friday Harbor • www.krystalacres.com • 360-378-6125 • Open April–October, daily 10 a.m.–5 p.m.; November–March, daily 11 a.m.–4 p.m.

Alpacas are funny looking, and you can see them living their best life on this scenic 80-acre farm. Walk down to the fields to say hi to the animals, then stop by the gift shop to peruse the selection of fresh-made alpaca sweaters, socks, scarves, sofa throws, and toys.

ZIP LINE WITH SAN JUAN ISLAND ZIP TOUR

www.zipsanjuan.com • 360-317-8434

Get picked up at the end of 1st Street in Friday Harbor, then strap on your helmet, gloves, and full-body harness and get ready to go on the only zip tour in the islands. Don't worry, the guides will show you how. On the eight zip lines of varying heights and the speeds they induce, experience the beauty of San Juan Island as you zip through forest canopy, across a glassy lake, and over protected wetlands. And yes, it's safe. Reservations required, $86.

PAY RESPECTS AT AFTERGLOW VISTA

692 Afterglow Drive, Friday Harbor

This burial could be considered family style, with its Roman column–ensconced, open-air rotunda of a mausoleum, under which the ashes of the McMillin family sit in thick stone chairs around the big limestone table, presumably having family dinner together for all of eternity.

// Whales near Lopez Island

VISIT THE WHALE MUSEUM

62 1st Street, Friday Harbor • whalemuseum.org • 360-378-4710 • Open May–October, daily
9 a.m.–6 p.m.; November–April, 10 a.m.–4 p.m.

Established in 1979, Friday Harbor's Whale Museum is the first of its kind in the country, with
heartfelt devotion to wild whales and the Salish Sea ecosystem they inhabit. Tour the Gallery
of Whales, learn about the human history of the area, and support conservation efforts. $9.

>> **Adopt an Orca** for only $35 a year through the Whale Museum. One-year adoption includes
a personalized adoption certificate; biography, photo, and genealogy chart of "your" whale;
education material about the orcas; and monthly updates. Also a neato "Orca Steward" patch
and a bumper sticker, if desired.

ABOVE & BEYOND

Dogs | A two-acre city park, **Eddie & Friends Dog Park** (Mullis Street and Argyle
Street, Friday Harbor; www.islandrec.org/eddie-and-friends-dog-park) has a larger
fenced-in grass and dirt area and small fenced-in area for small/nervous/old dogs.

Skates | A great spot for BMX bikers, **The Skate Park** (Argyle Avenue at San Juan
County Fairgrounds) has plenty of space to tool around in and plenty of elements for
practicing tricks.

Books | For a good selection of new books, highlighting those from San Juan Island
authors, visit **Griffin Bay Bookstore** (155 Spring Street, Friday Harbor; www.griffin
baybook.com; 360-378-5511). Good coffee shop, too, and a game area for kiddos,
meaning there will be kids. Open daily 10 a.m.–6 p.m.

With a wide selection and island vibes, **Serendipity Used Books** (223 A Street, Friday
Harbor; sanjuanupdate.com/serendipity; 360-378-2665) is a quaint bookstore near the
ferry; open daily 10 a.m.–6 p.m.

LOPEZ ISLAND

FROM SEATTLE: 3 HOURS · DAYS HERE: 2-PLUS

EAT	DRINK	DO	BUY
noodles at Setsunai	Best Ever Green Chile Sriracha Bacon Bloody Mary from Haven Kitchen	bike	a book at Lopez Bookshop

≡ *Plan Around*

TOUR DE LOPEZ

April · www.visitsanjuans.com/events/tour-de-lopez

The Lopez Island Chamber of Commerce is pretty adamant that this tour is noncompetitive, so leave the human growth hormones at home. Start the San Juan cycling season off by riding one of the four marked routes of differing lengths (5, 12, 18, and 31 miles) from Odlin County Park or Lopez Village to the Lopez Community Center on scenic country roads. A beer garden awaits your arrival. Barbecue lunch is included in the fee. $50.

// Biking the San Juan Islands

≡ *Eat & Drink*

Get Caffeinated

ISABEL'S ESPRESSO

308 Lopez Road, Lopez Island · isabelsespresso.com · 360-468-4114 · Open daily 7 a.m.–5 p.m.

A locals' favorite, Isabel keeps it simple and friendly. The flagship coffee is fair trade and organic, from Chiapas, Mexico, and the organic milk comes from Ferndale, Washington. Figure out a way to put whipped cream on something. Good pastries, too.

Farm Fresh

LOPEZ ISLAND FARMERS' MARKET

Lopez Village, Village Road, Lopez Island • www.lopezfarmersmarket.com • Open May–September, Saturday 10 a.m.-2 p.m.

For a comprehensive list of farm-to-market locales, check out www.lopezrocks.org.

LOPEZ ISLAND SHELLFISH & HATCHERY

203 Shoreland Drive, Lopez Island • www.jffarms.com • 360-468-2722 • Open daily 10 a.m.–4 p.m.

Jones Family Farms owns and operates a 3-acre tidal lagoon shellfish farm, a grass-based live-stock pasture farm, and a commercial fishing operation. Come to the farm stand and hatchery and get a tour, then pick up Pacific, Euro Flat, and Olympia oysters, Manila and butter clams, pink salmon, and fresh fish.

Dining

URSA MINOR

210 Lopez Road, Lopez Island • www.ursaminorlopez.com • 360-622-2730 • Summer hours: Thursday–Monday 5–9 p.m., Sunday brunch 10 a.m.–1 p.m.

Featuring "creative agrarian Northwest cuisine," which is another way of saying tasty farm-to-fork. The setting is casual, the drinks are amazing—get the barrel-aged negroni—and everything is produce-forward and uber colorful and fresh.

SETSUNAI

Lopez Village, 45 Eads Lane, Lopez Island • www.krautpleasers.com • 360-298-9052 • Open Thursday–Sunday 11 a.m.–8 p.m., Monday and Tuesday 11 a.m.–4 p.m.

A Japanese noodle bar in the historic Joinery building, using organic and locally sourced produce. The noodles and dumplings are handmade fresh daily, and 16-ounce jars of the kraut pleasers (kim chi and sauerkraut) are ready to go home with you.

HAVEN KITCHEN

9 Old Post Road, Lopez Island • www.lopezhaven.com • 360-468-3272 • Open Wednesday–Sunday for lunch noon–3 p.m., dinner 5–8 p.m.

Waterside casual in Lopez Village, with outdoor seating, great views, and a pan-global cuisine (guacamole, Thai fresh rolls, kale and Brussels sprout Caesar salad, etc.). Ridiculous specialty cocktails—the Best Ever Green Chile Sriracha Bacon Bloody Mary is a must-have.

Booze and Beyond

LOPEZ ISLAND VINEYARDS

724 Fisherman Bay Road, Lopez Island • lopezislandvineyards.com • 360-468-3644

San Juan County's oldest vineyard and winery, Lopez Island Vineyards (LIV) has grown grapes on its land since 1989. Their wines have won a bunch of awards during that time and go great with fresh-caught crab. Try their offerings at their summertime Lopez Island Farmers' Market tasting (May–September, Saturday 10 a.m.–2 p.m.) or call ahead to arrange a private tour and tasting. $10.

 *Stay Over*

Resort and Rest Inn

THE EDENWILD

132 Lopez Road, Lopez Island • theedenwild.com • 360-468-3238

A "friendly, not stuffy" boutique inn located in the center of Lopez Village was once owned by actor Tom Skerritt, the mustachioed gentleman in *Alien*, *Top Gun*, and a whole bunch of other things. The nine-room, TV-free inn is close to the amenities of town but is set apart by the pretty gardens. Features gorgeous views of Fisherman Bay and San Juan Channel and offers bike and kayak rentals and whale-watching tours through Edenwild Island Adventures. In-season $160–250, off-season $89–150.

// Edenwild Boutique Inn, Lopez Island

#farmlife

MIDNIGHT'S FARM

3042 Center Road, Lopez Island • www.midnightsfarm.com • 360-468-3269

Rent the sunny two-bedroom Field House on this 100-acre working farm, located next to a pond and a ways from the hubbub of farm life. If you want, you can feed a pig or milk a cow, dig in the garden, take a sauna, or drop in on a yoga class at Down Dog Studio. Stop by on-site Barn Owl Bakery for some bread fresh out the oven, and get a quarter cow or half a pig to take home with you. Reading a book by the window seat is highly recommended. $167.

Camping and Glamping

LOPEZ FARM COTTAGES AND TENT CAMPING

607 Fisherman Bay Road, Lopez Island • www.lopezfarmcottages.com • 360-468-3555

Proclaimed "One of the 10 Favorite Places to Woo in the United States" by MSNBC, this 27-acre oasis offers adorable Northwest Scandinavian–style cottages, two glamp sites with comfy premade tents, private campsites (with shower access!), and complimentary morning coffee. Pet-friendly accommodations available, but dogs must be on-leash at all time. $48–215.

SPENCER SPIT STATE PARK

521 A Bakeview Road, Lopez Island

Spencer Spit is a long sand thingy enclosing a saltchuck lagoon. This 200-acre park is one of the few marine and camping parks in the area that you can get to by car, and its waters are excellent for crabbing and clamming. You can prep your fresh catch at one of the three picnic shelters or at your campsite—there are 37 standard campsites, seven primitive campsites, three group camps, and two restrooms. To reserve your spot, go to washington.goingtocamp.com or call 888-CAMPOUT.

≡ *While You're Here*

BIKE LOPEZ

Bring your own or rent a bike on this bike-friendly island, which is not flat exactly—think slow burn, with fantastic scenery. Since there's a happy dearth of roads, the routes around the island's perimeter are fairly obvious; avoid the busier Center Road and Mud Bay Road. You can also mountain bike on Lopez Hill, a 400-acre property with 4 miles of trails. For maps and rentals, go to **Village Cycles** (214 Lopez Road, Lopez Island; villagecycles.net; 360-468-4013; open Monday–Saturday 10 a.m.–5 p.m., Sunday 10 a.m.–4 p.m.) or **Lopez Island Sea Kayak and Bicycle Works** (2820 Fisherman Bay Road, Lopez Island; www.lopezkayaks.com; 360-468-2847).

Hike

ICEBERG POINT AT AGATE BEACH

3 miles round-trip • Elevation gain: 50 feet

On the southern tip of Lopez Island, this sorta guarded kinda secret used to be a reef net post, where Slopezians could pick up fish straight off the boat. You have to park in Agate Beach County Park and (respectfully) walk up a gravel road, where a little sign will point the way. It's as quiet as a windswept, meadowed point can be. Look to the west and you'll see the foreign land of Victoria, BC! Dogs allowed on-leash.

FISHERMAN BAY PRESERVE

2 miles round-trip • End of Peninsula Road, Lopez Island

On the northwest side of the island, a 29-acre spit/preserve/park protects Fisherman Bay from the San Juan Channel. Hike the Tombolo, a bar of sand joining the mini-island of the preserve to the bigger island of Lopez, out to the spit and through its meadows, wetlands, and woodlands. Dogs allowed on-leash.

// Fisherman Bay, Lopez Island

ABOVE & BEYOND

Skate | The main ramp at **Lopez Island Skate Park** (204 Village Road, Lopez Island) is small and perfect for beginners. It's not the most epic of skateparks, but it is well loved by locals and visitors.

Books | With new mainstream releases, as well as work by local Lopez writers, musicians, and artists, **Lopez Bookshop** (211 Lopez Road, Lopez Island; www.lopezbookshop.com; 360-468-2132) is seriously cute, as well as being curated and to the point. It's open Monday–Saturday 9 a.m.–6 p.m., and Sunday 9 a.m.–5 p.m.

Good to Know |

· There are no traffic lights in the San Juan Islands.

· San Juan County was the first county in the country to ban jet skis.

· There's no hospital on Lopez Island, only a medical clinic in Lopez Village.

· Lopez Island has the highest volunteer per capita ratio in Washington State.

· Rumor has it that Friday Harbor was named after Hawaiian immigrant Peter Poalima, a sheepherder who worked for the Hudson Bay Company in the 1830s. *Poalima* means "Friday" in Hawaiian.

· President Theodore Roosevelt and John Wayne were once guests at the first hotel on San Juan Island, Hotel de Haro in Roche Harbor.

13

Mountains of Methow Valley

FROM SEATTLE: 4 HOURS · DAYS HERE: 2-PLUS

DO	EAT	DRINK	BUY
ski	breakfast in front of a roaring fire at Mazama Country Inn	hot chocolate	a ski pass

Methow Valley is a cluster of towns along the Methow River, about 180 miles northeast of Seattle, on the eastern foothills of the North Cascades mountain range. In the winter, ski novices and Olympic hopefuls flock to the region for the 124 miles of dedicated cross-country trails and hot chocolate in supercool backcountry cabins—often the Washington Pass portion of WA-20 is closed, so check pass conditions at wsdot.wa.gov.

During the warmer months, people of all stripes come for solid camping, fantastic biking, hiking, river rafting, and swimming. The North Cascades National Park is nearby to the west, with virtually unlimited activities to choose from. Stop in the Ross Lake National Recreation Area along WA-20, a.k.a. North Cascades Scenic Byway. Or take the southern, longer route on US-2, a.k.a. the Stevens Pass Greenway, through Okanogan-Wenatchee National Forest near Leavenworth. Or go counterclockwise through both Cascade regions by doing the Cascade Loop, a popular 470-plus-mile road trip with the Methow Valley and the city of Seattle as its east and west bookends.

Mazama, on the Methow River, is the northernmost town of the Methow Valley trio and the smallest in size. Most lodging and dining options are located farther south, but Mazama still claims the fame of the well-known general store, Mazama Store.

Winthrop, located at the junction of the Chewuch and Methow rivers, is a former prospector town, and though the building materials and technology have changed since the early 1800s, the Western look has not. Unlike Leavenworth's somewhat random Bavarian theme, Winthrop's cowboy style has roots in the presence of actual cowboys intent on finding their fortune. Alas, the gold rush ended with more empty pockets than full coffers, but still some folks decided to stick around. In 1972, as WA-20 was connecting the small towns to big cities, the Winthropians rallied for a townwide facelift to return the downtown's face to its days of glory.

Twisp, located at the junction of the Twisp and Methow rivers, is an artist community and has, at around 1,000 people, the biggest population out of the three. It's popular as a year-round vacation destination, with plenty of places to eat, sleep, shop, and do or see art.

☰ *Getting There*

BY CAR | During the winter, drive for approximately 64 miles on I-5, then take WA-20 for approximately 120 miles. During the summer, take Stevens Pass/US-2 or I-90 to US-97 N.

BY PLANE | Charter a plane from Boeing Field in Seattle, or from other Northwest airports, with Catlin Flying Service (www.catlinflyingservice.com; 509-429-2697). $100-plus.

☰ *Highlight Reel*

METHOW TRAILS

www.methowtrails.org

Methow Trails is touted far and wide as one of the best trail systems in North America. During the winter, you can hear the *swish swish* of Nordic skis for miles, and in the summer, the snow melts and people strap on their running shoes or hiking boots, or hop on their mountain bikes to explore the trails surrounded by over a million acres of wilderness. Check out the Methow Trails website for winter trails and summer trails maps and information. And be sure to check out the photo of the day and the trail report for daily recommendations. Dogs are welcome on 75 percent of the Methow Trails. Trail Pass required.

THE LOUP

97 FS 4200 100 Road, Okanogan • skitheloup.com • 509-557-3401

Located between Twisp and Okanogan on WA-20, the 300 acres of groomed terrain has a total of 1,240 vertical feet for skiing, snowboarding, tubing, and luge sledding, with 10 cut runs, chairlifts, and a beginner rope tow.

THE NORTH CASCADES

A half-million-acre alpine landscape with more than 300 glaciers, the North Cascades National Park is relatively remote and difficult to get to, especially during the winter, and so sees many fewer visitors than more accessible national parks. (In the spring, crews dig out the North Cascades Highway from under 10 to 15 feet of snow.) Sign up for a class at North Cascades Environmental Learning Center (ncascades.org), and hike, bike, swim, climb, ski, and camp. For more information, visit the National Park Service website at www.nps.gov/noca.

Get Guided

TAKE A SKI LESSON AT METHOW VALLEY SKI SCHOOL

427 Goat Creek Road, Winthrop • www.methownet.com/skischool • 509-996-3744

Learn cross-country skiing, one-one-one or with a group from a Professional Ski Instructors of America–certified instructor, then rent skis; Hok snowshoes, a wide snowshoe good for ungroomed snow; or pulks, small toboggans for lugging gear, dogs, or small humans.

HELI-SKIING WITH NORTH CASCADE HELI

heli-ski.com • 509-996-3272

There are multiple backcountry heli-ski trips to choose from, for those who have a little money to spend. Go on three-day, one-day, or custom assisted tours of the North Cascades, launching from the Freestone Inn in Mazama. Or heli up to the cozy 10-sleeper yurt, located just north of Hart's Pass at 6,000 feet—the yurt is warm and the meals are catered.

ROCK CLIMBING WITH MOUNTAIN MADNESS

www.mountainmadness.com • 1-800-328-5925

First-time climbers and those with some experience can take an intro course at Fun Rock. Learn techniques for friction climbing, crack climbing, and face climbing with the support of trusted guides. They offer a whole bunch of other outdoors courses all over the world, too.

HORSEBACK RIDING WITH THUNDERFOOT RIDING OR EARLY WINTERS OUTFITTING

Walking D Ranch, Hagermann Street, Twisp • www.thunderfootriding.com • 360-348-2144

18078 WA-20, Winthrop • www.earlywintersoutfitting.com • 509-996-2659

Take a one-hour to full-day excursion on the back of a horsie. You don't have to know what you're doing—you just have to pay attention during instruction and follow your guide. You can also take a private lesson, train your horse, or go hunting. Getting married? Ask Thunderfoot Riding about riding a horse to your wedding. $65.

GO FISH WITH GRIFF'S FLY FISHING ADVENTURES OR FLY FISHERS PRO SHOP

www.griffsflyfishing.com • 509-929-3813

www.flyfishersproshop.com • 509-429-7298

Hire an expert angler to curate the zones of Methow Valley's glacier-fed rivers and lakes for prime trout and salmon fishing. $150-plus.

RAFT WITH ALPINE ADVENTURES OR METHOW RIVER RAFT + KAYAK

alpineadventures.com • 1-800-RAFT-FUN or 360-863-6505

methowrafting.com • 360-318-5804

From May through July, take a three-, four-, or five-hour journey down the Methow River, braving rapids with names such as Cinder Block Drop and Black Cannon. There are more mellow trips as well as trips where you will experience turbulence. $60-plus.

Stay in Huts

RENDEZVOUS HUTS

www.rendezvoushuts.com • 509-996-8100

Located at 5-mile intervals, each of these five remote wood-framed huts can sleep up to 10 people. The huts are connected by groomed trails to the larger Methow Trails system via the Rendezvous ski trails. They all have a fully equipped though rustic kitchen, a woodstove, propane lights, and access to an outhouse. This is a backcountry situation, so you'll have to pack smart and ski it or haul it in. Pet-friendly accommodations available. $100–200.

ROLLING HUTS

18381 WA-20, Winthrop • rollinghuts.com • 509-996-4442

It's like camping minus the tent and plus a modular sleeping platform with mats, a floor-to-ceiling window, and walls. These huts are very photogenic but not super insulated, so in the winter bring the gear you need to stay warm and keep the fireplace roaring. The simple kitchenette includes a refrigerator and microwave, and there's a 12-person picnic table, a grill, and a water tap outside.

MAZAMA

FROM SEATTLE: 3.5 HOURS • DAYS HERE: 2-PLUS

EAT	DRINK	DO	BUY
bread and cheese from the Mazama Store	wine from the Mazama Store	hike Cedar Creek Falls	Goat's Beard merch from the Mazama Store

 Plan Around

There's not a whole lot going on; see Winthrop events (page 237).

Eat & Drink

There aren't too many food options in Mazama. For more dining options, see the Freestone Inn, or head down to Winthrop (page 238) and Twisp (page 243).

MAZAMA STORE

50 Lost River Road, Mazama • www.themazamastore.com • 509-996-2855 • Open daily 7 a.m.–6 p.m.

It's a grocery store, a coffee shop, a gas station, and a good ol'-timey place to shop and chat. Get ski gear, outdoor guides, gasoline, and locally made enamelware, as well as fresh bread, gourmet cheese, hot coffee, wine and beer, fresh pastries, and sandwiches—everything that you could need while in town. And, of course, the infamous Goat's Beard merch.

>> For hiking, climbing, and ski gear, check out **Goat's Beard Mountain Supplies** (goatsbeard mountainsupplies.com; 509-996-2515; open daily 8:30 a.m.–5:30 p.m.), located inside the Mazama Store. They also have clothing and guidebooks you might not find elsewhere, including pamphlets with insider information about local climbs and hats with bearded goats on them.

 Stay Over

FREESTONE INN & CABINS

31 Early Winters Drive, Mazama • www.freestoneinn.com • 509-996-3906

A large log building with 36 units, all of which have some kind of pretty view and a fireplace. The Sandy Butte Bistro & Bar offers French-style classics and a healthy wine list, while Jack's Hut Pizza & Bar features more casual dining with gourmet pizza and brews, and football fans can watch the game on any of their five big-screen TVs.

MAZAMA COUNTRY INN

15 Country Road, Mazama • www.mazamacountryinn.com • 509-996-2681

The inn has 18 guest rooms, some of which have private hot tubs, gas stoves, and mini-fridges. (They also rent out local cabins—see the website for details.) The hot tub is open year-round and the swimming pool is open Memorial Day through Labor Day. The restaurant serves organic and locally sourced foods, as well as hors d'oeuvres and drinks at the inn's Russian fireplace in the evening, and during the winter all three meals are included in the inn's rates. The coffee bar opens early, and breakfast starts daily at 7 a.m. so that you can get fueled up for your day on the mountain. There are no telephones or TVs, so go outside already.

MAZAMA RANCH HOUSE

10 Country Road, Mazama • www.mazamaranchhouse.com • 509-996-2040

Whether human or horse, creatures can find comfortable housing at Mazama Ranch House. Rent the five-bedroom main ranch house, one of the eight suites, or the detached longhorn cabin. $100-plus.

TIMBERLINE MEADOWS

45 Timerline Lane, Winthrop • www.timberlinemeadows.com • 1-844-430-8977

All cabins have direct access to the Methow Valley Sports Trail, so you can strap on your skis and go. There are a range of cabin sizes and amenities, though most are around 1,500 square feet or more and have multiple rooms, as well as other family-style amenities such as a flat-screen TV in the common room or bunkbeds in the bedrooms and in a loft off the landing. A great option for big groups. Pet-friendly accommodations available. $90-plus.

≡ *While You're Here*

HIKE CEDAR CREEK FALLS

3.5 miles round-trip • Elevation gain: 500 feet • Trailhead: 48.5792, -120.4787

An easy climb best done in the early spring, once the snow has melted and the creek is gushing. If timed right, there are lots of wildflowers and butterflies. From WA-20, turn south onto FR 200. The trailhead is about 0.8 mile in. Northwest Forest Pass required.

>> There are no off-leash dog parks in Mazama, but dogs are welcome on 75 percent of the trails of Methow Trails.

// Hot air balloons in Winthrop

WINTHROP

FROM SEATTLE: 3.75 HOURS · DAYS HERE: 2-PLUS

EAT	DRINK	DO
ice cream at Sheri's Sweet Shoppe	a whiskey and a beer at Three Fingered Jack's Saloon	visit Barron ghost town

Plan Around

SNOWSHOE SOFTBALL TOURNAMENT

February • winthropwashington.com

For the past 30-plus years, coed snowshoe softball teams arrive in Winthrop to engage in the world's most epic battle/a snow-to-the-face game of silliness. Come to watch, or join a snowshoe softball team so that you can compete.

WINTHROP BALLOON FESTIVAL

March • winthropwashington.com

For one weekend, watch dozens of brightly colored hot-air balloons drift in the sky above, a fantastic scene for photographers and people who like bright floaty things. Saturday night is Nightime Balloon Glow, where the balloons light up like lightning bugs.

WINTHROP RHYTHM AND BLUES FESTIVAL

July • winthropbluesfestival.com

Stellar R&B bands have been making the trek to Winthrop since 1988 to get the crowd's booty shaking or to make everyone cry. Camp on the Blues Ranch, right on the festival grounds (quiet time is 2 a.m. to 8 a.m.), or stay only 1 mile away in downtown Winthrop.

☰ *Eat & Drink*

Get Caffeinated

LARIAT COFFEE

265-B Riverside Avenue, Winthrop • lariatcoffee.com • 509-996-4260 • Open Monday–Friday 9 a.m.–4 p.m., Saturday 10 a.m.–2 p.m.

Their organic single-origin Arabica coffee won a Golden Bean Silver Medal in 2017—drink some in-house or pick up some beans to take with you to your backcountry lodging. Try the Black Colt, a cold-brewed, double-filtered coffee concentrate that will make you say *Whoa Nelly*.

ROCKING HORSE BAKERY

265 Riverside Avenue, Winthrop • rockinghorsebakery.com • 509-996-4241 • Open daily 7 a.m.– 4 p.m.

Get handcrafted from-scratch pastries, an egg scramble, and a black gold espresso for breakfast. For lunch, warm up with a cup of soup or cool down with a serious salad, then eat a sandwich. Pack up a slice of cake and a loaf of bread for later post-trail snacking.

>> While in the Rocking Horse Bakery, pick up some gorgeous pottery, glasswork, woodwork, and culinary creations from **Methow Masala**, located inside the store.

SHERI'S SWEET SHOPPE

207 Riverside Avenue, Winthrop • www.sherissweetshoppe.com • 509-996-3834 • Open daily 6:30 a.m. until the last customer comes calling

Sheri and company really, really want to make you happy. Give in by getting a fresh-baked cinnamon roll and a cup of coffee in the morning, then coming back for a sweet treat in the afternoon. After you choose from the 40 flavors of ice cream, get your scoop in a homemade waffle cone.

>> Although you can't stop by the farm and they don't have a stand at the farmers' market, the grains produced by Winthrop's plow-to-package **Bluebird Grain Farms** are worth ordering online. bluebirdgrainfarms.com

Dining

DUCK BRAND CANTINA

248 Riverside Avenue, Winthrop • www.duckbrandwinthrop.com • 509-996-2408 • Open daily
8 a.m.–9 p.m.

The original Duck Brand Saloon was established in 1891. Now a hotel and restaurant, the
cantina's long and eclectic menu features Mexi combos, salads, breakfasts, sandwiches, and
Pacific Northwest/Asian fusion entrées. Also Cajun jambalaya. Try the BBQ duck quesadilla
to go with your margaritas and tequila, beer on tap and in bottles and cans, hard cider, or glass
of wine. Decent rooms to stay in upstairs, too, and centrally located in the downtown area.

ARROWLEAF BISTRO

207 White Avenue, Winthrop • www.arrowleafbistro.com • 509-996-3919 • Open Wednesday–
Monday 4–10 p.m.

A natural blend of local and classic bistro cooking, with a constantly changing menu based on
what's in season, good beer and wine, and a romantic atmosphere for date night.

Booze and Beyond

THREE FINGERED JACK'S SALOON

176 Riverside Ave, Winthrop • www.3fingeredjacks.com • 509-996-2411 • Open daily 11 a.m.–closing

One of the bars that claims to be the oldest legal saloon in Washington State, named after a
cowboy by the name of Jack who accidentally cut off two of his fingers. Play a round of pool
and get a nationally produced beer (gasp!) and some classic pub fare.

OLD SCHOOLHOUSE BREWERY

Pub: 155 Riverside Avenue, Winthrop • 509-996-3183 • Open daily noon–10 p.m.

Taproom: 502 S Glover Street, Building 11 N, Twisp • 509-997-0902 • Open Monday–Friday 3–9
p.m., Saturday and Sunday noon–9 p.m. oldschoolhousebrewery.com

Self-proclaimed "the living room of the Methow Valley," the pub offers 15-plus beers on tap,
brewed from unfiltered North Cascades water and local hops, and fresh and locally sourced
salads, burgers, and veggie options. The Taproom, in Twisp, features beer and snacks, and you
are welcome to pick up food from the nearby food trucks and restaurants and bring it inside.

METHOW VALLEY CIDERHOUSE

28 WA-20, Winthrop • www.methowvalleyciderhouse.com • 509-341-4354 • Open Sunday–
Thursday noon–8 p.m., Friday and Saturday noon–10 p.m.

Taste cider made from organic apples grown on a 15-acre farm just outside town. It's recommended that you get the large sampler: Five 5-ounce pours of cider and/or beer, drinker's
choice. Eat local artisan sausages, the Ciderhouse potato salad, a sandwich, and a Ciderhouse
doughnut for dessert. During the summer, sit in their Apple Amphitheater for live music on
Friday and Saturday nights.

LOST RIVER WINERY

26 WA-20, Winthrop • lostriverwinery.com • 509-996-2888 • Winter hours: Thursday–Monday
11 a.m.–5 p.m. • Summer hours: daily 11 a.m.–5 p.m.

Do a complimentary tasting of the winery's fine wines, which were produced with grapes from
Columbia Valley. Then keep sipping a glassful in the tasting room or on the seasonal patio and
garden.

 **Stay Over**

Camping

PEARRYGIN LAKE STATE PARK

561 Bear Creek Road, Winthrop • 509-996-2370

A huge 1,186-acre campground with 150 campsites, two reservable group camps, two cabins,
and a vacation home. The lake itself is heavily stocked with rainbow trout—the best fishing
is around June and early September—and there are 6.5 miles of hiking trails. Reservations
recommended.

Hostel

NORTH CASCADES MOUNTAIN HOSTEL

209 Castle Avenue, Winthrop • www.northcascadesmountainhostel.com • 206-940-4507

Ski hard and sleep cheap at this downtown hostel. Get a single bunk or a double bed in one of the
mixed-gender bunk rooms, rent a private cabin, or rent out the entire main hostel for yourself
and 19 of your closest friends. Fee includes linens and towels, access to the kitchens, laundry
room, BBQ grill, and ski wax station. Pet-friendly accommodations available. $25-plus.

Inns and Lodges

WINTHROP INN

960 WA-20, Winthrop • winthropinn.com • 509-996-2217

Soak in the year-round hot tub after a long day of freezing your buns off. Pet-friendly accommodations available.

SUN MOUNTAIN LODGE

604 Patterson Lake Road, Winthrop • www.sunmountainlodge.com • 1-800-572-0493

Sitting among 3,000 acres of private wilderness, the view from whatever room you book in any of the four lodgings will be stunning. You won't have to leave the property if you don't want to: There's plenty of good food and wine, the spa will scrub away your cares, the list of activities goes on and on, and the amenities are cushy—private decks, gas fireplaces, jetted tubs, and bathrobes, to name a few.

RIVER'S EDGE RESORT

115 Riverside Avenue, Winthrop • www.riversedgewinthrop.com • 509-996-8000

Located along the Chewuch River in downtown Winthrop, this little resort provides easy access to the Old West town and all it has to offer. All but one cabin has a private hot tub on a private riverside deck, and all rooms have a fireplace, fully equipped kitchen, washing machine and dryer, and a TV.

#ranchlife

SPRING CREEK RANCH

22 Belsby Road, Winthrop • springcreekwinthrop.com • 509-996-2495

A 60-acre ranch with three private lodging options: the 2,000-square-foot, nine-sleeper ranch house; the 750-square-foot, four-sleeper ranch cabin; and the 250-square-foot, two-sleeper Owl's Nest. All are good options and come with a fully equipped kitchen, woodstove, good down duvet, and handcrafted local soap. The trailhead for the Methow Valley Sports Trails Association is located on the property. Board your horse for free; pet-friendly accommodations available. Two-night minimum. $100–370.

≡ *While You're Here*

RIDE IN A HOT-AIR BALLOON WITH MORNING GLORY BALLOON TOURS

960 WA-20, Winthrop • www.balloonwinthrop.com • 509-997-1700

See Methow Valley as the birds do. Float languorously for three hours or so—flight elevations depend on the wind and can be anywhere from treetop level to several thousand feet. Then, once you've reunited with the ground, enjoy the traditional picnic lunch at the launch site. $225 per person.

ABOVE & BEYOND

Dogs | There are no off-leash dog parks in Winthrop, but dogs are welcome on 75 percent of the trails of Methow Trails.

Skates | In the winter, ice skate or play hockey at **Winthrop Rink** (208 White Avenue, Winthrop; winthroprink.org; 509-996-4199), and in the summer, roller skate or play pickleball. $6–10 for a day pass, $2–4 for skate rental.

Books | The only bookstore in the area, **Trail's End Bookstore** (241 Riverside Avenue, Winthrop; www.trailsendbookstore.com; 509-996-2345) has a decent selection of books of all kinds, with a spotlight on books about Methow Valley and Methow Valley authors.

Gear | At **Methow Cycle and Sport** (29 WA-20, Winthrop; www.methowcyclesport .com; 509-996-3645) rent e-bikes, road bikes, or mountain bikes, standup paddleboards, river tubes, skis, or snowshoes—or get what you have tuned up. Check the website for the conditions of bike trails.

Buy or rent (or both) gear and equipment at **Winthrop Mountain Sports** (257 Riverside Avenue, Winthrop; www.winthropmountainsports.com; 509-996-2886). Don't forget to get your skis hot waxed.

The folks at **Nordic Ultratune** (134 Riverside Avenue, Winthrop; www.nordicultratune .com; 509-996-4145) have long studied the art of stone grinding, hot waxing, and flex testing. There's a few-day wait for any service, so plan ahead.

VISIT A GHOST TOWN

NF-374, Winthrop

With dreams of gold dancing in his head, prospector Alex Barron launched the town of Barron in the mid-1890s. He quickly sold it for no small fee, and soon more than 2,500 miners had arrived to find their fortunes. But apparently no one hit the jackpot, because soon they were abandoning their cabins, mine shafts, tavern, and store to follow the money. Today, many of the original structures are still standing, and some old-timey mining equipment is there, collecting 120-plus years of dust. Explore the town when there's no snow, and be aware that this is on private property, although the owners are friendly as long as you respect the area.

TWISP

FROM SEATTLE: 4 HOURS · DAYS HERE: 2

EAT	DRINK	DO	BUY
a cinnamon twist at Cinnamon Twisp Bakery	a smoothie at Glover Street Market	see art at Twispworks	art

Plan Around

There's not a lot going on in Twisp; see Winthrop events (page 237).

Eat & Drink

Get Caffeinated

BLUE STAR COFFEE ROASTERS

#3 Twisp Airport Road, Twisp · bluestarcoffeeroasters.com · 509-997-2583 · Open Monday–Saturday 7:30 a.m.–4:30 p.m.

See the entire production, from green bean to black magic. Drink some joe and eat a fresh pastry while you're at it.

// The Twisp River

116 N Glover Street, Twisp • 509-997-5030 • Open daily 6 a.m.–3 p.m.

The name is cute but the cinnamon twists are *beautiful*. In the summer, come for the most delectable apricot and peach pies and Danish. You can get the breakfast and specialty sandwiches, toasted bagels, smoothies, milkshakes, and juice year-round. And coffee, of course. They offer gluten-free delights, too.

Farm Fresh

201 WA-20, Twisp • www .methowvalleyfarmersmarket.com • Open April–October, Saturday 9 a.m.–noon.

124 N Glover Street, Twisp • www.gloverstreetmarket.com • 509-997-1320 • Open Monday–Saturday 9 a.m.–6 p.m.

Have a nice Northwest-style breakfast or all-day lunch, then pick up all the farm-fresh groceries you need. The organic smoothie and juice bar uses all-organic and seasonal produce for their colorful creations, and in the cool Cellar you can taste wines paired with cheese every Saturday between 2 and 6 p.m. They also have local microbrews, ciders, and bottles of wine to purchase.

Dining

125 N WA-20, Twisp • www.lafondalopez.com • 509-997-0247 • Open daily 11:30 a.m.–8 p.m.

It's a hodgepodge, with authentic Mexican fare offered alongside hamburgers, curry, and pasta. Get the Mexican—the veggies are fresh, the beans are well prepared, and the various sauces are well spiced.

TAPPI

201 Glover Street, Twisp • www.tappitwisp.com • 509-997-3345 • Open Thursday–Monday 5 p.m.–close

A rotating Italian country-style menu featuring fresh salads, wood-fired pizzas, and mouth-watering house-made pasta. A nightly wine pairing (with both food and weather) is a special treat.

 ## *Stay Over*

TWISP RIVER SUITES

140 W Twisp Avenue, Twisp • www.twispriversuites.com • 509-997-0100

Located near Twisp River, this modest hotel has a riverside fire pit, picnic tables, Adirondack chairs, and a hammock for enjoying the waters flowing by. Beds are comfy, the Twisp River Pub is next door, and there are flat-screen TVs and deep soaker tubs in each room for when you need a break from the great outdoors. Paws Awhile Pet Suites available. $139-plus.

ABOVE & BEYOND

Dogs | There are no off-leash dog parks in Twisp, but dogs are welcome on 75 percent of the trails of Methow Trails.

Good to Know |

- At 6,100 feet above sea level, Hart's Pass outside of Mazama is the highest car-accessible road in Washington. It's a crazy gravel-and-sand, one-lane climb that leads to Slate Pass Lookout. Drive at your own risk.
- Many credit Winthrop's founder's Harvard roommate for writing America's first western novel, *The Virginian*, after visiting the town.
- **Smokejumping**, a method of fighting forest fires, was first developed in 1939 by the US Forest Service, using an SR-10 Stinson Reliant aircraft. A gentleman by the name of Francis Lufkin was the first to jump out of the plane. www.northcascadessmoke jumperbase.com.

Been There, Done That |

- Take the Cascade Loop (www.cascadeloop.com) northwest on the North Scenic Byway through North Cascades National Park to Skagit Valley (page 50).
- Take the Cascade Loop (www.cascadeloop.com) southwest to Leavenworth (page 263). Then continue on Stevens Pass to Mukilteo to catch the ferry to Whidbey Island (page 249).

METHOW SUITES BED & BREAKFAST

620 Moody Lane, Twisp • methowsuites.com • 509-997-5970

Owned by a former Methow Valley educator and a smokejumper, this two-bedroom B&B offers a nummy locally sourced breakfast, private decks for watching the wildlife, a TV and DVD player, and a library. $125.

IDLE-A-WHILE MOTEL

505 N WA-20, Twisp • www.idle-a-while-motel.com • 509-997-3222

A hostel with a hot tub, sauna, and Tequila Fridays in walking distance of downtown Twisp. Rent a room in the motel or get a detached cabin. It's not the fanciest of locales, but the rooms are warm, dry, and cozy after a long day in the snow. $79-plus.

// Methow Valley

☰ *While You're Here*

SEE A PLAY AT THE MERC

101 S Glover Street, Twisp • www.mercplayhouse.org • 509-997-7529

A former mercantile, this 150-seat theater shows Shakespeare, kids' shows, Broadway classics, and more contemporary dirty-minded comedies, as well as musical performances from acclaimed musicians. Check the website for upcoming performances.

EXPLORE TWISPWORKS

502 S Glover Street, Twisp • twispworks.org • 509-997-3300

TwispWorks is on a mission to improve the economic vitality of the Methow Valley through art, education, technology, and agriculture, and they do this by supporting and promoting Methow-made goods and services. Stroll through the native plant garden, see how earth pigments and botanicals are used in the natural dye garden, learn Methow history in the interpretive center, listen to live music, and have a picnic on the lawn on this 6.4-acre campus in the heart of Twisp. Check out the open studios of silversmiths, metalworkers, glassblowers, stone carvers, textile and book artists, and painters on Saturdays during the summer, and see the website for schedules of community events.

Part Four
Quiet Time

Meditation and Contemplation on Whidbey Island

FROM SEATTLE: 1.5 TO 2.5 HOURS · DAYS HERE: 1 TO 3

DO	EAT	DRINK	BUY
contemplate	logan berry pie at Whidbey Pies & Café	coffee at Useless Bay	Cook-on Cookware at Cook on Clay and plants at Bayview Farm & Garden

Despite the fast-paced growth of the Seattle area, Whidbey Island has retained its slow-paced Island-style living. From Oak Harbor in the north down through Coupeville, Langley, Freeland, Greenbank, Clinton, and Bayview in the south, it's a lovely blend of rural and woodland, with a community avid about protecting the old-growth forests that have been there forever. Locals consider the area a sanctuary, and for good reason. The moment you step aboard the Mukilteo–Clinton ferry, you'll find yourself instinctively taking a deep, slow breath. There's something magical about the Pacific Northwest Island culture, and it's as though the quality of the air changes as you ride over the Puget Sound away from skyscrapers and traffic and toward farm stands, ocean bluffs, and forest labyrinths.

Parks on Whidbey Island are famously dog friendly. Businesses are small and family owned, with a penchant for local sourcing and organics. Roasteries are obsessed with the perfect espresso, and every restaurant boasts being *the* premier farm-to-fork eatery. Many of the farms feed communities only within a hundred-mile radius, and the rain shadow climate makes for some prime berries. If you haven't had berries fresh off the plant and still warm from a July sun, then come to Whidbey during the summer. And the best cure for the winter blues is a panoramic view of the sound, its waves dark and choppy, and the kind of quiet that distance from the city can bring.

>> If you and your dog will be camping on Whidbey Island, don't forget to bring a Seattle-made doggy sleeping bag from Barker Gear (www.barkergear.com).

Getting There

BY CAR/FERRY | Drive on I-5 N for 17 miles and take Exit 182 to WA-525 N to Clinton–Mukilteo. From the Mukilteo Terminal (614 Front Street, Mukilteo), take the Mukilteo–Clinton Ferry to Clinton (travel time: approximately 1.5 hours). You can check the wait at www.wsdot.wa.gov/ferries/vesselwatch.

BY BUS/FERRY | Take Bus #417 to the Mukilteo Terminal (travel time: approximately 2.5 hours), then take the ferry. For Island Transit bus routes and schedules, go to www.islandtransit.org.

BY CAR | Take the long but wonderfully scenic way around by driving north on I-5 N for 63 miles to Exit 230 to WA-20, then drive west on WA-520 for 17 miles through Fidalgo Island to Deception Pass Bridge. Once you cross the bridge over Deception Pass, drive south on WA-20. Views are stunning. You'll enter the island from the north side, in Oak Harbor.

Highlight Reel

YOGA LODGE

3475 Christie Road, Greenbank • www.yogalodge.com • 360-222-3749

On many weekends, yoga and meditation teachers from the Seattle area host retreats at the Yoga Lodge. It's an ideal place for that—set back into the forest, the lodge intentionally doesn't offer WiFi, so you have to leave your work/social media at home and just unplug.

You don't have to sign up for a group retreat to stay at the lodge. On weekends when

1 Earth Sanctuary, Whidbey Island
2 The Clinton-Mukilteo Ferry, Puget Sound
3 Earth Sanctuary, Whidbey Island

there's nothing going on or, more frequently, the weekdays, you can reserve a room and then use the lodge's grounds, contemplative space, and serene setting to get some peace and quiet. People come for their own self-driven yoga retreat—you can practice on your own, take one of the ongoing weekday classes with the Islanders, or ask in advance for a private class with the lodge's nice manager or the local teachers. Writers come and use the solitude to get some focus, too. But you don't have to do or be any particular thing—you just have to want quiet. The land surrounding the lodge has trails among old-growth gentle giants and a garden, and it's near many lovely hiking spots and fantastic restaurants.

EARTH SANCTUARY

www.earthsanctuary.org

2059 Newman Road, Langley • 360-331-6667

5536 Emil Road, Langley • 360-321-5465

The Earth Sanctuary retreat center is located on a 72-acre contemplation-inspiring nature reserve. You and/or your crew can rent the single-family house, then spend the day strolling the home of thousands of trees and native plants; 90 species of birds, including osprey, bald eagles and the great horned owl; and all kinds of happy mammals such as chipmunks and mountain beavers. Newts, bullfrogs, salamanders, and turtles blink slowly in the sanctuary's three ponds while trees live and die and replenish the earth. You can find a self-guided tour map, which points out the many sacred sites and artworks throughout the area, such as the labyrinth and prayer stone, the medicine wheel, the cottonwood stone circle, and the heart-stone seating area. This is an all-inclusive sacred symbols situation, with sculptures inspired by ancient Native American, French, and Tibetan Buddhist traditions. All this is to say that this is a hippy paradise, and even if you can't stay, you can visit the grounds during daylight hours (entrance fee: $7). Or schedule a sacred space and naturalist tour or a calm, abiding meditation tour.

THE WRITER'S REFUGE

writersrefuge.com • 206-799-0395

Whidbey Island is a mecca for writers. Let your writer's block melt away in this little cabin in the woods. It's got all the amenities a writer looking for peace and quiet might want: a comfy bed, wood-burning stove, a large screened-in porch, a recliner, bookshelves full of books on writing, and WiFi. This is a single-occupancy cabin because other people are distracting, but well-behaved dogs are welcome on a case-by-case basis. Three-night minimum, $90 per night.

≡ *Plan Around*

LANGLEY'S MYSTERY WEEKEND

February • visitlangley.com/lp/mystery-weekend

Every year for the last thirty-odd years, wannabe sleuthers come to Whidbey to solve a terrible fake crime. There's an original story featuring a bunch of clues to follow and weird suspects to interview. Solve the crime and win a prize!

THE GREAT NORTHWEST GLASS QUEST

February • www.thegreatnwglassquest.com

This 10-day treasure hunt takes place throughout Stanwood and Camano Island. Every morning, some sneaky person hides plastic replicas of hand-blown glass balls by world-renowned local artists Mark and Marcus Ellinger in parks and at local businesses. Scavengers use a treasure map to track down the fakes, which they exchange for the real McCoy.

PENN COVE MUSSELFEST

March • thepenncovemusselsfestival.com/mussel-mingle

Watch mussel-cooking demonstrations, see live music, judge a chowder-tasting competition (with your mouth), go on a boat tour of the Penn Cove mussels farm, and drink beer. You can compete in or watch a mussel-eating competition, too, if stuffing bivalve mollusks in your face or watching others stuffing bivalve mollusks in their faces seems like a good time to you.

WAG 'N' WALK

August • waifanimals.org/wagnwalk

Dress your dog up in a costume fitting the year's theme and walk them around Greenbank Farm. There are games and food vendors for people and pets, and the crowning of the King and Queen costume contest. Proceeds go to Whidbey Animals' Improvement Foundation and other nonprofit rescue groups.

OAK HARBOR MUSIC FESTIVAL

September • www.oakharborfestival.com

It's a music festival! It's free! It's a free music festival with more than 30 bands, beer and wine, and other festival-related vendors, held annually over Labor Day weekend.

WHIDBEY ISLAND KITE FESTIVAL

September • www.whidbeykites.org

Go fly a kite on Whidbey. Or watch the two mass ascensions of the Whidbey Island Sport Kite Championships.

WHIDBEY ISLAND GROWN WEEK

September • whidbeyislandgrown.com/whidbey-island-grown-week

A 10-day harvest celebration of all things hyperlocal and fresh, with lodging deals, hands-on farm and culinary adventures, and special tours and tastings.

>> Three times a year, wine- and boozemakers get together with local foodies and artists to celebrate with some **seasonal wine-tasting**. For more information, visit www.whidbeyisland vintners.org.
Red Wine & Chocolate in February
Savor Spring in May
Autumn on Whidbey in November

≡ *Eat & Drink*

Get Caffeinated

MUKILTEO COFFEE ROASTERS

5331 Crawford Road, Langley • mukilteocoffee.com • 360-321-5262 • Open Tuesday–Saturday 8 a.m.–4 p.m.

Mukilteo Coffee Roasters is a family-owned business that sources directly from family farms in Costa Rica, El Salvador, Guatemala, and Panama. They're super-nerds about small-batch roasting, and you'll be able to experience the results in the Café in the Woods, a funky way-off-the-beaten-path restaurant set back in the woods, with indoor and outdoor seating. Organic, farm-fresh, tasty breakfast and lunch is served all day. Be sure to get an espresso.

USELESS BAY COFFEE

121 Second Street, Langley • uselessbaycoffee.com • 360-221-4515 • Open daily 7:30 a.m.–4:30 p.m.

Watch the 1950s German Probat UG15 drum roaster do its magic as you sip espresso and eat fresh-baked pastry, a panini hot off the press, or a banh mi made with house-smoked pork.

KNEAD AND FEED BAKERY

4 Front Street NW, Coopeville • www.kneadandfeed.com • 360-678-5431 • Open Monday–Friday 9 a.m.–3 p.m., Saturday and Sunday 8 a.m.–3 p.m.

Knead and Feed Bakery has the best cinnamon rolls in town as well as other fresh-baked goods, a great view of Penn Cove, and scrumptious soups, salads, and sandwiches for lunch.

Farm Fresh

GLENDALE SHEPHERD

7616 Glendale Heights Road, Clinton • glendaleshepherd.com • Farm store and tasting hours: Saturday and Sunday 11 a.m.–4 p.m.

The Glendale Shepherd farm has been in the Swanson family for three generations. Little lambies nibble grass on the eastern coastline of Whidbey, living their best lives before being "humanely harvested," and the 70 milking sheep produce yogurt and award-winning cheese available in farmers' markets and grocery stores across the region. To see a small-scale, family-owned and -operated farm in action, come by for a taste. (Or to stay. See page 258.)

MUTINY BAY BLUES FARMSTAND

5598 Cameron Road, Freeland • mutinybayblues.com • 360-331-2331 • Open Monday–Saturday during blueberry season

You can't get these blueberries more than a hundred miles from this family-owned farm. They specialize in Duke, Draper, and Liberty varieties and do ongoing testing to find the next best blueberry. Check the website for information on which blueberry is ready to go into your mouth.

>> For more information on local farms, goods, and services, visit whidbeyislandgrown.com.

Farm to Fork

ISLAND NOSH

8898 WA-525, Clinton • www.islandnosh.com • 360-341-3828 • Open Tuesday–Saturday 11 a.m.–8 p.m.

Just a stone's throw from the Clinton ferry terminal, Island Nosh has an eclectic menu, with a focus on "ethnic noodles" such as mac 'n' cheese, ramen, curry, udon, and vermicelli. This inclusive sampling is seamlessly tied together by their use of fresh, locally sourced produce. Wrap up the meal with some fresh and gooey rice crispy treats.

ORCHARD KITCHEN

5574 Bayview Road, Langley • www.orchardkitchen.com • 360-321-1517 • Winter hours: October–June, Friday and Saturday dinner at 7 p.m.; summer hours: July–September, Thursday–Saturday dinner at 7 p.m.

Orchard Kitchen is serious about responsible local sourcing. They grow many of their ingredients on their organic farm, the prix fixe dinner is spendy but worth it, and you don't have to tip—they pay their employees a living wage! Since it is based strictly on the ongoing harvest, the "hyper seasonal" menu changes weekly. Reservations required. Dinner $75; additional wine pairing $44.

>> Want to learn how to cook farm-to-fork style? Check Orchard Kitchen's website for a schedule of cooking classes.

ROAMING RADISH

5417 Crawford Road, Langley • www.roamingradish.com • 360-331-5939 • Open Wednesday–Friday 5–10 p.m.

Dry-brined, maple-crusted, and slow-roasted 12-hour pork belly. Miso and Finn River dry-hopped, cider-marinated Pacific black cod. Carrot cake cupcake with cream cheese buttercream and pineapple gel. Created by an OG Islander returned from a culinary career in New Orleans, served in a renovated airplane hangar. Go there. Reservations required.

FLOWER HOUSE CAFE

2780 Marshview Avenue, Langley • www.bayviewfarmandgarden.com • 360-321-6789 • Open daily 8 a.m.–4 p.m.

Where avocado toast people and plant people come together to share their passions. Owned and operated by a mother-daughter duo, the café features a seasonal produce–forward menu, with local Useless Bay coffee and fresh-baked pastry. Bring your macchiato, chia pudding, chicken salad sandwich, and, of course, avocado toast to savor in the outdoor courtyard, which has been expertly planted for a lush, tropical atmosphere. Across the courtyard sits the Garden Shop, with its large glass greenhouse, jungle room, and 2 acres of nursery. This garden center was green before it was cool, having never once used or sold toxic chemicals. Mainlanders from near and far make the trip just to get some healthy trees, shrubs, perennials, vines, roses, and water plants. The gift shop is super cute and on trend, too.

WHIDBEY PIES & CAFE

765 Wonn Road, Greenbank • www.whidbeypies.com • 360-678-1288 • Open daily 11 a.m.–5 p.m.

Sit outside in the garden and enjoy a light and fresh soup, salad, sandwich, or savory, then satisfy your sweet tooth with a slice of homemade pie. The Gunn family elevates pie making to an art—get the loganberry. Or the marionberry. Or, if you've come in on a late summer day, the peach. Get a slice (or two or three or four) to eat there, then get a pie (or two or three or four) to go.

THE OYSTERCATCHER

901 Grace Street NW, Coupeville • www.oystercatcherwhidbey.com • 360-678-0683 • Open for lunch Friday–Monday noon–3 p.m., dinner Thursday–Sunday 5 p.m.–close

The fresh-out-of-the-oven bread alone is worth the visit. Everything else is delish, too. Get a dozen oysters on the half shell, some savory spreads, and a butcher's cut or catch of the day. They're happy to craft "vegetarian experiences," too.

FRASER'S GOURMET HIDEAWAY

1191 SE Dock Street #101, Oak Harbor • www.frasersgh.com • 360-279-1231

Combine a French training with Northwest sensibility and you have Fraser's Gourmet Hideaway. It goes without saying that the menu is seasonal and the seafood is good, and the housemade pasta will make you close your eyes and sit back in your chair.

Booze and Beyond

WHIDBEY ISLAND DISTILLERY

3466 Craw Road, Langley • www.whidbeyislanddistillery.com • 360-321-4715 • Open daily 11 a.m.–5 p.m.

Take a tour of the 9-acre farm, then taste the award-winning liqueurs, which are made from locally produced wines and the berries—black diamond blackberries, loganberry, raspberry, boysenberry—that the Pacific Northwest is known for. The Whidbey Island Distillery's blackberry liqueur is the highest rated spirit in North America. Try their new Bunker Rye whiskey, too.

SPOILED DOG WINERY

5881 Maxwelton Road, Langley • www.spoileddogwinery.com • 360-661-6226 • Open May–September, Wednesday–Friday 2–5 p.m., Saturday and Sunday noon–5 p.m.; October–April, Saturday and Sunday noon–5 p.m. and by appointment

The vintners at Spoiled Dog Winery love their dogs. They also love pinot noir, which was their primary reason for moving to Whidbey Island—to live under the rain shadow that makes an ideal clime for growing pinot noir grapes. Bring your own spoiled dogs and take photos.

>> Get your wine to go from **Greenbank Farm Wine Shop** (765 Wonn Road, Greenbank; greenbankfarmwineshop.com; 360-222-3797). Specializing in all things loganberry and award-winning local wines, ciders, and craft brews, the shop is located on the historic farm, which was once the world's leading producer of loganberries.

☰ *Stay Over*

#farmlife

GLENDALE SHEPHERD SHEEP CAMP

glendaleshepherd.com

The Glendale Shepherd Sheep Camp is perfect for counting sheep . . . because it's a sheep camp. Rent the camping site through Hipcamp.com and bring your tent, your hiking boots, and your appetite for cheese. Or rent the studio apartment through Airbnb. This clean, cozy space is located above the creamery. If you're lucky, you might see sheep having sex! Visit the Glendale Shepherd website for links to Hipcamp and Airbnb. Campsite: $40 per night; studio apartment: $52 per night.

LAVENDER WIND

2530 Darst Road, Coupeville • www.lavendarwind.com • 1-877-242-7716

Stay at a working lavender farm's guest house and wake up to panoramic views of the Puget Sound and the Olympic Mountains, lavender scones and tea for breakfast, and the scent of the lavender in the air. $75 per night.

Wine and Doze

COMFORTS OF WHIDBEY

5219 View Road, Langley • www.comfortsofwhidbey.com • 360-969-2961

As it says on the website: "Come for the wine, stay for the comfort." Open all year-round, the bed & breakfast portion of Comforts of Whidbey is located above the winery. Each of the six rooms has a view: either the Puget Sound or the pasture and vineyard. Guests get a continental breakfast during the week at 8:30 a.m. and a full farm-fresh breakfast on weekends. The rooms are sans TV but include a robe—in terms of max relaxation, that seems like a fair trade. On Thursdays, Fridays, and Mondays, wine tasting goes from noon to 5 p.m., and on Saturdays and Sundays you can get started earlier and spend more time drinking, with the tasting room open 11 a.m. to 6 p.m.

DANCING FISH VINEYARDS

1953 Newman Road, Freeland • www.dancingfishvineyards.com • 1-866-331-0129

Get away from it all and get onto 6 acres of vineyards, apple orchards, and a beautiful seventy-odd-year-old, newly renovated house. Tasting hours change seasonally, but the tasting room is open four days a week, giving you plenty of time to get your wine on and then stroll in a romantic fashion through the vines or walk up to the apple orchard's viewing deck to look out over the rolling green property. For foodies who know their way around a cookbook, the kitchen is fancy, with a La Cornue stove and plenty of room to put down your just-bought, hyperlocally grown produce, crack open a bottle of wine you got in the barrel room, and get cooking. Before going to bed, take a bath in the clawfoot tub, dry off, put on the complimentary bathrobe, and watch your favorite show on cable. The perfect getaway for a few friends who want some serious chill time. Pets allowed.

Camping and Glamping

CAMA BEACH CABINS AT CAMA BEACH STATE PARK

Cama Beach State Park, 1880 SW Camano Drive, Camano Island • parks.state.wa.us/407/Cama-Beach-State-Park • 360-387-1550

The cabins and bungalows from this 1930s-era fishing resort have been updated and refurbished with electricity, a refrigerator and freezer, a sink, and even a microwave! Cabins face the Saratoga Passage, in the 433-acre Cama State Park on the southwest shore of Camano Island, and you'll be able to see the neighboring Whidbey Island and the Olympic Mountains beyond that. Don't let the highfalutin electricity confuse you—this is closer to a wooden tent with appliances than to a hotel, and you'll need to bring all bedding, linen, cookware, and dishes. Don't expect any maid service, and you'll be sharing the bathhouse with your fellow cabin dwellers. It's usually pretty quiet, with grills and picnic tables near the water, a rocky beach to look for rocks on, and 15 miles of trails for hiking and biking. Cama Beach crabbing season starts July 1 and ends Labor Day (crabbers, don't forget to get your crab endorsement and catch record card from the Washington Department of Fish & Wildlife, wdfw.wa.gov). Pet-friendly cabins are available for a $15 fee. Rental fees depend on season, day of week, and type of cabin. Discover Pass required for vehicles.

>> Rent a boat or take a sailing lesson at the Center for Wooden Boats (cwb.org; 360-387-9361) in Cama State Park. Every Saturday the center hosts a toy boat–building free-for-all. Suggested donation: $3.

FORT EBEY STATE PARK

400 Hill Valley Drive, Coupeville

Pitch your tent on this former WWII fort, now a 651-acre state park with sweeping views of Admiralty Inlet, 25 miles of hiking and biking trails, and gun emplacements and underground rooms to explore. Bring your surfboard, paragliding gear, and seaweed-harvesting equipment (seaweed and shellfish license required). Reserve a spot at washington.goingtocamp.com or 1-888-CAMP-OUT.

≡ *While You're Here*

VISIT ORGANIC FARM SCHOOL

organicfarmschool.org

This working farm school teaches aspiring farmers how to . . . be farmers. Cultivated by the students and teachers, the 10-acre farm has vegetables, berries, bees, and livestock, growing together in a sunny swath of land. Visits and tours by reservation only.

SHOP COOK ON CLAY

640 Patmore Road, Coupeville • www.cookonclay.com • 360-678-1414 or 360-929-8121 • Open daily 10 a.m.–5 p.m.

Who knew there was such a thing as "flameproof" clay? Apparently, the artists at Cook on Clay did. They handmake gorgeous cookware, from casserole dishes to loaf pots, skillets to platters to pizza stones, all of which can be used where things get hot: the oven, microwave, grill—you name it. Call ahead to visit the showroom to buy stuff and to see how they do what they do.

KITEBOARD AND HIKE DOUBLE BLUFF BEACH

S Double Bluff Road, Freeland

Located to the south of Freeland, right off SR-525, Double Bluff Beach is known as a mecca for kiteboarding. October through March, intermediate to advanced kiteboarders harness the heavy winds coming down from the Strait of Juan de Fuca for some serious rippin' it up. Low tide is ideal for newbies.

// Farming on Whidbey Island

ABOVE & BEYOND

Dogs | Whidbey Island is very proud of its dog-friendly reputation (see Wag 'n' Walk on page 253). There are many areas where you can release your dog from its leash, such as the 13-acre **Marguerite Brons Memorial Park** (2837 Becker Road, Clinton), the 15-acre meadow of **Patmore Pit** (497 Patmore Road, Coupeville), or the working **Greenbank Farm** (765 Wonn Road, Greenbank). For more information, call 360-321-4049 or go to www.fetchparks.org.

Books | Not only do Whidbey Islanders love their dogs, they love their books. **Moonraker Bookstore** (209 1st Street, Langley; 360-221-6962; open Monday–Saturday 10:30 a.m.–5:30 p.m., Sunday 11 a.m.–5 p.m.) is a local favorite, with an adorable store-front and good selection of best-sellers, travel books, cookbooks, poetry, and more.

The claim to fame of the **Book Rack** (551 NE Midway Boulevard #3, Oak Harbor; www .bookrackwa.com; 360-675-6705; open Monday–Thursday 10 a.m.–7 p.m., Friday 10 a.m.–10 p.m., Saturday 10 a.m.–8 p.m., Sunday 11 a.m.–7 p.m.) is that it is the largest retailer of books, comics, and games on Whidbey Island. Stock up on Dungeons & Drag-ons, vintage comics, and new or used novels and nonfiction.

Wind & Tide Bookshop (790 SE Pioneer Way, Oak Harbor; www.windandtidebooks.net; 360-675-1342; open Tuesday–Saturday 11 a.m.–4 p.m.) has offered new and used books, graphic novels, and gift items since 1967.

Buy a book at **The Commons Café & Books** (124 2nd Street, Langley; southwhidbey commons.org; 360-221-2414; open Sunday–Thursday 8 a.m.–5 p.m., Friday and Saturday 8 a.m.–5 p.m.), then sit outside with your dog and eat some gluten-free, vegan, or normal pastries with a cup of joe.

At **Gregor Rare Books** (220 1st Street, Langley; www.gregorrarebooks.com; 360-221-8331; open Wednesday–Sunday 11 a.m.–5 p.m., Monday by chance or appointment) you can pick up a $3,000 Ernest Hemingway first edition or some less expensive but still amazing rare books and first editions.

Skates | **Oak Harbor Skate Park** (SE Glencoe Street and SE 3rd Avenue, Oak Harbor) has plenty of room and lots of elements to practice transitions and such. For photos and more information, go to www.northwestskater.com.

Rent bikes and mopeds at **Half Link Bicycle Shop** (5603 Bayview Road, Suite 1, Langley; bayviewbikes.com; 360-331-7980; open Tuesday–Saturday 10 a.m.–6 p.m.) and **Whidbey Island Moped** (308 1st Street, Langley; www.whidbeyislandmoped.com; 360-221-5152).

Not Ready to Go Home | Stop by the haunted **Oxford Saloon** (913 1st Street, Snohomish; www.oxfordsaloonsnohomish.com; 360-243-3060), established in 1910. This former dry goods store is rumored to have been a bordello along with a gaming house and bar where people fisticuffed one another on a not-irregular basis. One of the ghosts is named Henry, a policeman in life and an ass-pinching perv in death (possibly also in life). Two ghosts seen upstairs, in what are now offices, are believed to be the madam and one of her sex workers. The saloon now serves breakfast, burgers, and beers.

Good to Know |

- At 62 miles in length, Whidbey Island is the longest island in Washington State—*not* in the country, as some have mistakenly claimed.
- Washington's Island County includes Whidbey Island, Camano Island, Ben Ure Island, and six uninhabited islands. The county seat is in Coupeville.

Been There, Done That | Take the ferry to Mukilteo, then head east on the Cascade Loop (www.cascadeloop.com) to Leavenworth (page 263) and Methow Valley (page 230).

You could also watch those crazy kiteboarders catching air from the beach while taking a flat, sandy hike. The beach goes on for miles, with plenty of room for Fido to chase seagulls and roll in rotting seaweed. (If you aren't comfortable with dogs running free, their flappy dog lips pulled back in canine ecstasy, then this is not the beach for you. Double Bluff Beach is vying for *USA Today*'s #1 Dog-Friendly Beach.) Views are incredible and include the Cascade Range from Mount Baker to Mount Rainier and the Olympic Mountains to the west.

BIKE OR HIKE KETTLE TRAILS AT EBEY STATE PARK

400 Hill Valley Drive, Coupeville

The Kettles Trail System includes 35 miles of trails through old-growth forest and along ocean bluffs, and it is open to hikers, bikers, and horseback riders. You can park in Fort Ebey State Park or on WA-20 near Libbey Road. Pick up a map at Ebey State Park or download one at the National Park Service website (www.nps.gov). Discover Pass required.

>> Take a self-guided tour of Whidbey Island's visual artists' studios. You can see sculptors, photographers, glassblowers, painters, and basket weavers in their natural habitat by downloading the **Whidbey Art Trail** map at www.whidbeyarttrail.com.

15

Art and Music in Leavenworth

FROM SEATTLE: 3 HOURS · DAYS HERE: 2 TO 3

DO	EAT	DRINK	BUY
art	brats	beer	*The Art & Character of Nutcrackers*

It's true, Leavenworth has been called "Nazi Disneyland." But don't let that scare you—the Bavarian theme starts at the buildings' facades and ends at the dirndl, with a few stops at bratwurst and Oktoberfest in between. If drinking Hefeweizen and dancing to oompah is in your wheelhouse, then put visiting downtown Leavenworth during October on your itinerary.

But the town has so much more to offer than compressed meats and German cosplay. With its Alps-like setting, the Cascade Mountains create a hub for outdoor enthusiasts, artists, and solitude seekers. The Grunewald Guild is perfect for artists, with its art studios set on 14 acres of woodlands. Icicle Creek Center for the Arts caters to pianists, although you don't have to be a key tickler to enjoy the practice huts and cabins. Alpine Lakes High Camp and Loge Camps are ideal for those who want to get away from it all via the great outdoors.

≡ *Getting There*

Depending on the season, the trip to Leavenworth takes around 2.5 to 3.5 hours. If you're driving, take US-2 to go along the Stevens Pass Greenway, which follows the Skykomish River into the Cascade Range. Whether you drive or take the bus or train, the route is scenic, with stunning views of forest and mountains.

BY CAR | From Seattle, take I-5 to Everett, then get on WA-522 East to US-2. Continue on US-2 for approximately 117 miles.

BY SHUTTLE | The Leavenworth Shuttle (www.leavenworthshuttle.com; 509-548-7433) is a family-owned taxi service that serves the Seattle area. Cost: $2 per person and $3 per mile. Leavenworth is approximately 125 miles from Seattle.

BY BUS | Tickets on the Northwestern Trailways bus (northwesterntrailways.com) cost $36 one-way, and the trip takes approximately 3.5 hours.

BY TRAIN | The trip from King Street Station in the International District (303 Jackson Street, Seattle) to Leavenworth Icicle Station (11645 North Road, Leavenworth) takes around 3.5 hours and costs between $25 and $60 for a one-way ticket (www.amtrak.com). It's recommended that you arrange in advance for a shuttle to pick you up and take you to your destination.

>>   During December, you can take the snow train with Alki Tours (alkitours.com; 1-800-895-2554). This day trip includes a catered Amtrak train ride to Leavenworth, where you'll disembark to stroll the town's festivities and witness the famous lighting ceremony at dusk, after which you'll reboard for the ride back to Seattle.

≡ *Highlight Reel*

GRUNEWALD GUILD

19003 River Road, Leavenworth • grunewaldguild.com • 509-763-3693

Fifteen miles outside of Leavenworth proper, the Grunewald Guild is set back into 14 acres of woodlands outside the tiny town of Plain, next to the Wenatchee River. It's an arts education nonprofit retreat center that's a nice mix of quiet and groovy, earnest and open. Anytime between September and May you can take a personal retreat, with the cost of lodging dependent on availability and where you choose to rest your weary head: the three-season yurt, a single room, a shared room, or the dorm, located in the sleeping loft above the library. Whether your meals are served or self-prepped depends on programming or lack thereof. For a fee, you can use the arts studios and work spaces, of which there are many: the fiber arts studio, library, glass shop, paint shop, print shop, barn, and writer's studio.

1 Alpine Lakes High Camp, Leavenworth
2 Alpine Lakes High Camp, Leavenworth
3 Grunewald Guild, Leavenworth

The weeklong summer programs include food, lodging, and art classes, with offerings such as "Drawing for the Terrified," "Wade in Watercolor," "Stained Glass: Line, Color, and Light," and "Writing Workshop: The Medium of Memory." In the afternoons, you have a few hours of free time during which you can use any of the arts studios, take a nap in one of the hammocks spread throughout the campus, read a book in the library, leave the campus to visit Leavenworth, or go for a hike/ski/swim, depending on the season. There's ecumenical worship, too, but no presh if that's not your thing.

Whether you're in a program or on your own, check out the contemplative spaces: the labyrinth, the sculpture garden, the garden, the bridge over the chilly Wenatchee River. The Finisterre is extra trippy, made of steamed and stained trees set in a big steel ring.

ICICLE CREEK CENTER FOR THE ARTS

7409 Icicle Road, Leavenworth • icicle.org • 509-548-6347

Icicle Creek Center for the Arts is a haven for piano enthusiasts as well as other musicians, writers, or anyone looking for the kind of quiet that sparks creativity. You can attend any of the 100 performances featuring accomplished musicians and actors, set in a gorgeous theater, recital hall, or outside on the Meadows Stage, then spend the night in one of the eight charming cabins. There are two practice huts set in the woods, perfect for alone time. Or sign up for a four-day retreat for adult amateur pianists to get some training and practice in this peaceful place with perfect acoustics. Pet-friendly accommodations available.

ALPINE LAKES HIGH CAMP

Coulter Creek Road, Leavenworth • www.alpinelakeshighcamp.com • 509-763-3044

Located smack dab between Leavenworth and Stevens Pass, this all-seasons mountain getaway is 8.5 miles up a private road, accessible only by shuttle, which will pick you up at the parking lot off US-2. The nine backcountry huts are completely off the grid, though the lodge has two solar panels for charging devices. The beds are comfy and the kitchens are equipped, but you'll have to bring your own bedding and food. After a long day of backcountry cross-country skiing, snowshoeing, sledding, or fat tire biking, stoke up the wood-fired hot tub and sauna. In warmer weather, hike and mountain bike the trails that lead directly from Alpine Lakes High Camp. Dogs are allowed on weekdays for $30 per night. $170–600.

LOGE CAMPS

11798 US-2, Leavenworth • www.logecamps.com • 509-690-4106

Stay at a mountain village without breaking the bank. LOGE Camps were designed with outdoor enthusiasts in mind, with mountain bike storage, ski racks, and boot dryers. The cabins will afford you more privacy, whereas the hostel has more opportunities for post-exploration camaraderie. The hammocks, fire pits, outdoor-covered kitchen, and summer outdoor movies

// LOGE Leavenworth

and concerts make it both a social affair and a place to kick back and relax. Pet friendly. Hostel $55, cabin $150-plus.

≡ *Plan Around*

BAVARIAN ICEFEST

January • leavenworth.org

Come into town to smoosh or play ice cube scramble, watch live ice-carving and fire dancers, ride on a sled pulled by a snowmobile, then watch fireworks. $5.

TIMBRRR! WINTER MUSIC FESTIVAL IN LEAVENWORTH

January • winter.timbermusicfest.com

An outdoor music festival at which you will freeze your little bunsies off if you aren't wearing the proper attire. Between shows with fantastic musicians, warm up in the hot toddy garden, play a game of cornhole, compete in the bubble hockey tournament, or hit the slopes of Stevens Pass. This is not the time for camping—you'll want to book a room in one of Leavenworth's many lodgings.

WENATCHEE RIVER BLUEGRASS FESTIVAL

June • Chelan County Expo Center, 5700 Wescott Drive, Cashmere • www.wenatcheeriverbluegrass.com

The town of Cashmere is 10 miles southeast of downtown Leavenworth, and every year this little community hosts a bunch of award-winning bluegrass bands at the fairgrounds. Come for the workshops, food stands, and arts and crafts, too, as well as camping if you want to stay the night. Dogs allowed on the campgrounds only. $10–25; Camping $20 per night.

LEAVENWORTH INTERNATIONAL ACCORDION FESTIVAL

June • www.accordioncelebration.org

For twenty-odd years, accordionphiles have converged on this little Bavarian village to celebrate the squeezebox. There's a parade, a competition, workshops, jam sessions, and concerts during this three-day melodeon-o-rama. The accordion—it's not just for Weird Al anymore!

≡ Eat & Drink

The point of going to a retreat center, high camp, or resort is so that you don't have to deal with town and its townies and tourists. But just in case you want to spend time away from your time out, here are a few in-town dining options.

Get Caffeinated

J5 COFFEE

215 9th Street, Leavenworth • www.j5coffee.com • 509-470-9495 • Open Monday–Friday 7:30 a.m.–5:30 p.m., Saturday 7:30 a.m.–7 p.m., Sunday noon–5:30 p.m.

Organic fair-trade coffee, roasted in-house. Pick up a bag of the Emperor's Organic blend and, if you've forgotten yours at home, some chi-chi brewing equipment to take with you.

Farm Fresh

PREY'S FRUIT BARN

11007 US-2, Leavenworth • preysfruitbarn.com • 509-548-5771 • Winter hours: daily 10 a.m.–4 pm..

Right next to the Prey family orchard, Prey's Fruit Barn boasts being one of the largest fruit stands in Washington. It specializes in a seasonally rotating roster of over 40 varieties of apples and pears—call them to find out the current selection.

Dining

OLD MILL CAFE

18640 Beaver Valley Road, Leavenworth • www.oldmillcafeplain.com • 509-888-5102 • Open Monday and Thursday 6:30 a.m.–2 p.m., Friday–Sunday 6:30 a.m.–8 p.m.

The new owners of the Old Mill Cafe grew up in Texas and, after 20-plus years working in restaurants in the South, they decided to move to the Cascades and open a smokehouse in Plain. They're really, really into brisket. Also good: the loaded mac & cheese (loaded = add bacon bits, brisket, crispy chicken, pork, or "broccoli onion mushroom blend"), the baked tater, and the grits.

SOUTH RESTAURANT

913 Front Street, Leavenworth • www.southrestaurants.com • 509-888-HEAT • Open Monday–Thursday 11:30 a.m.–9 p.m., Saturday 11 a.m.–11 p.m., Sunday 11 a.m.–9 p.m.

When it's cold outside, get your Latin heat on at South. Try the spicy revolución shrimp burrito or street-style tomatillo chicken tacos. On hot days, go for house-made chips and guac followed by the flan. Year-round, get the Latin spirit samplers.

MANA

1033 Commercial Street, Leavenworth • www.manamountain.com • 509-548-1662 • Open Friday–Sunday for dinner at 6:30 p.m.

If you were a foodie living in Seattle before 2015, you probably knew about Sutra, a vegan fine dinery in Wallingford. The owners have since relocated to Leavenworth and opened Mana, a lovely hippy/foodie haven of wildly crafted organic goodness. The menu is prix fixe, with an optional wine or nonalcoholic tonic and elixir pairing, making dinner a leisurely three-hour event. Even if you love to booze it up, go for the nonalcoholic pairing: the drinks, such as rose-lime hawthorn-pomegranate sparkling elixir and basil-lemon-ginger-gingko tonic with ginger-coconut foam, may sound crazy, but once they're in your mouth, it'll all make sense. Dinner $85; wine pairing $47; nonalcoholic pairing $24.

Beers and Brats

It'd be a shame to visit Bavaria without getting a German beer and a brat. You can find some vegetarian "field roast" brats at most places, too.

MÜNCHEN HAUS BAVARIAN GRILL & BEER GARDEN

709 Front Street, Leavenworth • www.munchenhaus.com • 509-548-1158 • Open Monday–Friday 11 a.m.–10 p.m., Saturday and Sunday 11 a.m.–11 p.m.

Charbroiled Bavarian sausages, warm pretzels, close to a million specialty mustards, and apple cider kraut. Out of the list of beers on tap, try Dark Persuasion German Chocolate Cake Ale. Pet friendly.

DER HINTERHOF

321 9th Street, Leavenworth • www.derhinterhof.com • 509-888-4191 • Open Monday–Thursday 11 a.m.–10 p.m., Friday and Saturday 11 a.m.–11 p.m., Sunday 11 a.m.–9 p.m.

An indoor and outdoor venue, with craft beers, live music, and a ping-pong table. The BBQ is slow-cooked, so if you've had it up to here with sausage, get the brisket.

LEAVENWORTH SAUSAGE GARTEN

636 Front Street, Leavenworth • www.viscontis.com/sausage-garten • 509-888-4959 • Open Sunday–Thursday 10 a.m.–9 p.m., Friday and Saturday 10 a.m.–10 p.m.

Meet you at the sausage garden for a sausage fest. All meats are cured locally by Visconti's, an Italian restaurant group with a few locations in the Wenatchee area, and go perfectly with a German beer or local brew.

Booze and Beyond

DOGHAUS BREWERY

321 9th Street, Leavenworth • www.doghausbrewery.com • 509-393-3134 • Open Monday–Thursday 3–9 p.m., Friday 1–9 p.m., Saturday noon–10 p.m., Sunday noon–6 p.m.

Their life goals: 1. Pet dogs 2. Drink beer 3. Repeat. This tiny bar serves a rotation of eight brews, all named after our four-legged furry friends. No real food—just peanuts. Tasting room is dog and kid friendly.

BLEWETT BREWING

911 Commercial Street, Leavenworth • www.blewettbrew.com • 509-888-8809 • Open Monday–
Thursday noon–9 p.m., Friday noon–10 p.m., Saturday 11 a.m.–10 p.m., Sunday 11 a.m.–9 p.m.

IPAs and ales on tap, described in oenophilic language as "hazy with juicy notes of grape-
fruit and lemon zest" and "caramel and biscuit body with old and new world hops." The locally
sourced ingredients make the artisan pizza pop.

EAGLE CREEK WINERY AND D'VINERY TASTING ROOM

10037 Eagle Creek Road, Leavenworth • www.eaglecreekwinery.com • 509-548-7059 • Winery
May–October, Friday–Sunday 11 a.m.–5 p.m.

617-4A Front Street • Tasting room: year-round, Tuesday–Thursday noon–6 p.m., Friday and Saturday
11 a.m.–7 p.m., Sunday and Monday 11 a.m.–6 p.m.

A boutique winery where, in the late spring through early autumn, you can tour the grounds
and have a sip. The tasting room, open year-round, offers a four-wine sampling, including wines
made from Eagle Creek Winery grapes. $5.

>>   To stay at Eagle Creek Cottage overnight, request to book on VRBO.

Stay Over

SLEEPING LADY

7375 Icicle Road, Leavenworth • www.sleepinglady.com • 1-800-574-2123

Above the Narrow Bottom Canyon, a giant lady made of mountain sleeps. Or that's what
it looks like when you squint and look to the ridges of the Stuart Range. Hence the name
"Sleeping Lady." The amenities are pretty ridiculous—you never have to leave the resort at all.
In fact, just don't. Get a massage or facial at the Aspen Leaf Spa, swim in the Woodland Rock
pools, play a game of badminton, take a sauna, all within the resort. Eat all of your meals at one
of the restaurants, such as the Kingfisher Restaurant & Wine Bar, where much of the meal
comes straight out of the resort's own 2-acre organic garden. Want to see the source for yourself? The garden is open for daily strolling to all guests.

NATAPOC LODGING

12338 Bretz Road, Leavenworth • www.natapoc.com • 1-888-628-2762

Sit in a private hot tub, watch the Wenatchee River flowing by, and let your brain go soft. The
cabins come in different sizes, from a two-person with a queen-size bed, flat-screen TV, WiFi,
and wood-burning stove to an 18-person, three-story cabin with plenty of space to party. You

might bump into other people staying at Natapoc, but otherwise you'll be protected from the crush of humanity. Most of the cabins are surrounded by an acre or two of tall trees, with the river just a few steps out the door. $175–705.

☰ *While You're Here*

PET A REINDEER

10395 Chumstick Highway, Leavenworth • www.leavenworthreindeer.com • 509-885-3021

Who knew that reindeer were actual real-life animals? Apparently the owners of this endangered woodland caribou family farm did. Take a 30-minute tour to see the free-range chickens, say hello to draft horses Sven and Aksel, climb a tractor, and then, the pièce de résistance: feed the reindeer! Tours are offered year-round, but if for some sick reason you dig Santa, then you can book a super special Santa tour. $12.

SKI/SNOWBOARD OR BIKE/HIKE STEVENS PASS

www.stevenspass.com/site

Mountain bikers go berserk for Berserker, as well as the other biking trails, and skiers and snowboarders love the many downhill and Nordic skiing runs, as well as the backcountry

// Snowboarding at Stevens Pass

access. (Stevens Pass tends to be less crowded than other Washington ski areas, which makes it perfect for those who want to be outside but don't want to wait in line for an hour to get on the lift.) Hikers can take a bite out of the 2,650-mile Mexico-to-Canada Pacific Coast Trail and take a ride on the scenic chairlift. Whatever your outdoor enthusiasm, Stevens Pass has got you covered all year-round.

SIP AND PAINT

www.sipandpaint.org

Perhaps you've always thought that you were bad at art. But maybe you just needed a little creative lubricant. Choose from acrylic and watercolor, beer or wine. Like a drunken artiste, this class roves between wineries, bars, farmers' markets, and lodges, so visit the website to find the schedule and location. Aprons included. $35–40.

VISIT THE NUTCRACKER MUSEUM

735 Front Street, Leavenworth • www.nutcrackermuseum.com • 509-548-4573 • Open daily 1–5 p.m.

If you don't find dolls that crack nuts absolutely terrifying, then stop by the Nutcracker Museum. With over 7,000 kinds of implements—from antique, carved wooden levers to utilitarian, handheld, cast-iron nutcrackers in the shape of soldiers, crocodiles, clowns and, of course, ladies' legs—there's a cracker for every nut. As the museum says: "You will be amazed at the many different ways that a nut can be cracked!" $5.

// The Nutcracker Museum, Leavenworth

GO ON A NORTHWEST DOGSLED ADVENTURE

www.northwestdogsledadventuresllc.com • Open mid-December–April, weather permitting

Go on a one-hour, 7-mile dogsled ride, starting from the Fish Lake/Lake Wenatchee Trailhead, just 45 minutes west of Leavenworth. The team is made up of Alaskan and Siberian Husky rescues, Iditarod racers, and Iditarod retirees. $165.

ABOVE & BEYOND

Skates | **Pump Track at Enchantment Park** (300 Enchantment Parkway, Leavenworth; www.bluelotusfoundation.org/leavenworth-pump-track) is a shared bike and skate park and one of the few asphalt-paved tracks on the West Coast. BMXers and skaters come from far and wide to make the loop. Epic. For photos and more information, go to www .northwestskater.com.

Books | **A Book For All Seasons** (703 US-2, Leavenworth; www.abookforallseasons.com; 509-548-1451; open daily 9 a.m.–8 p.m.) is so cozy that Debbie Macomber included it in her book *When Christmas Comes*. Located below Innsbrucker Inn.

Not Ready to Go Home | Drive east approximately 22 miles to Wenatchee (wenatchee.org), another hub of outdoor adventure.

Good to Know |

· Leavenworth's transformation into a Bavarian enclave occurred in the 1960s, after the logging industry moved away and the city was flailing. The makeover was an orches- trated effort to attract a new source of income: tourism.

· Arlene Wagner, one of the founders of the Nutcracker Museum, was the first guest on the *Conan* show in 2010.

· One of the nation's worst train disasters happened in 1910 near Leavenworth, in what was then called Wellington. After the avalanche-caused calamity, the townsfolk decided they needed to rebrand and so renamed the unincorporated area Tye. You can still find pieces of the wreckage along Iron Goat Trail.

Been There Done That |

· Drive east on the Cascade Loop (www.cascadeloop.com) for more mountain fun in Methow Valley (page 230).

· Drive west to get to Mukilteo and the ferry to Whidbey Island (page 249).

16

DIY Retreat in Trout Lake

FROM SEATTLE: 4.5 HOURS · DAYS HERE: 2-PLUS

DO	EAT	DRINK
meditate and whitewater raft	sandwich at Feast Market and Delicatessen	beer at Everybody's Brewing

☰ *Getting There*

BY CAR | Drive on I-5 S for approximately 230 miles to I-84 E. Take Exit 64 to WA-141 N and drive for 22.6 miles. Or drive on I-90 E and I-82 E for approximately 147 miles, then take Exit 37 onto US-97. Drive for another 112 miles.

≡ *Highlight Reel*

TROUT LAKE ABBEY

46 Stoller Road, Trout Lake • www.tlabbey.com • 509-395-2030

Trout Lake Abbey is a unique space 250 miles east of Seattle and 21 miles north of White Salmon on the Washington side and Hood River on the Oregon side of the Columbia Gorge. It's a bed & breakfast, an organic farm, an alpaca farm, and a fruit orchard. It's also a collaboration between a Zen Buddhist and a Druid. What's a Druid, you ask? A Druid is someone who reveres nature and forms relationships with spirits and people through gift exchange. You can think of it as, "I give so you may give."

The property is expansive, with a beautiful temple, a cloistered garden, and Buddhist statues on one side and, on the other, a walking labyrinth and small-scale Stonehenge made of basalt towers brought in from Eastern Washington. Up above it all, Mount Adams pokes its summit into the sky.

You don't have to identify as a Buddhist or a Druid to stay here. Everyone is welcome, including the Buddhist- or Druid-ignorant but curious. You can sign up for a guided group retreat or come for a DIY personal retreat, whatever that means for you. Stay in a private room or a bunk room in the B&B; in a dorm-style hut in the cloistered garden; or in one of the simple meditation huts, an 8-by-8-foot room with a futon on the floor, a meditation heater, and a fan or heater, depending on the season. Or pitch a tent on the abbey's grounds. Be silent, or not. Meditate, or don't. Attend Buddhist services at 6:30 a.m. and 6:30 p.m. Monday through Friday and 9 a.m. on Sundays, or don't. Work on the organic farm, pace the labyrinth, go drink a beer in White Salmon, or all of the above. Or none of the above. The only requirement is to be respectful and quiet. And also to rinse off in the outdoor shower with the view of Mount Hood—that's an experience you won't want to miss. $25–126.

// Trout Lake Abbey, Trout Lake

≡ *Plan Around*

HIGH DAYS

Come for the eight high days of the winter and summers solstices, the spring and fall equi-
noxes, and the four days that are halfway in between. During these times, there are Druid
celebrations in which Kirk, the theatrical Druid priest, builds a bonfire in the basalt stone circle
and makes sacrifices of oils, gold, flowers, and whatever else appeases the Celtic gods.

MOUNT ADAMS ENDURANCE RIDE

June • mtadamsride.wordpress.com

Ride 12, 30, 55, 75, or 100 miles through the forested trails of Gifford–Pinchot National Forest. Open to beginners, world-class competitors, and everyone in between.

HUCKLEBERRY FESTIVAL

September • Daubenspeck Park, Bingen • huckleberry-fest.com

A one-weekend extravaganza of huckleberry deliciousness, with live entertainment and a
small-town parade featuring horses and a marching band.

// Trout Lake Abbey, Trout Lake

≡ *Eat & Drink*

The abbey will serve you a light organic breakfast, but otherwise you're on your own. There's a kitchenette you can use for your own cooking, so bring groceries from home or pick some up in nearby White Salmon. Or go into town for a meal at Trout Lake Country Inn.

Get Caffeinated

HEAVENLY GROUNDS AND STATION CAFE

247 WA-141, Trout Lake • troutlakewashington.com/heavenly-grounds-and-station-cafe • 509-395-2211

Get a nice coffee drink and some snacks at Heavenly Grounds. If you want more of a meal, walk over to the other side of the building to the Station Café. If there's anything huckleberry related, such as a huckleberry smoothie or piece of huckleberry pie, then get that.

Dining

TROUT LAKE COUNTRY INN

15 Guler Road, Trout Lake • troutlakewashington.com/trout-lake-country-inn • 509-395-3667 • Open Monday 5–9 p.m., Thursday 11:30 a.m.–9 p.m., Friday and Saturday 11:30 a.m.–11 p.m., Sunday 11:30 a.m.–9 p.m.

"A true honky-tonk surrounded by breathtaking beauty," claims the website. The restaurant serves burgers, sandwiches, and salads using locally sourced, organic, and seasonal ingredients when possible. Come on a Saturday night for dinner and dancing.

Farm Fresh

WHITE SALMON FARMERS' MARKET

Rhinegarten Park, Main Street at NW Lincoln and NW Washington, White Salmon • Open June–October, Tuesday 4–7 p.m.

FEAST MARKET AND DELICATESSEN

151 E Jewett, White Salmon • feastmarket.org • 509-637-6886 • Open Monday–Saturday 9 a.m.–7 p.m., Sunday 10 a.m.–6 p.m.

A small, family-owned market, perfect for stocking up for your stay at Trout Lake Abbey. Eat a sandwich and drink a beer while you're there, then shop groceries and fresh produce.

Booze and Beyond

EVERYBODY'S BREWING

177 E Jewett Boulevard, White Salmon • everybodysbrewing.com • 509-637-2774

Core beers, small-batch, and local harvest series. Burgers and entrées are made with Carlton Farms pork, Imperial Stock Ranch lamb, Mary's organic chicken, and Painted Hills and Cascade natural beef. Bread comes from local bakeries Flour Garden and Blue Sky. Get a kosher salt soft pretzel followed by a pulled pork burrito. Check the website for hours.

≡ *While You're Here*

RAFT THE WHITE SALMON RIVER

The White Salmon River is a well-known yet secret-ish spot for kayaking and whitewater rafting. Take a trip down its crystal clear waters that, depending on the season, can hit Class III–IV rapids, with glorious names such as Deadman's Corner and Corkscrew. Take in the views of Mount Adams, undeveloped shoreline, and the various animals of the riverside forest. Both tours offer half-day and full-day trips, guaranteed to induce some adrenaline.

RIVER DRIFTERS (riverdrifters.com; 1-800-972-0430; Open March–October; $60–125)

WET PLANET RAFTING AND KAYAKING (wetplanetwhitewater.com; 1-877-390-9445; June–October; $65–130)

VISIT BZ FALLS

WA-141, White Salmon • www.fs.usda.gov

Make the short hike to this 12-foot plunging punchbowl waterfall along the path of White Salmon River. Rumor has it that, when the time is right, cliff jumping can occur. As always with water sports, check the water's depth and the surrounding terrain, and put safety first.

Rural Retreats

NORTHWEST VIPASSANA CENTER IN ONALASKA

445 Gore Road, Onalaska • www.kunja.dhamma.org • 360-978-5434

The tiny town of Onalaska is rural, without a lot going on according to city slicker standards. Which is the point—you come out here to be bored. Or angry. Or proud, jealous, worried, wounded; whatever it is your feeling is what's happening, and there's no distraction from all that hoopla. The Northwest Vipassana Center—the oblivious star of the show—is located on 50 acres in the middle of nowhere, where people go to shut up for a second and just sit. It's trial by fire: brand-new students are barred from the shorter one-, two-, or three-day courses, instead required to take the full 10-day course. That means, for 10 days straight, you will learn vipassana meditation step by step, how to see things as they really are, to self-observe to self-purify, and then do it. Or not *do* it. Or whatever, you get it.

The center stays open and the courses are run by donation, so you can go for free. If you are one of the Amazonians balling on tech money and driving up housing costs, please pay something, for Pete's sake. Be forewarned: This is not some kind of spa experience, where you leave Seattle an exhausted shell of a person and return a glowing god fit for the cover of some yoga magazine. If you arrive an unbearable asshole, chances are good you will leave an unbearable asshole. But maybe a calmer, kinder unbearable asshole. Your time there will probably be difficult and painful, and hopefully it will give you the tools to continue the discipline. This is a silent situation, all meals are prepared for you, and you are required to stay on the property for the whole 10 days. All retreats require preregistration. Curious but not ready to commit? Check out Seattle Vipassana Hall, Seattle Insight Meditation Society at seattleinsight.org.

☰ *Getting There*

BY CAR | Drive on I-5 S for approximately 97 miles, then take US-12 E for 11 miles. Travel time: approximately two hours. Check Northwest Vipassana Center's Rideboard for ridesharing options.

BY TRAIN | Take Amtrak Coast Starlight 11 to Centralia Station. From Centralia, call Quality Taxi Service (360-807-3923) to get to the center.

>> Before going home, get back on I-5 and head south for approximately 7 miles. There you'll find **Gospodor Monument Park** (370 Camus Road, Toledo), a strange pet project involving 87- to 108-foot-tall monuments in haphazard honor of Mother Teresa, victims of the Holocaust, and American Indians. The towers light up at night and are visible from miles away.

CLOUD MOUNTAIN RETREAT CENTER IN CASTLE ROCK

373 Agren Road, Castle Rock; www.cloudmountain.org • 360-274-4859

Cloud Mountain Retreat Center is a beautiful, forested enclave in Castle Rock, located between Olympia and Portland. With a range of offerings and a solid roster of teachers, it's an ideal space for both beginners and experienced practitioners to study meditation. Residential retreats run between five days and two weeks, with a couple beginner weekends throughout the year. All retreats **require preregistration.**

☰ *Getting There*

BY CAR | Drive on I-5 S for 106 miles to WA-506 W. Continue on WA-506 W for approximately 6 miles. Travel time: approximately 1 hour, 45 minutes.

>> Not Ready to Go Home | Head east to Mount St. Helens National Volcanic Monument in Gifford Pinchot National Forest (www.fs.usda.gov).

Part Five

Itineraries

Woodinville Ropes Course and Wine Itinerary

≡ The One-Day Itinerary

The best way to wake up is on a ropes course, 40 feet above the ground, so pick up a coffee and head over to **Adventura**. After you've defied gravity, check in at **Willows Lodge** (14580 NE 145th Street, Woodinville; www .willowlodge.com; 425-424-3900) and take a shower, then have lunch at the Lodge's **Barking Frog** or order room service. The afternoon is devoted to wine tasting, followed by a massage at the **Willow Lodge Spa** (at Willow Lodge) or a soak in your private two-person tub. Have dinner and see a show at either **Chateau Ste. Michelle** (14111 NE 145th Street, Woodinville; www.ste-michelle .com; 425-488-1133) or **Teatro ZinZanni** (14300 NE 145th Street, Woodinville; zinzanni.com; 206-802-0015)

// Teatro ZinZanni, Woodinville

≡ The Two-Day Itinerary

Bike the **Burke–Gilman Trail** to the Sammamish River Trail (or drive your car via I-90 or WA-520) to Woodinville. Check in to your room at **Willows Lodge** (see above) so you can change out of your sweaty bike shorts and freshen up. Attend a **Chateau Ste. Michelle** (see above) summer concert in the evening, getting dinner from one of the food vendors there, then go back to your room with a bottle of wine to **soak in the two-person tub**. In the morning, head over to nearby **Adventura** (14300 NE 145th Street, Woodinville; adventuraplay.com; 866-892-5632) for an adrenaline-provoking but wholly safe elevated ropes course experience. After you've made your zip line exit, shower back in your room and take a self-directed or guided **wine tour**, followed by an afternoon nap. Wake up with a dip in the heated pool, then go to **Teatro ZinZanni** (see above) for a dinner theater/circus and cabaret show. Once the show is over, head back to your room at Willows Lodge for a deep sleep.

Whidbey Island Itinerary

☰ One to Two Days: Do Nothing While Doing Something

Take a ferry ride from Mukilteo in the morning and feel the tension drop away. Spend the morning walking the long, sandy stretch of **Double Bluff Beach** (S Double Bluff Road, Freeland), then have lunch and a slice of berry pie at **Whidbey Pies & Cafe** (765 Wonn Road, Greenbank; www .whidbeypies.com; 360-678-1288). Head over to **Earth Sanctuary** (2059 Newman Road or 5536 Emil Road, Langley; www.earthsanctuary.org; 360-331-6667) for a contemplative stroll, this time under old-growth forest, stopping at the sacred sites to catch your breath. Dine at **Island Nosh** (8898 WA-525, Clinton; www.islandnosh.com; 360-341-3828) before catching the ferry home. Or . . .

Have a long, leisurely meal at **Orchard Kitchen** (5574 Bayview Road, Langley; www.orchard kitchen.com; 360-321-1517), then spend the night at **Yoga Lodge** (3475 Christie Road, Green-bank; www.yogalodge.com; 360-222-3749). Take a yoga class in the morning or arrange in advance for a private yoga session, then get a lunch at **Flower House Café** (2780 Marshview Avenue, Langley; www.bayviewfarmandgarden.com; 360-321-6789). Buy a plant or plants from **Bayview Farm and Garden** while you're there. Go for wine tasting at **Spoiled Dog Winery** (5881 Maxwelton Road, Langley; www.spoileddogwinery.com; 360-661-6226) before heading home.

Vanagon Bainbridge Island Itinerary

☰ Day One

Walk onto the Seattle–Bainbridge Ferry and meet your **PacWesty** Vanagon (pacwesty.com; 888-212-3546) at the Bainbridge Island ferry terminal. Drive to **Sweet Dahlia Baking** (9720 Coppertop Loop, Suite 103, Bainbridge Island; sweetdahliabaking.com; 206-201-3297) for a scone and then go next door to **Storyville** (9459 Coppertop Loop NE, Bainbridge Island; www.storyville.com; 206-780-5777) to get a cup of coffee and see the roastery. Hold hands as you stroll the romantic grounds of **Bloedel Reserve** (7571 NE Dolphin Drive, Bainbridge Island; bloedelreserve.org; 206-842-7631), then have a late, leisurely lunch at **SuBI** (403

Madison Avenue N, #150, Bainbridge Island; www.sushibi.com; 206-855-7882), followed by another romantic stroll along the waterfront in **Waterfront Park**. Backtrack and pick up a bottle of wine at **Eagle Harbor Wine Co.** (278 Winslow Way E, Suite 106, Bainbridge Island; eagleharbor.wine; 206-842-4669), then go down to the Harbor Marina, where you'll catch a **sailboat** for a sunset sail (sailbainbridge.com; 206-788-6512). Drink the wine in a classy fashion as you cruise Elliot Bay. Back on dry land, eat at **Hitchcock Restaurant** (133 Winslow Way E #100, Bainbridge Island; www.hitchcockrestaurant.com; 206-201-3789), then bunk down for the night in your Vanagon. The next day, you can return the Vanagon and head home or . . .

≡ Day Two and Beyond

Drive north on WA-3 to the Olympic Peninsula for another day of fun. See the Biking the Olympic Discovery Trail Itinerary (below).

Biking the Olympic Discovery Trail Itinerary

The 130-mile Olympic Discovery Trail runs from Port Townsend along the northeast edge of the Olympic Peninsula to La Push on the Pacific Coast (or vice versa). In partnership with the Clallam Tribe, this trail has been painstakingly reclaimed and reworked for ease of use. Today, more than half of the route is motorized vehicle–free.

Riding the Olympic Discovery Trail can be a four-day trip, with overnights at each quarter of the ODT. Or it can take less time, depending on how far you want to go each day and how many stops you want to make. Every 5 to 10 miles there's a kiosk with maps and info, and there's a bathroom every 2 to 3 miles. Between the four main stops there's little by way of restaurants; it's recommended that you pick up a sandwich and a drink to take with you, then stop by whatever pretty point along the trail strikes your fancy for a picnic. Check out the interactive map and get more information at olympicdiscoverytrail.org.

>> For bike shops along the way, visit the **Olympic Peninsula Bicycle Alliance** at olympicpeninsula cycling.com.

☰ *Day One: East End*

27 MILES, PORT TOWNSEND TO SEQUIM

From Port Townsend Boatyard (N Lincoln Street at E Railroad Avenue) to Jamestown S'Klallam Campus in Blyn at the south tip of Sequim Bay.

Get a good night's rest in Port Townsend at **Quimper Inn** (1306 Franklin Street, Port Townsend; www.quimperinn.com; 360-385-1060), then have breakfast at **Pane d'Amore Artisan Bakery** (617 Tyler Street, Port Townsend; www.panedamore.com; 360-385-1199). Take some scones to go or head over to **Lehani's Eat Local Café** (221 Taylor Street, Port Townsend; 360-385-3961) to pick up a sandwich. Get on your bike and ride. Once you arrive in Sequim, eat dinner at **Nourish Sequim** (101 Provence View Lane, Sequim; nourishsequim .com; 360-797-1480) and hit the hay at **Clark's Chambers B&B** (322 Clark Road, Sequim; clarkschambersbandb.com; 360-683-4431).

☰ *Day Two: East Central*

26.4 MILES, SEQUIM TO PORT ANGELES

From Jamestown S'Klallam Campus in Blyn, at the south tip of Sequim Bay to Port Angeles City Pier (Lincoln Street at W Front Street).

If you want to get a jump on the day, wake up with **Adagio Bean & Leaf** (981 E Washington Street, Sequim; m.adagiobeanandleaf.com; 360-582-0024), which opens at 6 a.m. and has great coffee and tea drinks and pastries, as well as sandwiches you can get to go. You can also wash your butt while there—they have a bidet, a rare treat in any American locale. Or get an espresso and a homemade muffin at **Rainshadow Coffee Roasting Company** (157 W Cedar Street, Sequim; www .rainshadowcoffee.com; 360-681-0650). Visit the **Dungeness Spit** (Dungeness National Wildlife Refuge, 554 Voice of America Road, Sequim) in the morning, then grab a sandwich at **Pacific Pantry Artisan Deli** (229 S Sequim Avenue, Sequim; 360-797-1221) before heading out. Once you get to Port Angeles proper, sleep like a forefather at **George Washington Inn & Estate** (939 Finn Hall Road, Port Angeles; georgewashingtoninn.com; 360-452-5207).

☰ *Day Three: West Central*

31.7 MILES, PORT ANGELES TO LAKE CRESCENT

From Port Angeles City Pier (Lincoln Street at W Front Street) to Fairholme Hill at Highway 101.

Get a slice of blackberry pie and a cup of coffee at **Blackberry Café** (50530 WA-112, Port Angeles; 360-928-0141), then ride to Lake Crescent. You're going to want to spend a lot of time there, gazing at the stunning blue waters and, of course, swimming. Stay at **Lake Crescent Lodge** (416 Lake Crescent Road, Port Angeles; www.olympicnationalparks.com/lodging/lake-crescent-lodge; 1-888-896-3818), where you can get all your meals and max out your time in the water.

☰ *Day Four: West End*

41.6 MILES, LAKE CRESCENT TO FORKS OR LA PUSH

From Fairholme Hill at Highway 101 to La Push.

End your day in Forks, grabbing dinner at **Plaza Jalisco** (90 N Forks Avenue, Forks; 360-374-3108) and a room at **Kalaloch Lodge** (157151 Highway 101, Forks; www.thekalalochlodge.com; 1-866-662-9928). Or continue on the 12 miles to the remote town of La Push, right on the edge of the world. Have dinner at the only restaurant in town, **River's Edge Restaurant** (41 Main Street, La Push; 360-374-5777) and then spend the evening listening to the sound of waves crashing from a cabin at **Quileute Oceanside Resort** (330 Ocean Front Drive, La Push; quileuteoceanside.com; 1-800-487-1267).

Cascade Loop Itinerary

Take a 470-plus-mile road trip on the Cascade Loop (www.cascadeloop.com), stopping off in **Leavenworth, Methow Valley, Skagit Valley, Whidbey Island**, and other towns along the way to see an incredible swath of the great state of Washington. You can make it a quick trip or really spend some time (more than the four days of this itinerary). Go in the fall to see the leaves change and eat some apples; in the winter for quiet and snow sports (if you're willing to risk road closures); in the summer for sunny driving and warm stopovers; in the spring for wildflower blooms and snowmelt. Be sure to make reservations in advance.

☰ *Day One*

Wake up early and drive the approximately 135 miles to **Leavenworth**, get beers and brats for lunch at **München Haus Bavarian Grill and Beer Garden** (709 Front Street, Leavenworth; www.munchenhaus.com; 509-548-1158), and then stop in at the **Nutcracker Museum** (735 Front Street, Leavenworth; www.nutcrackermuseum.com; 509-548-4573). Go for a 4-mile hike along **Icicle Creek**, then have a fancy dinner at **Mana** (1033 Commercial Street, Leavenworth; www.manamountain.com; 509-548-1662). Sleep at **Loge Camps** (11798 US-2, Leavenworth; www.logecamps.com/leavenworth-wa; 509-690-4106). Take the next day to hike, bike, ski, stroll, or swim. Or . . .

☰ *Day Two*

Drive 122 miles to Winthrop. Get lunch at **Mazama Store** (50 Lost River Road, Mazama; www.themazamastore.com; 509-996-2855), then head into **North Cascades National Park** (www.nps.gov/noca/index.htm; 360-854-7200) for a day of hiking. Have dinner at **Arrowleaf Bistro** (207 White Avenue, Winthrop; www.arrowleafbistro.com; 509-996-3919), stroll the Western-themed town, then eat an ice cream cone at **Sheri's Sweet Shoppe** (207 Riverside Avenue, Winthrop; www.sherissweetshoppe.com; 509-996-3834) before bunking down at **Rolling Huts** (18381 WA-20, Winthrop; rollinghuts.com; 509-996-4442). Take the next day to hike, bike, ski, stroll, or swim. Or . . .

☰ *Day Three*

Drive the approximately 150 miles to **La Conner**. Time it for the **Daffodil Festival** in March or **Birds of Winter**, and be sure to make a stop or two at one of the spots along the **Skagit Farm to Pint Ale Trail** (skagitfarmtopint.com). Stay over at the **La Conner Lodge** (107 S 2nd Street, La Conner; www.laconnerlodging.com; 360-466-1500). Take the next day to hike, bike, ski, stroll, or swim. Or . . .

☰ *Day Four*

Drive the approximately 56 miles to **Whidbey Island** and take a hike at **Double Bluff Beach**. Get lunch at **The Oystercatcher** (901 Grace Street NW, Coupeville; www.oystercatcher whidbey.com; 360-678-0683), then take a self-guided tour on the **Whidbey Art Trail** (www .whidbeyarttrail.com; 925-787-1692 or 360-929-7477). Be sure to have a piece of pie at **Whidbey Pies & Cafe** (765 Wonn Road, Greenbank; www.whidbeypies.com; 360-678-1288) before heading to catch the ferry home. Or, if you want one more quiet night on the road, sleep over at **Earth Sanctuary** (2059 Newman Road, Langley; earthsanctuary.org; 360-331-6667).

Resources

Acknowledgments

For the real intel, I went to the locals, and there were too many helpful people across this great state of Washington for me to name them all. Thank you, Shane Robinson, Keeman Wong, Claire Feigal, Wendy Dion, Norm James, Skater Dan Hughes, Julie Burgmeier, Jed Holmes, Claire Donahue, Chris Mueller at Visit Bainbridge, Scott Chreist, Mike Hanson, Nora Phillips, Barbara Marrett, and the folks at the San Juan Islands Visitor Bureau.

Thank you, Cara Bilodeau, Rosebud Eustace, Arielle Farina Williams, and Laura Ascolese, for being in the same boat with me all these years.

Thank you to my wonderful agent, Amy Levenson of Blue Heron Literary. Thank you to my brilliant mentor, Jenna Land Free.

Thank you to the editorial and design teams at The Countryman Press. Thank you, Róisín Cameron, Senior Editor at The Countryman Press, for your expert guidance. Thanks to Natalie Eilbert and Kathryn Flynn for your essential editorial contributions and Amanda Kreutzer at Faceout Studio for the beautiful design.

Thank you, as always, to Paul Burstein and Florence Katz Burstein.

And special thanks to Troy Lucero, who somehow manages to keep everything afloat and look good while doing it.

Index

Page numbers in *italics* refer to photographs.